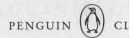
THE *BOUNTY* MUTINY

William Bligh was born near Plymouth, England, in 1754. In 1762, at the age of seven, he was entered on the books of the *Monmouth* as captain's servant, although he may not have actually served. In 1776, at age twenty-two, he was appointed master of the *Resolution*, under the command of the celebrated James Cook. Shortly after Cook's death and the return of his expedition in 1780, Bligh married Elizabeth Betham. In 1787, after several voyages in naval and merchant vessels, Bligh was offered command of an expedition to transplant breadfruit plants from Tahiti to the West Indies in the *Bounty*. In 1791 he undertook a more successful breadfruit voyage in the *Providence*. After being incidentally involved in the mutiny at the Nore, Bligh commanded the *Director* at the Battle of Camperdown in 1797 and the *Glatton* at the Battle of Copenhagen in 1801. In 1805 Bligh was offered the governorship of New South Wales. He died in 1817 in London and was buried in Lambeth.

Edward Christian, brother of mutineer Fletcher Christian, was born in 1758 near Cockermouth in the Lake District. Counsel for William and Dorothy Wordsworth in their famous suit against James Lowther, he became chief justice of the Isle of Ely and professor of law at Cambridge. He died in 1823.

R. D. Madison teaches English at the U.S. Naval Academy in Annapolis, Maryland. He has edited several volumes of military and naval history, including Robert Southey's *Life of Nelson*, David Porter's *Journal of a Cruise*, and Thomas Wentworth Higginson's *Army Life in a Black Regiment and Other Writings* (Penguin Classics, 1997).

THE *BOUNTY* MUTINY

WILLIAM BLIGH

EDWARD CHRISTIAN

WITH AN
INTRODUCTION BY
R. D. MADISON

PENGUIN BOOKS

PENGUIN BOOKS
Published by the Penguin Group
Penguin Putnam Inc., 375 Hudson Street,
New York, New York 10014, U.S.A.
Penguin Books Ltd, 27 Wrights Lane,
London W8 5TZ, England
Penguin Books Australia Ltd, Ringwood,
Victoria, Australia
Penguin Books Canada Ltd, 10 Alcorn Avenue,
Toronto, Ontario, Canada M4V 3B2
Penguin Books (N.Z.) Ltd, 182–190 Wairau Road,
Auckland 10, New Zealand

Penguin Books Ltd, Registered Offices:
Harmondsworth, Middlesex, England

This edition with an introduction by Robert D. Madison
published in Penguin Books 2001

1 3 5 7 9 10 8 6 4 2

LIBRARY OF CONGRESS CATALOGING-IN PUBLICATION DATA

Bligh, William, 1754–1817.
The Bounty mutiny / William Bligh, Edward Christian ;
with an introduction by R. D. Madison.
p. cm.
Includes bibliographical references.
ISBN 0-14-043916-1
1. Bounty Mutiny, 1789. 2. Oceania—Description and travel—
Early works to 1800. 3. Bligh, William, 1754–1817—Journeys—Oceania.
4. Christian, Fletcher, 1764–1793—Journeys—Oceania. 5. Bounty (Ship)
I. Christian, Edward, d. 1823. II. Title.
DU20 .B49 2001
919.504—dc21
00-049207

Printed in the United States of America
Set in Stempel Garamond

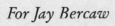

For Jay Bercaw

CONTENTS

INTRODUCTION

The names of William Bligh, Fletcher Christian, and the *Bounty* have belonged to the popular culture of the English-speaking world for over two hundred years. The story of the most famous mutiny has many beginnings and many endings—all of which intersected on an April morning in 1789 near the Pacific island group we now call Tonga. On that morning, William Bligh and a handful of barely loyal supporters, put off the *Bounty* into a small launch, began the greatest boat voyage in history, while Fletcher Christian and the *Bounty* sailed off into a mystery which has never been entirely resolved, despite the discovery of the *Bounty* colony on Pitcairn Island some twenty years later.

I

Perhaps the story is best begun with a look at the life of the commanding officer. William Bligh was born in or near Plymouth, England, on 9 September 1754. Destined for the navy, he was entered on the books of the *Monmouth* as captain's servant in 1762, at the age of seven, although he may not actually have served. Such an entry was useful to give young aspirants for a naval career a head start—at least on paper if not in actual service. Perhaps such a custom was the more welcome if the captain in question merely pocketed any wages due to the mythical apprentices. By 1770, however, Bligh was regularly entered in the *Hunter* as an able-bodied seaman—a suitable designation for a youngster waiting for a commission. He must have been extraordinarily talented at seamanship and navigation, for at age twenty-two he was appointed sailing-master of the *Resolution* under the celebrated English navigator and explorer James Cook. As the officer in charge of the day-to-day management of the vessel, Bligh must have thought himself especially blessed by the sea gods. In any event, the voyage with Cook was to provide him with a hero and a patron.

James Cook (1728–1779) had himself quickly gained a reputation in piloting and surveying while on voyages to the coast of North America, and was in the right place at the right time when the Royal Society initiated an expedition to observe the transit of the planet Venus. Given command of the *Endeavour,* he sailed in 1768 for the other end of the earth, having on board a remarkable assemblage of scientific talent in the persons of Joseph Banks, Daniel Solander, and Sydney Parkinson. In April 1769 they arrived at Tahiti. During the homeward passage the expedition engaged in much discovery and charting, arriving home in 1771. In 1772 Cook sailed on a second expedition of discovery in *Resolution,* skirting the fogs and ice of the Antarctic seas in search of a continent, and keeping his men remarkably free from disease.

It was this team that the young Bligh joined when Cook sailed again, this time for the Arctic regions, in 1776. Their route to the north was circuitous, sailing around the world by way of the Cape of Good Hope and spending a year among the islands of the Pacific. After discovering the Sandwich Islands—now Hawaii—they made their way north until stopped by the ice. Returning to the Sandwich Islands, they recuperated and continued surveying until deteriorating relations with the Sandwich Islanders brought on an outburst of savage fury in which Cook was bludgeoned and stabbed to death on the beach of Karakakoa Bay. Bligh was on a boat mission nearby; he had to defend himself against the native attacks while witnessing the cowardice of another boat that failed to come to the aid of Cook. It is likely that Bligh also was involved with recovering Cook's remains (there was no intact body). The death of Cook powerfully affected Bligh, who did not conceal his displeasure at the behavior of his fellow officers. At the return of the expedition to England in 1780, most were promoted. Bligh was not.

In the following months Bligh assisted with the publication of Cook's journals. While visiting the Isle of Man, he met Elizabeth Betham, who would become his wife early in 1781. Bligh also took temporary employment with her relative Duncan Campbell, a West Indian trader, and alternated this work with his naval service as a lieutenant. He finally received command of his own vessels, which were West-Indiamen, including the *Britannia.* In about 1786 or 1787, he took on to the *Britannia* a volunteer apprentice named Fletcher Christian, in the same arrangement in which he himself had entered service: as an able-bodied seaman until such time as a vacancy should occur among the officers. Christian was about ten years younger than Bligh, and apparently just as eager for a career at sea.

Meanwhile, Bligh's friends at the Royal Society had not been idle. One of Cook's discoveries was the abundance of breadfruit on the island of Tahiti (see Appendix A, page 197). The breadfruit was primarily a botanical and dietary curiosity, but, in light of the partial loss to Britain of the supply of dried fish from the newly independent colonies in North America, the breadfruit emerged as a possible alternative source of food for English slaves on sugar plantations in Jamaica and the Lesser Antilles. At the center of the breadfruit speculation were two of Bligh's allies—Duncan Campbell and Joseph Banks, the scientist.

Joseph Banks (1743–1820) had life advantages shared by neither Cook nor Bligh. Studies at Harrow and Eton prefaced those at Oxford, where Banks embraced the study of botany. Inheriting his father's fortune in 1764, he was elected to the Royal Society in 1766 at a remarkably young age. He found a place on Cook's first expedition through the influence of Lord Sandwich, and he organized its scientific complement. Disagreements about accommodations led Banks to decline an invitation to join Cook's second expedition, but in 1778 Banks nevertheless was named president of the Royal Society, a post he held to his death. Under his influence the society renewed its interest in natural history, and he himself was made a baronet in 1781. Thus he was in a remarkably good position to help—or hinder—a young officer's pursuit of a scientific command.

By 1787 there was enough commercial and scientific interest in the breadfruit to justify Banks's petitioning the king to undertake—at government expense—an expedition to transplant the breadfruit. In fairly rapid succession, a vessel was obtained—the *Bethia,* belonging to Duncan Campbell—and its commander selected: William Bligh. Whatever family connections Bligh may have benefited from, he was also perfect for the command: he had extensive service in the name of science and trade in both Pacific and West Indian waters; he was favorably known to Banks; and the admiralty viewed him as an able young navigator and chartmaker. He took command at Deptford on 20 August 1787.

The new commander oversaw the fitting-out and manning of the vessel, now renamed *Bounty.* His enthusiasm was remarked upon at the time, as no doubt it should have been. Here was Bligh's opportunity to follow in the wake of his hero Cook. Already he may have begun thinking of himself as the "son of Captain Cook," a fiction he later allowed to pass at Tahiti.

Bligh could have had no unusual concerns as he put together the crew of the *Bounty*. As a lieutenant himself, he was limited in the number and rank of officers he could bring along: there would be no other lieutenants, and only two regular midshipmen; other young gentlemen would have to fill lesser billets if they wanted to go along. Bligh did not have much choice about the ship's surgeon: the appointment of the besotted Thomas Huggan to the *Bounty* may indicate that the vessel was viewed by the admiralty as a harmless place for dead-end talent. After all, the *Bounty*, though armed, was not a vessel of war—it carried no marines, and the duties of the gunner must have been light. The voyage must have been viewed as something of a lark by Bligh's friends: in the end, several of the young crewmembers, including twenty-four-year-old Fletcher Christian, fourteen-year-old Peter Heywood, twenty-one-year-old George Stewart, Thomas Hayward, and John Hallet were all friends of the extended Bligh family and all except Christian sailed as midshipmen. If there was an excessive number of boys in the junior officership, the remaining dozen able-bodied seamen should have been sufficient to man the vessel under ordinary circumstances—but probably not under Bligh's more enlightened three-watch system. No doubt Bligh needed the boys as acting lieutenants to head up his watches, too.

Although Bligh's orders directed him to sail to Tahiti by way of Cape Horn, delays in the shipyard and at the admiralty slowed the *Bounty*'s departure until late in the season. Already Bligh's plan for a speedy reenactment of Cook's success was falling apart. Finally, on 23 December 1787, the *Bounty* left Spithead in a gale of wind.

By April 1788 the *Bounty* had reached the vicinity of Cape Horn, but despite heroic efforts to make the passage to the west, the vessel was tossed back continuously. Realizing the season was too far advanced to make the passage, Bligh turned the *Bounty*'s head eastward toward the Cape of Good Hope and the high latitudes of the Indian Ocean—the right way to go the wrong way around the world.

Bligh made Table Mountain near the Cape by 22 May, and lay over in Table Bay for over a month. On 19 August *Bounty* made the

Mewstone on the coast of Van Dieman's Land—now Tasmania. Bligh felt an enormous sense of relief—he was decidedly on his own turf now, having visited with Cook in 1777—and it wasn't long before he had instituted a full program of exploration and natural history research. Nor did Bligh neglect to provide for the next Cook avatar, planting fruit trees, pumpkins, and Indian corn.

By late October the *Bounty* had made its way to Tahiti, where Bligh found Cook and Banks to be well remembered. After formalities with the chief inhabitants, Bligh sent botanist David Nelson to scout for breadfruit, keeping his mission a secret from the Tahitians. It was apparently the Tahitian leader, Tinah, himself who first broached the idea of sending breadfruit as a gift to King George. "This was the exact point to which I wished to bring the conversation," Bligh wrote; "I told him the bread-fruit-trees were what King George would like" (Bligh, *Voyage,* p. 73).

The business of transplanting breadfruit occupied the next several months, interrupted by minor thefts and much cultural exchange, led by Bligh himself—who, despite his anthropological enlightenment, must have found some of the ceremonies unpleasant to a self that he increasingly reveals as fastidious. In October he was "incommoded by the heat" of a press of Tahitians (ibid., p. 63), and Bligh must have found it difficult to join noses, "the customary manner of saluting" (ibid., p. 65); later he "collected such a crowd that the heat was scarce bearable . . . they however carefully avoided pressing against me" (ibid., p. 68). Despite being assured of the protocol, Bligh declined to denude himself from the waist up as a prerequisite to meeting a Tahitian dignitary. It was perhaps not merely the thievery but also prudery that convinced Bligh to establish boundaries "within which the natives were not to enter without leave" (ibid., p. 77).

On 4 April 1789, the *Bounty,* with something over a thousand breadfruit plants, weighed anchor and sailed out of Toahroah Harbor. Bligh must have been elated. He had successfully turned the geographical and scientific discoveries of Cook to the economic benefit of the British Empire, he had kept the health of his men (by and large), and minor squabbles (to be expected on a long voyage) seemed well under control. Bligh had everything to look forward to: a speedy voyage to the West Indies, followed by promotion, fame, and fortune. With a signal victory over some islanders to atone for

Cook's death, Bligh would have exceeded the achievement of Cook himself. He was not, however, to receive this minor blessing, although he did his best to create such an incident.

On 23 April the *Bounty* sighted Nomuka, another island Bligh had visited with Cook a decade earlier. Bligh seems to have viewed these islanders through the eyes of his former commander and perhaps from a heightened sense of self-congratulation. In any case, he belittled the warnings of his two chief officers—by then John Fryer and Fletcher Christian—and determined to bully the natives into returning a stolen grapnel. He took prisoners and, in a scenario laid out by Cook on the shore of Hawaii ten years before, Bligh had better luck: he got his native hostages on board and succeeded in humiliating them. But he could not get them to produce a stolen article that by now was probably miles away in the Tongan archipelago. Reluctantly, Bligh moved the Nomukans overboard into waiting canoes, and turned the *Bounty* toward Tofua.

What does it take to cause a mutiny? In a calm sea somewhere near Tofua, a cat's-paw reaches out of the east and stirs up the slightest of swells. With a barely audible creak of rigging, the *Bounty* rolls ever so slightly leeward and returns to an upright keel. On deck, a pile of coconuts settles, and a sleepy midshipman dreams of wind and home while the helmsman is hypnotized by the glare of a distant volcano.

II

Fletcher Christian was born on 25 September 1764 near Cockermouth in the Lake District of England. He attended the same school as William Wordsworth, but at that time the much younger Wordsworth was decades from being the well-known poet he would become. Like other boys in the Free Grammar School, Fletcher may have entertained the dream of university: certainly he continued to study at St. Bees School near Whitehaven. He even may have studied there when the celebrated pirate John Paul Jones made his assault on Whitehaven.

Like the Wordsworths, the Christians fell upon hard times. It did not seem likely that further schooling was in store for Fletcher. In 1780 his bankrupt mother, age thirty-nine, took Fletcher and a younger brother to live on the Isle of Man. The Christians had many relations there, and it was perhaps as early as this that Fletcher met the Bethams—and subsequently the Blighs—and determined to follow a career at sea. At any rate, in April 1783 Christian signed on as a midshipman on the *Eurydice,* then at Spithead. On the *Eurydice,* Christian's behavior was exemplary, and he was given the position of acting lieutenant. He returned in 1785 and began casting about for a berth on an Indiaman. One way or another, within two years, he ended up with Bligh on the *Britannia.* Bligh, Christian learned in his months on *Britannia,* could be very passionate—but Christian flattered himself that he knew how to get along. And apparently Bligh was more easygoing in the merchant service than he was when wearing the king's button halfway around the world.

So it was perfectly natural that Bligh should enroll Fletcher Christian on the *Bounty* voyage, although Christian did not join the vessel until early September, a fortnight after Bligh arrived. He signed as master's mate, although in March 1788 he was made acting lieutenant—the same position he had held on the *Eurydice.* His promotion seems to have elevated him over his peers, including those regularly signed on as midshipmen. But Bligh apparently knew his man, and certainly never demoted Christian. Perhaps Bligh appreciated someone who could put up with him: although Christian was frequently the object of Bligh's ragging after leaving Tahiti, Bligh's butts before that had primarily been John Fryer, the master, and William Purcell, the carpenter—both apparently competent individuals whose position on board may have somehow threatened Bligh. Nevertheless, after the mutiny both of them ended up in the *Bounty*'s launch with their commander.

In the days following the incident at Nomuka, Bligh was clearly irritable. His frustration found an outlet in Christian, whom Bligh accused in front of the ship's company of stealing coconuts in the night. Only the most recent of Bligh's humiliations of his officers, it was the final insult for Christian—who determined to leave the *Bounty* on a hastily built raft and take his chances in the wide Pacific.

On the night before the mutiny, Bligh no doubt turned in with only slightly punctured delusions of grandeur. Christian turned in in a state of suicidal depression. Neither one of them at the time had the least thought of mutiny.

III

Just a little less than a year later, in March 1790, Bligh stepped ashore in Portsmouth, England. Of the survivors of the mutiny, he was the first back to England; some would return only later and others never: the Far East, especially Batavia (now Jakarta), was a deadly place for Europeans, and took its toll (the naturalist Nelson was dead even before Bligh left for England). Despite his desire to return home quickly, Bligh had a lengthy period of travel time to contemplate the events that had transpired. A model breadfruit voyage had been frustrated by a deeply laid but widespread mutiny. Through the assistance of divine Providence, Bligh subsequently navigated the *Bounty's* launch approximately four thousand miles to safety. It was the greatest boat voyage on record, and Bligh knew it. He could almost, he wrote at the end of his narrative, bear the failure of the expedition with "resignation and chearfulness." And why not? He had done something even Cook had not. He had insured his immortality not by dying on a foreign shore, but by surviving against odds which he was careful to measure and publish.

Bligh did not hesitate to let the world, as well as the admiralty, know of his exploit. His *Narrative of the Mutiny*, published within the year, contains a half-dozen pages devoted to the mutiny and eighty to the subsequent boat journey. He had collaborated on the publication of Cook's journals, and he knew what made a good story. Bligh let his public know that, without charts and with sights taken under extraordinarily difficult circumstances, he was able to sail his launch westward from Tofua through known and unknown islands to the coast of New Holland (Australia), through the Great Barrier Reef, and ultimately to civilization at Coupang on the island of Timor. He had lost only one man—to natives at the very start of his journey. He had had to put up with surly crewmembers, spoiled and insufficient food, a cramped and overburdened vessel. Remarkably, he did not lack fresh water—nearly incessant rains saw to that. Bligh prided himself on bringing home so quickly and by himself the account of the villainy of the mutineers. Perhaps he thought his was the only version of the story that would ever return.

For the time being, there was no reason to suspect Bligh of being anything other than a hero. A court-martial found Bligh innocent of the loss of his vessel; he was introduced to the king, promoted twice, and within a year was given the captaincy of another breadfruit expedition—this time in the *Providence,* with a suitable complement of lieutenants and marines. The *Providence,* with another vessel in company, sailed in August 1791.

Even before Bligh's court-martial, the admiralty had taken measures to find the mutineers and the missing *Bounty.* In August 1790 Captain Edward Edwards was given command of the frigate *Pandora* with orders to seek the mutineers at Tahiti or wherever they might be found in the Pacific archipelago (see Appendix B, page 205). As far as anyone at the admiralty was concerned, everyone who sailed off with the *Bounty* was a mutineer and, if captured, was to be treated as such.

In March 1791 the *Pandora* reached Tahiti, and Edwards must have been somewhat surprised when several members of the *Bounty*'s crew began to come aboard voluntarily. Nevertheless, he followed his orders with precision and manacled the prisoners and confined them to a special cabin constructed on deck. In all, he rounded up fourteen men who had been brought back to Tahiti in September 1789 after Fletcher Christian had tried unsuccessfully to colonize Tubuai in an island group to the south. Now, a year and a half later, the survivors were ready to return to England—but hardly under the conditions granted by Edwards.

In May the *Pandora* left Tahiti and for several months searched fruitlessly for signs of the *Bounty.* In August the *Pandora* headed for home, only to fetch up on the same Great Barrier Reef Bligh had navigated through so brilliantly. When the *Pandora* broke up and went down, four of the prisoners went down with her. Four boats—with ten of the *Bounty* prisoners—traced Bligh's route to safety in Coupang. They finally reached England—and a prison ship—in March 1792. That summer the survivors were tried for mutiny.

On 29 October three mutineers were hanged. The others, for one reason or another, were found not guilty, were pardoned, or had their verdicts set aside. Now that the free were free and the dead were dead, stories that had circulated only privately slowly became public. Foremost in the efforts to make the full story of the mutiny public was Edward Christian, Fletcher's older brother. Edward was a brilliant, if underachieving, attorney. He knew how to gather evidence, how to arrange it, and how to make it stick. Alerted by the recently pardoned Peter Heywood, Edward gathered a group of unimpeachable witnesses and systematically interviewed both the surviving mutineers and the survivors of Bligh's open-boat voyage. He lobbied to have the trial record made public, and when he was denied this he collaborated with Stephen Barney, attorney for one of the mutineers, to publish a partial transcript made for the defense. To this he added an extensive analysis, and published the whole in 1794 as *Minutes of the Proceedings of the Court-Martial held at Portsmouth, August 12, 1792. On Ten Persons charged with Mutiny on Board His Majesty's Ship the* Bounty. *With an Appendix, Containing A full Account of the real Causes and Circumstances of that unhappy Transaction, the most material of which have hitherto been withheld from the Public.* It was a masterpiece, and, in defending the character of his brother Fletcher, Edward also exposed Bligh as a tyrant—not of the flogging kind, but a foul-mouthed, arbitrary, vain perfectionist who consistently drove his men to the very edge of insubordination.

Bligh had been out of the country on his successful voyage in the *Providence* until late 1793, and was no doubt surprised at the turn his reputation had taken during his absence. On his return he attended to loose ends and, since the full narrative of the *Bounty* voyage had been published in his absence in 1792 by friends Joseph Banks and the naval chronicler James Burney, he began to prepare the narrative of his second voyage for the press. But although he was granted the Royal Society's gold medal for transplanting the breadfruit to the West Indies, Bligh found he still needed to turn his attention to Edward Christian's accusation. This he did in a modest pamphlet, *An Answer to Certain Assertions* (1794). While this was not all Bligh had to say on the subject, it was nevertheless too much, and Edward Christian defended his rebuttal deftly in *A Short Reply to Capt. William Bligh's Answer* (1795). Though brief, the pamphlets are extraordinarily valuable in demonstrating Bligh's view of his former shipmates and Edward's methods of building his case.

Bligh's career was damaged but hardly ruined, and Fletcher Christian's reputation was salved if not purified. Nothing further was heard of the *Bounty* or her mutineers, and the whole incident threatened to disappear into obscurity in the wake of new mutinies at the Nore and Spithead (in which Bligh had only a minor role). The breadfruit experiment itself failed: the West Indian slaves refused to eat it, and the whole question of black slavery so altered the philosophical landscape that science and commercialism no longer walked hand in hand through the breadfruit groves.

What had become of the *Bounty* and the remainder of her crew? With a reduced crew made up of eight mutineers, six Polynesian men, twelve women, and one child, Fletcher Christian sailed the *Bounty* among the islands to the west of Tahiti before turning her southward and eastward in search of obscurity. They were to find it on Pitcairn Island.

IV

During the first quarter of the nineteenth century there was no dearth of interest in maritime exploration. The journal *Quarterly Review*, with close ties to the admiralty, became a strong proponent of the navy in general and exploration in particular. One of its experts on naval affairs was the journal's founder and Tory essayist John Wilson Croker, secretary of the admiralty after 1809. In 1810 the *Quarterly Review* ran the first version of Robert Southey's *Life of Nelson.* It is not surprising then that tucked away in a review of *Voyage de Dentrecasteaux* in that same year should be a notice that the American sealing vessel *Topaz,* under a Captain Folger, stopped at Pitcairn Island and found an Englishman who claimed to be the last surviving member of the *Bounty* mutineers. With some skepticism, the *Quarterly* acknowledged that the story, though coming from an American, must be true, since the name of the sailor, Alexander Smith, appeared on the *Bounty*'s books and a chronometer returned by him proved to be one assigned to the *Bounty* (see Appendix C, page 213).

This was the first public notice of the discovery of the mutineers. Five years passed before the *Quarterly* could provide a more detailed account, which it did as an appendage to a review of David Porter's *Journal of a Cruise* (see Appendix D, page 215). By this time the *Quarterly* writer—William Gifford, editor of the journal—had information gathered by the officers of the vessels *Briton* and *Tagus,* which had been sent out in pursuit of Porter during the War of 1812. By the time of their arrival at Pitcairn Island, Smith had resumed an earlier name, John Adams, and, not surprisingly, he convinced the British officers that Christian had been the "leader and sole cause" of the mutiny. Their readiness to believe Adams was heightened by the apparently pious community that greeted them—not the anarchic afterleavings of mutiny the officers might have supposed to find. In fact, Gifford was the first to hint that Fletcher Christian might have founded a paradise. The *Quarterly* article was a remarkable tour de force of turning the Americans into pirates while canonizing the *Bounty* descendants.

The next public utterance concerning the *Bounty* mutineers came from an unlikely source—so unlikely that it was largely overlooked at the time. Among the Polynesian consorts of the mutineers was one Jenny, wife of mutineer Isaac Martin. Her wanderings alone were even more far-flung than those she shared with the mutineers, for she was able to return to Tahiti by way of South America and the Marquesas Islands. Her story (see Appendix E, page 228) ought to have carried considerable weight, since the process of oral transmission was so central to her culture and since the inconsistent accounts of Smith/Adams were raising eyebrows. But the relative insignificance of the *United Service Journal,* in which her story appeared in 1829 (compared to the clout of the *Quarterly*), coupled with her status as a woman—and a native woman at that—perhaps distanced her story from the mainstream. In any case, it was totally eclipsed by the publication of the first deliberate inquiry into the status of the *Bounty* survivors on Pitcairn undertaken by Frederick W. Beechey in the ship *Blossom,* the results of which were published in his very successful *Narrative of a Voyage* in 1831 (see Appendix F, page 235). This work completed the picture of old Adams as benevolent patriarch and gave the fullest report of his version of events on Pitcairn.

Meanwhile, there were now enough pieces available to make a fairly complete picture of the mutiny from beginning to end, and there were still enough rumblings about where the blame should be laid to interest Sir John Barrow (1764–1848), himself a *Quarterly* essayist and second secretary of the admiralty. Barrow, no friend of either mutiny or tyranny, was a prolific writer on exploration, with a special interest in the Arctic regions that would dominate geographical attention after the age of Cook. In writing the book he would publish in 1831 as *The Eventful History of the Mutiny and Piratical Seizure of* H.M.S. Bounty: *Its Causes and Consequences,* Barrow did not have to worry about personal controversy. Fletcher Christian was supposed to have died around 1793. His brother Edward had died in 1823, and Bligh five years before that, in 1817. However, there were still those living whose part Barrow might take, particularly *Bounty* crew member Peter Heywood. After the court-martial,

Heywood continued in favor with the public and even those who had found him guilty. His rank was restored and he received further promotion to the rank of captain. He died early in 1831, and may or may not actively have collaborated with Barrow on his book. Remarkably, years before, Heywood believed he had spotted a fugitive Fletcher Christian in Devonport, and Barrow was the first to make public this otherwise unconfirmed sighting—only after Heywood's death.

For forty years—and perhaps more—the version of the *Bounty* story published by Barrow exclusively held the literary field. Even Lady Diana Belcher—stepdaughter of Peter Heywood and the second great *Bounty*phile—did not rival Barrow's popularity when she published her *Mutineers of the Bounty and Their Descendants* in 1870. Only with the publication of Charles Nordhoff's and James Norman Hall's fictionalized *Bounty* trilogy—*Mutiny on the Bounty* (1932), *Men Against the Sea* (1934), and *Pitcairn's Island* (1934)—did a distinct twentieth-century *Bounty* paradigm emerge. But even the influence of Barrow's book could not entirely shape the popular response to the *Bounty* mutiny. For the nineteenth century as a whole, one's view of the mutiny still grew out of one's own belief in either the overarching importance of the stability of civilization on one hand, or in the inalienable rights of man on the other. James Fenimore Cooper, writing in 1844 about an abortive mutiny on a navy training vessel named the *Somers,* took Bligh's view:

> Mutinies have two general characters, the one of *disaffection,* the other of *conspiracy.* That of the *Hermione* was of the first class, that of the *Bounty* of the last. (From *Proceedings of the Naval Court Martial in the Case of Alexander Slidell Mackenzie* [1844], p. 273.)

For Herman Melville, who reflects in chapter 18 of *Omoo* (1847) on the celebrity of Tahiti, it was "Here the memorable mutiny of the Bounty afterward had its origin." Melville, if anyone, was able to tell the difference between the seductions of the land and the tyranny of the quarterdeck, yet there is no allusion to Bligh or the *Bounty* in his own fictionalized mutinous agony in chapter 67 of *White-Jacket* (1850). A third notable sailor-author of the nineteenth century, Richard Henry Dana, Jr., writes in the third part of *The Seaman's Friend* (1841), "In all these cases of revolt, mutiny, endeavors to commit the same, and confinement of the master, it is to be remembered that the acts are excusable if done from a sufficient justifying cause." But a year earlier, in describing in *Two Years Before the Mast* his own encounter with quarterdeck tyranny, which must have been very similar to Fletcher Christian's, Dana invokes neither Bligh nor *Bounty,* and seems to have had no thought of murder or mutiny.

In the twentieth century, the *Bounty* story has been thoroughly mythologized. It is only a short step from Fletcher Christian to Billy Budd, and no step at all from Lieutenant Bligh to Captain Queeg. In fact, it may be Herman Wouk's *Caine Mutiny* (1951) that most dispassionately examines the nature of the failure of command, even as it applies to the *Bounty.* In any case, modern historians of the mutiny still find themselves thrust into the roles of defenders and accusers. For those great spirits William Bligh and Fletcher Christian, two stars still keep not their motion in one sphere.

R. D. Madison
Annapolis, Maryland

SUGGESTIONS FOR FURTHER READING

The volume of *Bounty* literature is enormous. The following list is limited but may provide helpful starting points. Works by Kennedy and Christian contain the most up-to-date surveys of the literature.

Barrow, Sir John. *The Mutiny of the* Bounty. 1831. Reprint (Gavin Kennedy, ed.), Boston: David R. Godine, 1980.

Beechey, F. W. *Narrative of a Voyage to the Pacific and Beering's Strait.* London: Colburn and Bentley, 1831.

Belcher, Diana. *The Mutineers of the* Bounty *and Their Descendants in Pitcairn and Norfolk Islands.* London: John Murray, 1870.

Bligh, William. *A Voyage to the South Sea.* London: George Nicol, 1792.

Christian, Glynn. *Fragile Paradise: The Discovery of Fletcher Christian,* Bounty *Mutineer.* Boston: Little, Brown, 1982.

Kennedy, Gavin. *Captain Bligh: The Man and His Mutinies.* London: Duckworth, 1989.

Mackaness, George. *The Life of Vice-Admiral William Bligh.* London: Angus and Robertson, 1951.

Maude, H. E. "In Search of a Home," *Journal of the Polynesian Society.* Vol. 67, no. 2 (June 1958), 104–131.

Rutter, Owen, ed. *The Court-Martial of the* Bounty *Mutineers.* Notable British Trials. London: Hodge, 1931.

———. *The Journal of James Morrison Boatswain's Mate of the* Bounty *describing the Mutiny and subsequent Misfortunes of the Mutineers together with an account of the Island of Tahiti.* London: Golden Cockerel Press, 1935.

A NOTE ON THE TEXTS

The texts for the four major documents included in this Penguin edition are based on the first editions:

William Bligh, *A Narrative of the Mutiny, on Board His Majesty's Ship* Bounty; *and the Subsequent Voyage of Part of the Crew, in the Ship's Boat, from Tofoa, one of the Friendly Islands, to Timor, a Dutch Settlement in the East Indies* (London: George Nicol, 1790).

Edward Christian and Stephen Barney, *Minutes of the Proceedings of the Court-Martial held at Portsmouth, August 12, 1792. On Ten Persons charged with Mutiny on Board His Majesty's Ship the* Bounty. *With an Appendix, Containing A full Account of the real Causes and Circumstances of that unhappy Transaction, the most material of which have hitherto been withheld from the Public* (London: J. Deighton, 1794).

William Bligh, *An Answer to Certain Assertions contained in the Appendix to a Pamphlet, entitled* Minutes of the Proceedings on the Court-Martial held at Portsmouth, August 12th, 1792, on Ten Persons charged with Mutiny on Board his Majesty's Ship the Bounty (London: G. Nicol, 1794).

Edward Christian, *A Short Reply to Capt. William Bligh's Answer* (London: J. Deighton, 1795).

A facsimile edition of these four texts was published for the Australiana Society by Georgian House, Melbourne, Australia, in 1952.

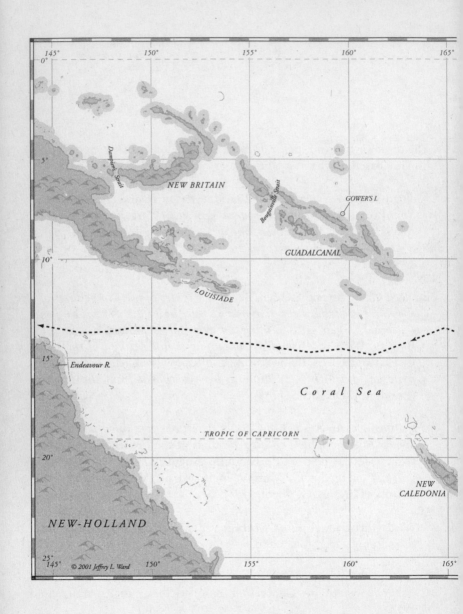

145°   150°   155°   160°   165°

0°

5°

Dampier Strait

NEW BRITAIN

Bougainville Strait

GOWER'S I.

GUADALCANAL

10°

LOUISIADE

15°
Endeavour R.

Coral Sea

TROPIC OF CAPRICORN

20°

NEW
CALEDONIA

NEW-HOLLAND

25°
145°   150°   155°   160°   165°

© 2001 Jeffrey L. Ward

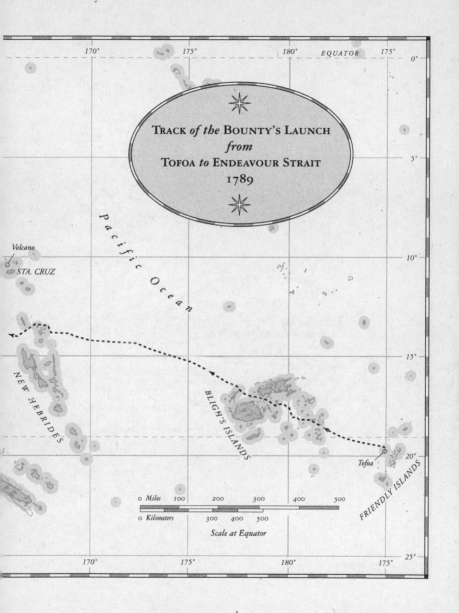

170°

EQUATOR

TRACK *of the* BOUNTY'S LAUNCH
from
TOFOA *to* ENDEAVOUR STRAIT
1789

Volcano

STA. CRUZ

P a c i f i c   O c e a n

NEW HEBRIDES

BLIGH'S ISLANDS

Tofoa

FRIENDLY ISLANDS

o *Miles*   100   200   300   400   500

o *Kilometers*   300   400   500

Scale at Equator

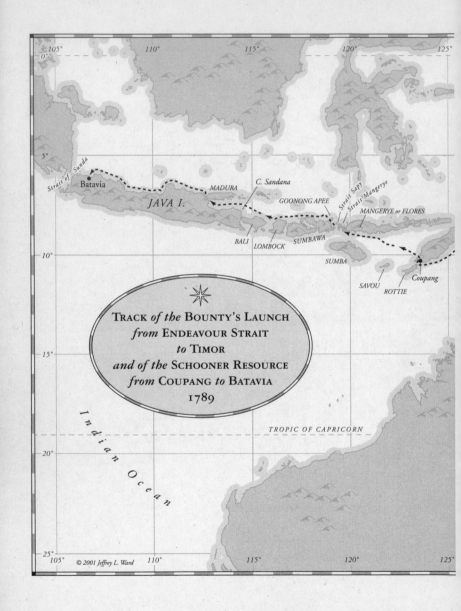

Track *of the* Bounty's Launch
from Endeavour Strait
to Timor
and of the Schooner Resource
from Coupang *to* Batavia
1789

© 2001 Jeffrey L. Ward

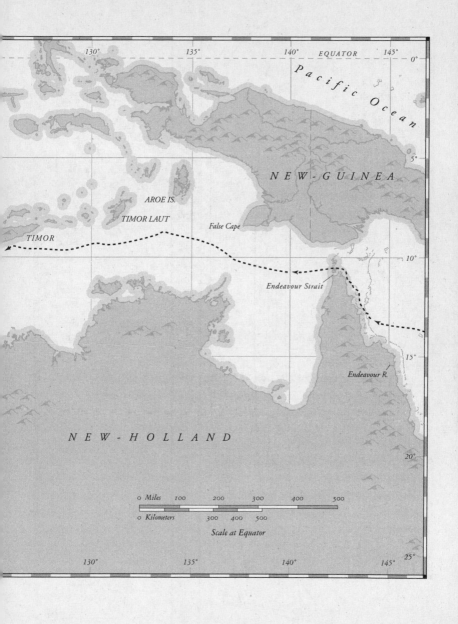

130°   135°   140°   EQUATOR   145°   0°

Pacific Ocean

5°

N E W - G U I N E A

AROE IS.

TIMOR LAUT   *False Cape*

TIMOR

10°

Endeavour Strait

15°

Endeavour R.

N E W - H O L L A N D   20°

o Miles   100   200   300   400   500
o Kilometers   300   400   500
Scale at Equator

130°   135°   140°   145°   25°

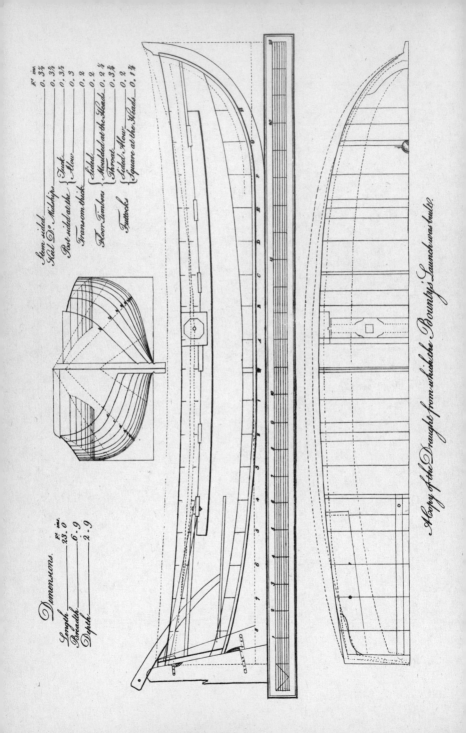

A Copy of the Draught from which the Bounty's Launch was built.

Dimensions. Ft. in.
Length ———— 23. 0
Breadth ———— 6. 9
Depth ———— 2. 9

Stem sided ———————— 0. 3½
Keel Dʳ. Midships ———————— 0. 3½
Post sided at the { Head ———— 0. 3½
{ Heel ———— 0. 3

Transom thick ———————— 0. 2

Floor Timbers { Sided ———— 0. 2
{ Moulded at the Head 0. 2½

Futtocks { Throat ———— 0. 3½
{ Sided. Floor ———— 0. 2
{ Square at the Head 0. 1¾

A
NARRATIVE

OF THE

MUTINY,

ON BOARD

HIS MAJESTY's SHIP *BOUNTY*;

AND THE

SUBSEQUENT VOYAGE OF PART OF THE CREW,

IN THE SHIP's BOAT,

From Tofoa, one of the Friendly Iſlands,

To Timor, a Dutch Settlement in the Eaſt Indies.

———

Written by Lieutenant WILLIAM BLIGH.

Advertisement

THE FOLLOWING NARRATIVE is only a part of a voyage undertaken for the purpose of conveying the Bread-fruit Tree from the South Sea Islands to the West Indies. The manner in which this expedition miscarried, with the subsequent transactions and events, are here related. This part of the voyage is not first in the order of time, yet the circumstances are so distinct from that by which it was preceded, that it appears unnecessary to delay giving as much early information as possible concerning so extraordinary an event. The rest will be laid before the Public as soon as it can be got ready; and it is intended to publish it in such a manner, as, with the present Narrative, will make the account of the voyage compleat.

At present, for the better understanding the following pages, it is sufficient to inform the reader, that in August, 1787, I was appointed to command the Bounty, a ship of 215 tons burthen, carrying 4 sixpounders, 4 swivels, and 46 men, including myself and every person on board. We sailed from England in December, 1787, and arrived at Otaheite the 26th of October, 1788. On the 4th of April, 1789, we left Otaheite, with every favourable appearance of completing the object of the voyage, in a manner equal to my most sanguine expectations. At this period the ensuing Narrative commences.

A Narrative, &c.

I SAILED FROM OTAHEITE on the 4th of April 1789, having on board 1015 fine bread-fruit plants, besides many other valuable fruits of that country, which, with unremitting attention, we had been collecting for three and twenty weeks, and which were now in the highest state of perfection.

On the 11th of April, I discovered an island in latitude 18° 52′ S. and longitude 200° 19′ E. by the natives called Whytootackee. On the 24th we anchored at Annamooka, one of the Friendly Islands; from which, after completing our wood and water, I sailed on the 27th, having every reason to expect, from the fine condition of the plants, that they would continue healthy.

On the evening of the 28th, owing to light winds, we were not clear of the islands, and at night I directed my course towards Tofoa. The master had the first watch; the gunner the middle watch; and Mr. Christian, one of the mates, the morning watch. This was the turn of duty for the night.

Just before sun-rising, Mr. Christian, with the master at arms, gunner's mate, and Thomas Burket, seaman, came into my cabin while I was asleep, and seizing me, tied my hands with a cord behind my back, and threatened me with instant death, if I spoke or made the least noise: I, however, called so loud as to alarm every one; but they had already secured the officers who were not of their party, by placing centinels at their doors. There were three men at my cabin door, besides the four within; Christian had only a cutlass in his hand, the others had muskets and bayonets. I was hauled out of bed, and forced on deck in my shirt, suffering great pain from the tightness with which they had tied my hands. I demanded the reason of such violence, but received no other answer than threats of instant death, if I did not hold my tongue. Mr. Elphinston, the master's mate, was kept in his birth; Mr. Nelson, botanist, Mr. Peckover, gunner, Mr. Ledward, surgeon, and the master, were confined to their cabins; and also the clerk, Mr. Samuel, but he soon obtained leave to come on deck. The fore hatchway was guarded by centinels; the boatswain and carpenter were, however, allowed to come on deck, where they saw me standing abaft the mizen-mast, with my hands tied behind my back, under a guard, with Christian at their head.

The boatswain was now ordered to hoist the launch out, with a threat, if he did not do it instantly, to take care of himself.

The boat being out, Mr. Hayward and Mr. Hallet, midshipmen, and Mr. Samuel, were ordered into it; upon which I demanded the cause of such an order, and endeavoured to persuade some one to a sense of duty; but it was to no effect: "Hold your tongue, Sir, or you are dead this instant," was constantly repeated to me.

The master, by this time, had sent to be allowed to come on deck, which was permitted; but he was soon ordered back again to his cabin.

I continued my endeavours to turn the tide of affairs, when Christian changed the cutlass he had in his hand for a bayonet, that was brought to him, and, holding me with a strong gripe by the cord that tied my hands, he with many oaths threatened to kill me immediately if I would not be quiet: the villains round me had their pieces cocked and bayonets fixed. Particular people were now called on to go into the boat, and were hurried over the side: whence I concluded that with these people I was to be set adrift.

I therefore made another effort to bring about a change, but with no other effect than to be threatened with having my brains blown out.

The boatswain and seamen, who were to go in the boat, were allowed to collect twine, canvas, lines, sails, cordage, an eight and twenty gallon cask of water, and the carpenter to take his tool chest. Mr. Samuel got 150 lbs of bread, with a small quantity of rum and wine. He also got a quadrant and compass into the boat; but was forbidden, on pain of death, to touch either map, ephemeris, book of astronomical observations, sextant, time-keeper, or any of my surveys or drawings.

The mutineers now hurried those they meant to get rid of into the boat. When most of them were in, Christian directed a dram to be served to each of his own crew. I now unhappily saw that nothing could be done to effect the recovery of the ship: there was no one to assist me, and every endeavour on my part was answered with threats of death.

The officers were called, and forced over the side into the boat, while I was kept apart from every one, abaft the mizen-mast; Christian, armed with a bayonet, holding me by the bandage that secured my hands. The guard round me had their pieces cocked, but, on my daring the ungrateful wretches to fire, they uncocked them.

Isaac Martin, one of the guard over me, I saw, had an inclination to assist me, and, as he fed me with shaddock, (my lips being quite parched with my endeavours to bring about a change) we explained our wishes to each other by our looks; but this being observed, Martin was instantly removed from me; his inclination then was to leave the ship, for which purpose he got into the boat; but with many threats they obliged him to return.

The armourer, Joseph Coleman, and the two carpenters, McIntosh and Norman, were also kept contrary to their inclination; and they begged of me, after I was astern in the boat, to remember that they declared they had no hand in the transaction. Michael Byrne, I am told, likewise wanted to leave the ship.

It is of no moment for me to recount my endeavours to bring back the offenders to a sense of their duty: all I could do was by speaking to them in general; but my endeavours were of no avail, for I was kept securely bound, and no one but the guard suffered to come near me.

To Mr. Samuel I am indebted for securing my journals and commission, with some material ship papers. Without these I had nothing to certify what I had done, and my honour and character might have been suspected, without my possessing a proper document to have defended them. All this he did with great resolution, though guarded and strictly watched. He attempted to save the time-keeper, and a box with all my surveys, drawings, and remarks for fifteen years past, which were numerous; when he was hurried away, with "Damn your eyes, you are well off to get what you have."

It appeared to me, that Christian was some time in doubt whether he should keep the carpenter, or his mates; at length he determined on the latter, and the carpenter was ordered into the boat. He was permitted, but not without some opposition, to take his tool chest.

Much altercation took place among the mutinous crew during the whole business: some swore "I'll be damned if he does not find his way home, if he gets any thing with him," (meaning me); others, when the carpenter's chest was carrying away, "Damn my eyes, he will have a vessel built in a month." While others laughed at the helpless situation of the boat, being very deep, and so little room for those who were in her. As for Christian, he seemed meditating instant destruction on himself and every one.

I asked for arms, but they laughed at me, and said I was well acquainted with the people where I was going, and therefore did not want them; four cutlasses, however, were thrown into the boat, after we were veered astern.

When the officers and men, with whom I was suffered to have no communication, were put into the boat, they only waited for me, and the master at arms informed Christian of it; who then said—"Come, captain Bligh, your officers and men are now in the boat, and you must go with them; if you attempt to make the least resistance you will instantly be put to death": and, without any farther ceremony, holding me by the cord that tied my hands, with a tribe of armed ruffians about me, I was forced over the side, where they untied my hands. Being in the boat we were veered astern by a rope. A few pieces of pork were then thrown to us, and some cloaths, also the cutlasses I have already mentioned; and it was now that the armourer and carpenters called out to me to remember that they had no hand in the transaction. After having undergone a great deal of ridicule, and been kept some time to make sport for these unfeeling wretches, we were at length cast adrift in the open ocean.

I had with me in the boat the following persons:

Names.	Stations.
JOHN FRYER	Master.
THOMAS LEDWARD	Acting Surgeon.
DAVID NELSON	Botanist.
WILLIAM PECKOVER	Gunner.
WILLIAM COLE	Boatswain.
WILLIAM PURCELL	Carpenter.
WILLIAM ELPHINSTON	Master's Mate.
THOMAS HAYWARD	}Midshipmen.
JOHN HALLET	

John Norton ....⎫
Peter Linkletter ....⎬Quarter Masters.

Lawrence Lebogue .....Sailmaker.

John Smith ....⎫
Thomas Hall ....⎬Cooks.

George Simpson ....Quarter Master's Mate.

Robert Tinkler ....A boy.

Robert Lamb ....Butcher.

Mr. Samuel ....Clerk.

There remained on board the Bounty, as pirates,

Fletcher Christian .....Master's Mate.

Peter Haywood ....⎫
Edward Young ....⎬Midshipmen.
George Stewart ....⎭

Charles Churchill .....Master at Arms.

John Mills ....Gunner's Mate.

James Morrison ....Boatswain's Mate.

Thomas Burkitt ....Able Seaman.

Matthew Quintal ......Ditto.

John Sumner ....Ditto.

John Millward ....Ditto.

William McKoy ....Ditto.

Henry Hillbrandt ......Ditto.

Michael Byrne ....Ditto.

William Musprat ....Ditto.

Alexander Smith ....Ditto.

John Williams ....Ditto.

Thomas Ellison ....Ditto.

Isaac Martin ....Ditto.

Richard Skinner ....Ditto.

Matthew Thompson ....Ditto.

William Brown ....Gardiner.

Joseph Coleman ....Armourer.

Charles Norman ....Carpenter's Mate.

Thomas McIntosh ......Carpenter's Crew.

In all 25 hands, and the most able men of the ship's company.

Having little or no wind, we rowed pretty fast towards Tofoa, which bore NE about 10 leagues from us. While the ship was in sight she steered to the WNW, but I considered this only as a feint; for when we were sent away—"Huzza for Otaheite," was frequently heard among the mutineers.

Christian, the captain of the gang, is of a respectable family in the north of England. This was the third voyage he had made with me; and, as I found it necessary to keep my ship's company at three watches, I gave him an order to take charge of the third, his abilities being thoroughly equal to the task; and by this means my master and gunner were not at watch and watch.

Haywood is also of a respectable family in the north of England, and a young man of abilities, as well as Christian. These two were objects of my particular regard and attention, and I took great pains to instruct them, for they really promised, as professional men, to be a credit to their country.

Young was well recommended, and appeared to me an able stout seaman; therefore I was glad to take him: he, however, fell short of what his appearance promised.

Stewart was a young man of creditable parents, in the Orkneys; at which place, on the return of the Resolution from the South Seas, in 1780, we received so many civilities, that, on that account only, I should gladly have taken him with me: but, independent of this recommendation, he was a seaman, and had always borne a good character.

Notwithstanding the roughness with which I was treated, the remembrance of past kindnesses produced some signs of remorse in Christian. When they were forcing me out of the ship, I asked him, if this treatment was a proper return for the many instances he had received of my friendship? he appeared disturbed at my question, and answered, with much emotion, "That,—captain Bligh,—that is the thing;—I am in hell—I am in hell."

As soon as I had time to reflect, I felt an inward satisfaction, which prevented any depression of my spirits: conscious of my integrity, and anxious solicitude for the good of the service in which I was engaged, I found my mind wonderfully supported, and I began to conceive hopes, notwithstanding so heavy a calamity, that I should one day be able to account to my King and country for the misfortune.— A few hours before, my situation had been peculiarly flattering. I had a ship in the most perfect order, and well stored with every necessary both for service and health: by early attention to those particulars I had, as much as lay in my power, provided against any accident, in case I could not get through Endeavour Straits, as well as against what might befal me in them; add to this, the plants had been successfully preserved in the most flourishing state: so that, upon the whole, the voyage was two thirds completed, and the remaining part in a very promising way; every person on board being in perfect health, to establish which was ever amongst the principal objects of my attention.

It will very naturally be asked, what could be the reason for such a revolt? in answer to which, I can only conjecture that the mutineers had assured themselves of a more happy life among the Otaheiteans, than they could possibly have in England; which, joined to some female connections, have most probably been the principal cause of the whole transaction.

The women at Otaheite are handsome, mild and chearful in their manners and conversation, possessed of great sensibility, and have sufficient delicacy to make them admired and beloved. The chiefs were so much attached to our people, that they rather encouraged their stay among them than otherwise, and even made them promises of large possessions. Under these, and many other attendant circumstances, equally desirable, it is now perhaps not so much to be wondered at, though scarcely possible to have been foreseen, that a set of sailors, most of them void of connections, should be led away; especially when, in addition to such powerful inducements, they imagined it in their power to fix themselves in the midst of plenty, on the finest island in the world, where they need not labour, and where the allurements of dissipation are beyond any thing that can be conceived. The utmost, however, that any commander could have supposed to have happened is, that some of the people would have been tempted to desert. But if it should be asserted, that a commander is to guard against an act of mutiny and piracy in his own ship, more than by the common rules of service, it is as much as to say that he must sleep locked up, and when awake, be girded with pistols.

Desertions have happened, more or less, from many of the ships that have been at the Society Islands; but it ever has been in the commanders power to make the chiefs return their people: the knowledge, therefore, that it was unsafe to desert, perhaps, first led mine to consider with what ease so small a ship might be surprized, and that so favourable an opportunity would never offer to them again.

The secrecy of this mutiny is beyond all conception. Thirteen of the party, who were with me, had always lived forward among the people; yet neither they, nor the mess-mates of Christian, Stewart, Haywood, and Young, had ever observed any circumstance to give them suspicion of what was going on. With such close-planned acts of villainy, and my mind free from any suspicion, it is not wonderful that I have been got the better of. Perhaps, if I had had marines, a centinel at my cabin-door might have prevented it; for I slept with the door always open, that the officer of the watch might have access to me on all occasions. The possibility of such a conspiracy was ever the farthest from my thoughts. Had their mutiny been occasioned by any grievances, either real or imaginary, I must have discovered symptoms of their discontent, which would have put me on my guard: but the case was far otherwise. Christian, in particular, I was on the most friendly terms with; that very day he was engaged to have dined with me; and the preceding night he excused himself from supping with me, on pretence of being unwell; for which I felt concerned, having no suspicions of his integrity and honour.

It now remained with me to consider what was best to be done. My first determination was to seek a supply of bread-fruit and water at Tofoa, and afterwards to sail for Tongataboo, and there risk a solicitation to Poulaho, the king, to equip my boat, and grant a supply of water and provisions, so as to enable us to reach the East Indies.

The quantity of provisions I found in the boat was 150 lb. of bread, 16 pieces of pork, each piece weighing 2 lb. 6 quarts of rum, 6 bottles of wine, with 28 gallons of water, and four empty barrecoes.

Wednesday, April 29th.* Happily the afternoon kept calm, until about 4 o'clock, when we were so far to windward, that, with a moderate easterly breeze which sprung up, we were able to sail. It was nevertheless dark when we got to Tofoa, where I expected to land; but the shore proved to be so steep and rocky, that I was obliged to give up all thoughts of it, and keep the boat under the lee of the island with two oars; for there was no anchorage. Having fixed on this

---

*It is to be observed, that the account of time is kept in the nautical way, each day ending at noon. Thus the beginning of the 29th of April is, according to the common way of reckoning, the afternoon of the 28th.

mode of proceeding for the night, I served to every person half a pint of grog, and each took to his rest as well as our unhappy situation would allow.

In the morning, at dawn of day, we set off along shore in search of landing, and about ten o'clock we discovered a stony cove at the NW part of the island, where I dropt the grapnel within 20 yards of the rocks. A great deal of surf ran on the shore; but, as I was unwilling to diminish our stock of provisions, I landed Mr. Samuel, and some others, who climbed the cliffs, and got into the country to search for supplies. The rest of us remained at the cove, not discovering any way to get into the country, but that by which Mr. Samuel had proceeded. It was great consolation to me to find, that the spirits of my people did not sink, notwithstanding our miserable and almost hopeless situation. Towards noon Mr. Samuel returned, with a few quarts of water, which he had found in holes; but he had met with no spring, or any prospect of a sufficient supply in that particular, and had only seen signs of inhabitants. As it was impossible to know how much we might be in want, I only issued a morsel of bread, and a glass of wine, to each person for dinner.

I observed the latitude of this cove to be 19° 41′ S.

This is the NW part of Tofoa, the north-westernmost of the Friendly Islands.

Thursday, April 30th. Fair weather, but the wind blew so violently from the ESE that I could not venture to sea. Our detention therefore made it absolutely necessary to see what we could do more for our support; for I determined, if possible, to keep my first stock entire: I therefore weighed, and rowed along shore, to see if any thing could be got; and at last discovered some cocoa-nut trees, but they were on the top of high precipices, and the surf made it dangerous landing; both one and the other we, however, got the better of. Some, with much difficulty, climbed the cliffs, and got about 20 cocoa-nuts, and others slung them to ropes, by which we hauled them through the surf into the boat. This was all that could be done here; and, as I found no place so eligible as the one we had left to spend the night at, I returned to the cove, and, having served a cocoa-nut to each person, we went to rest again in the boat.

At dawn of day I attempted to get to sea; but the wind and weather proved so bad, that I was glad to return to my former station; where, after issuing a morsel of bread and a spoonful of rum to each person, we landed, and I went off with Mr. Nelson, Mr. Samuel, and some others, into the country, having hauled ourselves up the precipice by long vines, which were fixed there by the natives for that purpose; this being the only way into the country.

We found a few deserted huts, and a small plantain walk, but little taken care of; from which we could only collect three small bunches of plantains. After passing this place, we came to a deep gully that led towards a mountain, near a volcano; and, as I conceived that in the rainy season very great torrents of water must pass through it, we hoped to find sufficient for our use remaining in some holes of the rocks; but, after all our search, the whole that we found was only nine gallons, in the course of the day. We advanced within two miles of the foot of the highest mountain in the island, on which is the vol-cano that is almost constantly burning. The country near it is all cov-ered with lava, and has a most dreary appearance. As we had not been fortunate in our discoveries, and saw but little to alleviate our distresses, we filled our cocoa-nut shells with the water we found, and returned exceedingly fatigued and faint. When I came to the precipice whence we were to descend into the cove, I was seized with such a dizziness in my head, that I thought it scarce possible to effect it: however, by the assistance of Mr. Nelson and others, they at last got me down, in a weak condition. Every person being returned by noon, I gave about an ounce of pork and two plantains to each, with half a glass of wine. I again observed the latitude of this place 19° 41′ south. The people who remained by the boat I had directed to look for fish, or what they could pick up about the rocks; but nothing eat-able could be found: so that, upon the whole, we considered our-selves on as miserable a spot of land as could well be imagined.

I could not say positively, from the former knowledge I had of this island, whether it was inhabited or not; but I knew it was con-sidered inferior to the other islands, and I was not certain but that the Indians only resorted to it at particular times. I was very anxious to ascertain this point; for, in case there had only been a few people here, and those could have furnished us with but very moderate sup-plies, the remaining in this spot to have made preparations for our voyage, would have been preferable to the risk of going amongst multitudes, where perhaps we might lose every thing. A party, there-fore, sufficiently strong, I determined should go another route, as soon as the sun became lower; and they cheerfully undertook it.

Friday, May the 1st: stormy weather, wind ESE and SE. About two o'clock in the afternoon the party set out; but, after suffering much fatigue, they returned in the evening, without any kind of success.

At the head of the cove, about 150 yards from the water-side, was a cave; across the stony beach was about 100 yards, and the only way from the country into the cove was that which I have already described. The situation secured us from the danger of being surprised, and I determined to remain on shore for the night, with a part of my people, that the others might have more room to rest in the boat, with the master; whom I directed to lie at a grapnel, and be watchful, in case we should be attacked. I ordered one plantain for each person to be boiled; and, having supped on this scanty allowance, with a quarter of a pint of grog, and fixed the watches for the night, those whose turn it was, laid down to sleep in the cave; before which we kept up a good fire, yet notwithstanding we were much troubled with flies and musquitoes.

At dawn of day the party set out again in a different route, to see what they could find; in the course of which they suffered greatly for want of water: they, however, met with two men, a woman, and a child; the men came with them to the cove, and brought two cocoa-nut shells of water. I immediately made friends with these people, and sent them away for bread-fruit, plantains, and water. Soon after other natives came to us; and by noon I had 30 of them about me, trading with the articles we were in want of: but I could only afford one ounce of pork, and a quarter of a bread-fruit, to each man for dinner, with half a pint of water; for I was fixed in not using any of the bread or water in the boat.

No particular chief was yet among the natives: they were, notwithstanding, tractable, and behaved honestly, giving the provisions they brought for a few buttons and beads. The party who had been out, informed me of having discovered several neat plantations; so that it became no longer a doubt of there being settled inhabitants on the island; and for that reason I determined to get what I could, and sail the first moment the wind and weather would allow me to put to sea.

Saturday, May the 2d: stormy weather, wind ESE. It had hitherto been a weighty consideration with me, how I was to account to the natives for the loss of my ship: I knew they had too much sense to be amused with a story that the ship was to join me, when she was not in sight from the hills. I was at first doubtful whether I should tell the real fact, or say that the ship had overset and sunk, and that only we were saved: the latter appeared to me to be the most proper and advantageous to us, and I accordingly instructed my people, that we might all agree in one story. As I expected, enquiries were made after the ship, and they seemed readily satisfied with our account; but there did not appear the least symptom of joy or sorrow in their faces, although I fancied I discovered some marks of surprise. Some of the natives were coming and going the whole afternoon, and we got enough of bread-fruit, plantains, and cocoa-nuts for another day; but water they only brought us about five pints. A canoe also came in with four men, and brought a few cocoa-nuts and bread-fruit, which I bought as I had done the rest. Nails were much enquired after, but I would not suffer one to be shewn, as I wanted them for the use of the boat.

Towards evening I had the satisfaction to find our stock of provisions somewhat increased: but the natives did not appear to have much to spare. What they brought was in such small quantities, that I had no reason to hope we should be able to procure from them sufficient to stock us for our voyage. At sunset all the natives left us in quiet possession of the cove. I thought this a good sign, and made no doubt that they would come again the next day with a larger proportion of food and water, with which I hoped to sail without farther delay: for if, in attempting to get to Tongataboo, we should be blown away from the islands altogether, there would be a larger quantity of provisions to support us against such a misfortune.

At night I served a quarter of a bread-fruit and a cocoa-nut to each person for supper; and, a good fire being made, all but the watch went to sleep.

At day-break I was happy to find every one's spirits a little revived, and that they no longer regarded me with those anxious looks, which had constantly been directed towards me since we lost sight of the ship: every countenance appeared to have a degree of cheerfulness, and they all seemed determined to do their best.

As I doubted of water being brought by the natives, I sent a party among the gullies in the mountains, with empty shells, to see what they could get. In their absence the natives came about us, as I expected, but more numerous; also two canoes came in from round the north side of the island. In one of them was an elderly chief, called Maccaackavow. Soon after some of our foraging party returned, and with them came a good-looking chief, called Eegijeefow, or perhaps more properly Eefow, Egij or Eghee, signifying a chief. To both these men I made a present of an old shirt and a knife, and I soon found they either had seen me, or had heard of my being at Annamooka. They knew I had been with captain Cook, who they enquired after, and also captain Clerk. They were very inquisitive to know in what manner I had lost my ship. During this conversation a young man appeared, whom I remembered to have seen at Annamooka, called Nageete: he expressed much pleasure at seeing me. I now enquired after Poulaho and Feenow, who, they said, were at Tongataboo; and Eefow agreed to accompany me thither, if I would wait till the weather moderated. The readiness and affability of this man gave me much satisfaction.

This, however, was but of short duration, for the natives began to increase in number, and I observed some symptoms of a design against us; soon after they attempted to haul the boat on shore, when I threatened Eefow with a cutlass, to induce him to make them desist; which they did, and every thing became quiet again. My people, who had been in the mountains, now returned with about three gallons of water. I kept buying up the little bread-fruit that was brought to us, and likewise some spears to arm my men with, having only four cutlasses, two of which were in the boat. As we had no means of improving our situation, I told our people I would wait until sun-set, by which time, perhaps, something might happen in our favour: that if we attempted to go at present, we must fight our way through, which we could do more advantageously at night; and that in the mean time we would endeavour to get off to the boat what we had bought. The beach was now lined with the natives, and we heard nothing but the knocking of stones together, which they had in each hand. I knew very well this was the sign of an attack. It being now noon, I served a cocoa-nut and a bread-fruit to each person for dinner, and gave some to the chiefs, with whom I continued to appear intimate and friendly. They frequently importuned me to sit down, but I as constantly refused; for it occurred both to Mr. Nelson and myself, that they intended to seize hold of me, if I gave them such an opportunity. Keeping, therefore, constantly on our guard, we were suffered to eat our uncomfortable meal in some quietness.

Sunday, 3d May. Fresh gales at SE and ESE, varying to the NE in the latter part, with a storm of wind.

After dinner we began by little and little to get our things into the boat, which was a troublesome business, on account of the surf. I carefully watched the motions of the natives, who still increased in number, and found that, instead of their intention being to leave us, fires were made, and places fixed on for their stay during the night. Consultations were also held among them, and every thing assured me we should be attacked. I sent orders to the master, that when he saw us coming down, he should keep the boat close to the shore, that we might the more readily embark.

I had my journal on shore with me, writing the occurrences in the cave, and in sending it down to the boat it was nearly snatched away, but for the timely assistance of the gunner.

The sun was near setting when I gave the word, on which every person, who was on shore with me, boldly took up his proportion of things, and carried them to the boat. The chiefs asked me if I would not stay with them all night, I said, "No, I never sleep out of my boat; but in the morning we will again trade with you, and I shall remain until the weather is moderate, that we may go, as we have agreed, to see Poulaho, at Tongataboo." Maccaackavow then got up, and said, "You will not sleep on shore? then Mattie," (which directly signifies we will kill you) and he left me. The onset was now preparing; every one, as I have described before, kept knocking stones together, and Eefow quitted me. We had now all but two or three things in the boat, when I took Nageete by the hand, and we walked down the beach, every one in a silent kind of horror.

When I came to the boat, and was seeing the people embark, Nageete wanted me to stay to speak to Eefow; but I found he was encouraging them to the attack, and I determined, had it then begun, to have killed him for his treacherous behaviour. I ordered the carpenter not to quit me until the other people were in the boat. Nageete, finding I would not stay, loosed himself from my hold and went off, and we all got into the boat except one man, who, while I was getting on board, quitted it, and ran up the beach to cast the stern fast off, notwithstanding the master and others called to him to return, while they were hauling me out of the water.

I was no sooner in the boat than the attack began by about 200 men; the unfortunate poor man who had run up the beach was knocked down, and the stones flew like a shower of shot. Many Indians got hold of the stern rope, and were near hauling us on shore, and would certainly have done it if I had not had a knife in my pocket, with which I cut the rope. We then hauled off to the grapnel, every one being more or less hurt. At this time I saw five of the natives about the poor man they had killed, and two of them were beating him about the head with stones in their hands.

We had no time to reflect, before, to my surprise, they filled their canoes with stones, and twelve men came off after us to renew the attack, which they did so effectually as nearly to disable all of us. Our grapnel was foul, but Providence here assisted us; the fluke broke, and we got to our oars, and pulled to sea. They, however, could paddle round us, so that we were obliged to sustain the attack without being able to return it, except with such stones as lodged in the boat, and in this I found we were very inferior to them. We could not close, because our boat was lumbered and heavy, and that they knew very well: I therefore adopted the expedient of throwing overboard some cloaths, which they lost time in picking up; and, as it was now almost dark, they gave over the attack, and returned towards the shore, leaving us to reflect on our unhappy situation.

The poor man I lost was John Norton: this was his second voyage with me as a quarter-master, and his worthy character made me lament his loss very much. He has left an aged parent, I am told, whom he supported.

I once before sustained an attack of a similar nature, with a smaller number of Europeans, against a multitude of Indians; it was after the death of captain Cook, on the Morai at Owhyhee, where I was left by lieutenant King: yet, notwithstanding, I did not conceive that the power of a man's arm could throw stones, from two to eight pounds weight, with such force and exactness as these people did. Here unhappily I was without arms, and the Indians knew it; but it was a fortunate circumstance that they did not begin to attack us in the cave: in that case our destruction must have been inevitable, and we should have had nothing left for it but to die as bravely as we could, fighting close together; in which I found every one cheerfully disposed to join me. This appearance of resolution deterred them, supposing they could effect their purpose without risk after we were in the boat.

Taking this as a sample of the dispositions of the Indians, there was little reason to expect much benefit if I persevered in my inten-

tion of visiting Poulaho; for I considered their good behaviour hitherto to proceed from a dread of our fire-arms, which, now knowing
us destitute of, would cease; and, even supposing our lives not in
danger, the boat and every thing we had would most probably be
taken from us, and thereby all hopes precluded of ever being able to
return to our native country.

We were now sailing along the west side of the island Tofoa, and
my mind was employed in considering what was best to be done,
when I was solicited by all hands to take them towards home: and,
when I told them no hopes of relief for us remained, but what I
might find at New Holland, until I came to Timor, a distance of full
1200 leagues, where was a Dutch settlement, but in what part of the
island I knew not, they all agreed to live on one ounce of bread, and
a quarter of a pint of water, per day. Therefore, after examining our
stock of provisions, and recommending this as a sacred promise for
ever to their memory, we bore away across a sea, where the navigation is but little known, in a small boat, twenty-three feet long from
stem to stern, deep laden with eighteen men; without a chart, and
nothing but my own recollection and general knowledge of the situation of places, assisted by a book of latitudes and longitudes, to
guide us. I was happy, however, to see every one better satisfied with
our situation in this particular than myself.

Our stock of provisions consisted of about one hundred and fifty
pounds of bread, twenty-eight gallons of water, twenty pounds of
pork, three bottles of wine, and five quarts of rum. The difference between this and the quantity we had on leaving the ship, was principally owing to loss in the bustle and confusion of the attack. A few
cocoa-nuts were in the boat, and some bread-fruit, but the latter was
trampled to pieces.

It was about eight o'clock at night when I bore away under a
reefed lug fore-sail: and, having divided the people into watches, and
got the boat in a little order, we returned God thanks for our miraculous preservation, and, fully confident of his gracious support, I
found my mind more at ease than for some time past.

At day-break the gale increased; the sun rose very fiery and red, a
sure indication of a severe gale of wind. At eight it blew a violent
storm, and the sea ran very high, so that between the seas the sail was
becalmed, and when on the top of the sea it was too much to have set:

but I was obliged to carry to it, for we were now in very imminent danger and distress, the sea curling over the stern of the boat, which obliged us to bale with all our might. A situation more distressing has, perhaps, seldom been experienced.

Our bread was in bags, and in danger of being spoiled by the wet: to be starved to death was inevitable, if this could not be prevented: I therefore began to examine what cloaths there were in the boat, and what other things could be spared; and, having determined that only two suits should be kept for each person, the rest was thrown overboard, with some rope and spare sails, which lightened the boat considerably, and we had more room to bale the water out. Fortunately the carpenter had a good chest in the boat, into which I put the bread the first favourable moment. His tool chest also was cleared, and the tools stowed in the bottom of the boat, so that this became a second convenience.

I now served a tea-spoonful of rum to each person, (for we were very wet and cold) with a quarter of a bread-fruit, which was scarce eatable, for dinner; but our engagement was now strictly to be carried into execution, and I was fully determined to make what provisions I had last eight weeks, let the daily proportion be ever so small.

At noon I considered my course and distance from Tofoa to be WNW$\frac{3}{4}$W. 86 miles, my latitude 19° 27′ S. I directed my course to the WNW, that I might get a sight of the islands called Feejee, if they laid in the direction the natives had pointed out to me.

Monday, 4th May. This day the weather was very severe, it blew a storm from NE to ESE. The sea ran higher than yesterday, and the fatigue of baling, to keep the boat from filling, was exceedingly great. We could do nothing more than keep before the sea; in the course of which the boat performed so wonderfully well, that I no longer dreaded any danger in that respect. But among the hardships we were to undergo, that of being constantly wet was not the least: the nights were very cold, and at day-light our limbs were so benumbed, that we could scarce find the use of them. At this time I served a tea-spoonful of rum to each person, which we all found great benefit from.

As I have mentioned before, I determined to keep to the WNW, until I got more to the northward, for I not only expected to have better weather, but to see the Feejee Islands, as I have often under-

stood, from the natives of Annamooka, that they lie in that direction;
Captain Cook likewise considers them to be NW by W from Tongataboo. Just before noon we discovered a small flat island of a
moderate height, bearing WSW, 4 or 5 leagues. I observed in latitude
18° 58′ S; our longitude, by account, 3° 4′ W from the island Tofoa,
having made a N 72° W course, distance 95 miles, since yesterday
noon. I divided five small cocoa-nuts for our dinner, and every one
was satisfied.

Tuesday, 5th May. Towards the evening the gale considerably
abated. Wind SE.

A little after noon, other islands appeared, and at a quarter past
three o'clock we could count eight, bearing from S round by the west
to NW by N; those to the south, which were the nearest, being four
leagues distant from us.

I kept my course to the NW by W, between the islands, and at six
o'clock discovered three other small islands to the NW, the westernmost of them bore NW½W 7 leagues. I steered to the southward of
these islands, a WNW course for the night, under a reefed sail.

Served a few broken pieces of bread-fruit for supper, and performed prayers.

The night turned out fair, and, having had tolerable rest, every one
seemed considerably better in the morning, and contentedly break-
fasted on a few pieces of yams that were found in the boat. After
breakfast we prepared a chest for our bread, and got it secured: but
unfortunately a great deal was damaged and rotten; this nevertheless
we were glad to keep for use.

I had hitherto been scarcely able to keep any account of our run;
but we now equipped ourselves a little better, by getting a log-line
marked, and, having practiced at counting seconds, several could do
it with some degree of exactness.

The islands I have passed lie between the latitude of 19° 5′ S and
18° 19′ S, and, according to my reckoning, from 3° 17′ to 3° 46′ W
longitude from the island Tofoa: the largest may be about six leagues
in circuit; but it is impossible for me to be very exact. To show where
they are to be found again is the most my situation enabled me to
do. The sketch I have made, will give a comparative view of their extent. I believe all the larger islands are inhabited, as they appeared
very fertile.

At noon I observed, in latitude 18° 10′ S, and considered my course and distance from yesterday noon, NW by W$\frac{1}{2}$W, 94 miles; longitude, by account, from Tofoa 4° 29′ W.

For dinner, I served some of the damaged bread, and a quarter of a pint of water.

Wednesday, 6th May. Fresh breezes ENE, and fair weather, but very hazy.

About six o'clock this afternoon I discovered two islands, one bearing W by S 6 leagues, and the other NW by N 8 leagues; I kept to windward of the northernmost, and passing it by 10 o'clock, I resumed my course to the NW and WNW. At day-light in the morning I discovered a number of other islands from SSE to the W, and round to NE by E; between those in the NW I determined to pass. At noon a small sandy island or key, 2 miles distant from me, bore from E to S$\frac{3}{4}$W. I had passed ten islands, the largest of which may be 6 or 8 leagues in circuit. Much larger lands appeared in the SW and N by W, between which I directed my course. Latitude observed 17° 17′ S; course since yesterday noon N 50° W; distance 84 miles; longitude made, by account, 5° 37′ W.

Our supper, breakfast, and dinner, consisted of a quarter of a pint of cocoa-nut milk, and the meat, which did not exceed two ounces to each person: it was received very contentedly, but we suffered great drought. I dared not to land, as we had no arms, and were less capable to defend ourselves than we were at Tofoa.

To keep an account of the boat's run was rendered difficult, from being constantly wet with the sea breaking over us; but, as we advanced towards the land, the sea became smoother, and I was enabled to form a sketch of the islands, which will serve to give a general knowledge of their extent. Those I have been near are fruitful and hilly, some very mountainous, and all of a good height.

To our great joy we hooked a fish, but we were miserably disappointed by its being lost in getting into the boat.

Thursday, 7th May. Variable weather and cloudy, wind north-easterly, and calms. I continued my course to the NW, between the islands, which, by the evening, appeared of considerable extent, woody, and mountainous. At sun-set the southernmost bore from S to SW by W, and the northernmost from N by W$\frac{1}{2}$W to NE$\frac{1}{2}$E. At six o'clock I was nearly mid-way between them, and about 6 leagues distant from each shore, when I fell in with a coral bank, where I had only four feet water, without the least break on it, or ruffle of the sea to give us warning. I could only see that it extended about a mile on each side of us; but, as it is probable that it extends much farther, I have laid it down so in my sketch.

I now directed my course W by N for the night, and served to each person an ounce of the damaged bread, and a quarter of a pint of water, for supper.

It may readily be supposed, that our lodgings were very miserable and confined, and I had only in my power to remedy the latter defect by putting ourselves at watch and watch; so that one half always sat up while the other lay down on the boat's bottom, or upon a chest, with nothing to cover us but the heavens. Our limbs were dreadfully cramped, for we could not stretch them out, and the nights were so cold, and we so constantly wet, that after a few hours sleep we could scarce move.

At dawn of day we again discovered land from WSW to WNW, and another island NNW, the latter a high round lump of but little extent; and I could see the southern land that I had passed in the night. Being very wet and cold, I served a spoonful of rum and a morsel of bread for breakfast.

As I advanced towards the land in the west, it appeared in a variety of forms; some extraordinary high rocks, and the country agreeably interspersed with high and low land, covered in some places with wood. Off the NE part lay two small rocky islands, between which and the island to the NE, 4 leagues apart, I directed my course; but a lee current very unexpectedly set us very near to the shore, and I could only get clear of it by rowing, passing close to the reef that surrounded the rocky isles. We now observed two large sailing canoes coming swiftly after us along shore, and, being apprehensive of their intentions, we rowed with some anxiety, being sensible of our weak and defenceless state. It was now noon, calm and cloudy weather, my latitude is therefore doubtful to 3 or 4 miles; my course since yesterday noon N 56 W, distance 79 miles; latitude by account, 16° 29′ S, and longitude by account, from Tofoa, 6° 46′ W. Being constantly wet, it was with the utmost difficulty I could open a book to write, and I am sensible that what I have done can only serve to point out where these lands are to be found again, and give an idea of their extent.

Friday, 8th May. All the afternoon the weather was very rainy, attended with thunder and lightning. Wind NNE.

Only one of the canoes gained upon us, and by three o'clock in the afternoon was not more than two miles off, when she gave over chase.

If I may judge from the sail of the vessels, they are the same as at the Friendly Islands, and the nearness of their situation leaves little room to doubt of their being the same kind of people. Whether these canoes had any hostile intention against us is a matter of doubt; perhaps we might have benefited by an intercourse with them, but in our defenceless situation it would have been risking too much to make the experiment.

I imagine these to be the islands called Feejee, as their extent, direction, and distance from the Friendly Islands, answers to the description given of them by those Islanders. Heavy rain came on at four o'clock, when every person did their utmost to catch some water, and we increased our stock to 34 gallons, besides quenching our thirst for the first time since we had been at sea; but an attendant consequence made us pass the night very miserably, for, being extremely wet, and no dry things to shift or cover us, we experienced cold and shiverings scarce to be conceived. Most fortunately for us, the forenoon turned out fair, and we stripped and dried our cloaths. The allowance I issued to-day, was an ounce and a half of pork, a teaspoonful of rum, half a pint of cocoa-nut milk, and an ounce of bread. The rum, though so small in quantity, was of the greatest service. A fishing-line was generally towing, and we saw great numbers of fish, but could never catch one.

At noon, I observed, in latitude 16° 4′ S, and found I had made a course, from yesterday noon, N 62° W, distance 62 miles; longitude, by account, from Tofoa, 7° 42′ W.

The land I passed yesterday, and the day before, is a group of islands, 14 or 16 in number, lying between the latitude of 16° 26′ S and 17° 57′ S, and in longitude, by my account, 4° 47′ to 7° 17′ W from Tofoa; three of these islands are very large, having from 30 to 40 leagues of sea-coast.

Saturday, 9th May. Fine weather, and light winds from the NE to E by S.

This afternoon we cleaned out the boat, and it employed us till sun-set to get every thing dry and in order. Hitherto I had issued the allowance by guess, but I now got a pair of scales, made with two cocoa-nut shells; and, having accidentally some pistol-balls in the boat, 25* of which weighed one pound, or 16 ounces, I adopted one, as the proportion of weight that each person should receive of bread at the times I served it. I also amused all hands, with describing the situation of New Guinea and New Holland, and gave them every information in my power, that in case any accident happened to me, those who survived might have some idea of what they were about, and be able to find their way to Timor, which at present they knew nothing of, more than the name, and some not that.

At night I served a quarter of a pint of water, and half an ounce of bread, for supper. In the morning, a quarter of a pint of cocoa-nut milk, and some of the decayed bread, for breakfast; and for dinner, I divided the meat of four cocoa-nuts, with the remainder of the rotten bread, which was only eatable by such distressed people.

At noon, I observed the latitude to be 15° 47′ S; course since yesterday N 75° W; distant 64 miles; longitude made, by account, 8° 45′ W.

Sunday, May the 10th. The first part of this day fine weather; but after sun-set it became squally, with hard rain, thunder, and lightning, and a fresh gale; wind E by S, SE, and SSE.

In the afternoon I got fitted a pair of shrouds for each mast and contrived a canvass weather cloth round the boat, and raised the quarters about nine inches, by nailing on the seats of the stern sheets, which proved of great benefit to us.

About nine o'clock in the evening, the clouds began to gather, and we had a prodigious fall of rain, with severe thunder and lightning. By midnight we had caught about twenty gallons of water. Being miserably wet and cold, I served to each person a tea-spoonful of rum, to enable them to bear with their distressed situation. The weather continued extremely bad, and the wind increased; we spent a very miserable night, without sleep, but such as could be got in the midst of rain. The day brought us no relief but its light. The sea was constantly breaking over us, which kept two persons baling; and we had no choice how to steer, for we were obliged to keep before the waves to avoid filling the boat.

The allowance which I now regularly served to each person was one 25th of a pound of bread, and a quarter of a pint of water, at sun-set, eight in the morning, and at noon. To-day I gave about half an

*It weighed 272 grains.

ounce of pork for dinner, which, though any moderate person would have considered but a mouthful, was divided into three or four.

The rain abated towards noon, and I observed the latitude to be 15° 17′ S; course N 67° W; distance 78 miles; longitude made 10° W.

Monday, May the 11th. Strong gales from SSE to SE, and very squally weather, with a high breaking sea, so that we were miserably wet, and suffered great cold in the night. In the morning at day-break I served to every person a tea-spoonful of rum, our limbs being so cramped that we could scarce feel the use of them. Our situation was now extremely dangerous, the sea frequently running over our stern, which kept us baling with all our strength.

At noon the sun appeared, which gave us as much pleasure as in a winter's day in England. I issued the 25th of a pound of bread, and a quarter of a pint of water, as yesterday. Latitude observed 14° 50′ S; course N 71° W; distance 102 miles; and longitude, by account, 11° 39′ W. from Tofoa.

Tuesday, May the 12th. Strong gales at SE, with much rain and dark dismal weather, moderating towards noon, and wind varying to the NE.

Having again experienced a dreadful night, the day showed to me a poor miserable set of beings full of wants, without any thing to relieve them. Some complained of a great pain in their bowels, and all of having but very little use of their limbs. What sleep we got was scarce refreshing, we being covered with sea and rain. Two persons were obliged to be always baling the water out of the boat. I served a spoonful of rum at day-dawn, and the usual allowance of bread and water, for supper, breakfast, and dinner.

At noon it was almost calm, no sun to be seen, and some of us shivering with cold. Course since yesterday W by N; distance 89 miles; latitude, by account, 14° 33′ S; longitude made 13° 9′ W. The direction of my course is to pass to the northward of the New Hebrides.

Wednesday, May the 13th. Very squally weather, wind southerly. As I saw no prospect of getting our cloaths dried, I recommended it to every one to strip, and wring them through the salt water, by which means they received a warmth, that, while wet with rain, they could not have, and we were less liable to suffer from colds or rheumatic complaints.

In the afternoon we saw a kind of fruit on the water, which Mr.

Nelson knew to be the Barringtonia of Forster, and, as I saw the same again in the morning, and some men of war birds, I was led to believe we were not far from land.

We continued constantly shipping seas, and baling, and were very wet and cold in the night; but I could not afford the allowance of rum at day-break. The twenty-fifth of a pound of bread, and water I served as usual. At noon I had a sight of the sun, latitude 14° 17′ S; course W by N 79 miles; longitude made 14° 28′ W.

Thursday, May the 14th. Fresh breezes and cloudy weather, wind southerly. Constantly shipping water, and very wet, suffering much cold and shiverings in the night. Served the usual allowance of bread and water, three times a day.

At six in the morning, we saw land, from SW by S eight leagues, to NW by W¾W six leagues, which I soon after found to be four islands, all of them high and remarkable. At noon discovered a rocky island NW by N four leagues, and another island W eight leagues, so that the whole were six in number; the four I had first seen bearing from S½E to SW by S; our distance three leagues from the nearest island. My latitude observed was 13° 29′ S, and longitude, by account, from Tofoa, 15° 49′ W; course since yesterday noon N 63° W; distance 89 miles.

Friday, May the 15th. Fresh gales at SE, and gloomy weather with rain, and a very high sea; two people constantly employed baling.

At four in the afternoon I passed the westernmost island. At one in the morning I discovered another, bearing WNW, five leagues distance, and at eight o'clock I saw it for the last time, bearing NE seven leagues. A number of gannets, boobies, and men of war birds were seen.

These islands lie between the latitude of 13° 16′ S and 14° 10′ S: their longitude, according to my reckoning, 15° 51′ to 17° 6′ W from the island Tofoa.* The largest island may be twenty leagues in circuit, the others five or six. The easternmost is the smallest island, and most remarkable, having a high sugar-loaf hill.

The sight of these islands served but to increase the misery of our situation. We were very little better than starving, with plenty in

---

*By making a proportional allowance for the error afterwards found in the dead reckoning, I estimate the longitude of these islands to be from 167° 17′ E to 168° 34′ E from Greenwich.

view; yet to attempt procuring any relief was attended with so much danger, that prolonging of life, even in the midst of misery, was thought preferable, while there remained hopes of being able to surmount our hardships. For my own part, I consider the general run of cloudy and wet weather to be a blessing of Providence. Hot weather would have caused us to have died with thirst; and perhaps being so constantly covered with rain or sea protected us from that dreadful calamity.

As I had nothing to assist my memory, I could not determine whether these islands were a part of the New Hebrides or not: I believed them perfectly a new discovery, which I have since found to be the case; but, though they were not seen either by Monsieur Bougainville or Captain Cook, they are so nearly in the neighbourhood of the New Hebrides, that they must be considered as part of the same group. They are fertile, and inhabited, as I saw smoke in several places.

Saturday, May the 16th. Fresh gales from the SE, and rainy weather. The night was very dark, not a star to be seen to steer by, and the sea breaking constantly over us. I found it necessary to act as much as possible against the southerly winds, to prevent being driven too near New Guinea; for in general we were forced to keep so much before the sea, that if we had not, at intervals of moderate weather, steered a more southerly course, we should inevitably, from a continuance of the gales, have been thrown in sight of that coast: in which case there would most probably have been an end to our voyage.

In addition to our miserable allowance of one 25th of a pound of bread, and a quarter of a pint of water, I issued for dinner about an ounce of salt pork to each person. I was often solicited for this pork, but I considered it better to give it in small quantities than to use all at once or twice, which would have been done if I had allowed it.

At noon I observed, in 13° 33′ S; longitude made from Tofoa, 19° 27′ W; course N 82° W; distance 101 miles. The sun gave us hopes of drying our wet cloaths.

Sunday, May the 17th. The sunshine was but of short duration. We had strong breezes at SE by S, and dark gloomy weather, with storms of thunder, lightning, and rain. The night was truly horrible, and not a star to be seen; so that our steerage was uncertain. At dawn of day I found every person complaining, and some of them soliciting extra allowance; but I positively refused it. Our situation was extremely miserable; always wet, and suffering extreme cold in the night, without the least shelter from the weather. Being constantly obliged to bale, to keep the boat from filling, was, perhaps, not to be reckoned an evil, as it gave us exercise.

The little rum I had was of great service to us; when our nights were particularly distressing, I generally served a tea-spoonful or two to each person: and it was always joyful tidings when they heard of my intentions.

At noon a water-spout was very near on board of us. I issued an ounce of pork, in addition to the allowance of bread and water; but before we began to eat, every person stript and wrung their cloaths through the sea-water, which we found warm and refreshing. Course since yesterday noon WSW; distance 100 miles; latitude, by account, 14° 11′ S, and longitude made 21° 3′ W.

Monday, May the 18th. Fresh gales with rain, and a dark dismal night, wind SE; the sea constantly breaking over us, and nothing but the wind and sea to direct our steerage. I now fully determined to make New Holland, to the southward of Endeavour straits, sensible that it was necessary to preserve such a situation as would make a southerly wind a fair one; that I might range the reefs until an opening should be found into smooth water, and we the sooner be able to pick up some refreshments.

In the morning the rain abated, when we stripped, and wrung our cloaths through the sea-water, as usual, which refreshed us wonderfully. Every person complained of violent pain in their bones: I was only surprised that no one was yet laid up. Served one 25th of a pound of bread, and a quarter of a pint of water, at supper, breakfast, and dinner, as customary.

At noon I deduced my situation, by account, for we had no glimpse of the sun, to be in latitude 14° 52′ S; course since yesterday noon WSW 106 miles; longitude made from Tofoa 22° 45′ W. Saw many boobies and noddies, a sign of being in the neighbourhood of land.

Tuesday, May the 19th. Fresh gales at ENE, with heavy rain, and dark gloomy weather, and no sight of the sun. We past this day miserably wet and cold, covered with rain and sea, from which we had no relief, but at intervals by pulling off our cloaths and wringing them through the sea water. In the night we had very severe lightning, but otherwise it was so dark that we could not see each other.

The morning produced many complaints on the severity of the weather, and I would gladly have issued my allowance of rum, if it had not appeared to me that we were to suffer much more, and that it was necessary to preserve the little I had, to give relief at a time we might be less able to bear such hardships; but, to make up for it, I served out about half an ounce of pork to each person, with the common allowance of bread and water, for dinner. All night and day we were obliged to bale without intermission.

At noon it was very bad weather and constant rain; latitude, by account, 14° 37′ S; course since yesterday N 81° W; distance 100 miles; longitude made 24° 30′ W.

Wednesday, May the 20th. Fresh breezes ENE with constant rain; at times a deluge. Always baling.

At dawn of day, some of my people seemed half dead: our appearances were horrible; and I could look no way, but I caught the eye of some one in distress. Extreme hunger was now too evident, but no one suffered from thirst, nor had we much inclination to drink, that desire, perhaps, being satisfied through the skin. The little sleep we got was in the midst of water, and we constantly awoke with severe cramps and pains in our bones. This morning I served about two teaspoonfuls of rum to each person, and the allowance of bread and water, as usual. At noon the sun broke out, and revived every one. I found we were in latitude 14° 49′ S; longitude made 25° 46′ W; course S 88° W; distance 75 miles.

Thursday, May the 21st. Fresh gales, and heavy showers of rain. Wind ENE.

Our distresses were now very great, and we were so covered with rain and salt water, that we could scarcely see. Sleep, though we longed for it, afforded no comfort: for my own part, I almost lived without it: we suffered extreme cold, and every one dreaded the approach of night. About two o'clock in the morning we were overwhelmed with a deluge of rain. It fell so heavy that we were afraid it would fill the boat, and were obliged to bale with all our might. At dawn of day, I served a large allowance of rum. Towards noon the rain abated and the sun shone, but we were miserably cold and wet, the sea breaking so constantly over us, that, notwithstanding the heavy rain, we had not been able to add to our stock of fresh water. The usual allowance of one 25th of a pound of bread and water was served at evening, morning, and noon. Latitude, by observation,

14° 29´ S, and longitude made, by account, from Tofoa, 27° 25´ W; course, since yesterday noon, N 78° W, 99 miles. I now considered myself on a meridian with the east part of New Guinea, and about 65 leagues distant from the coast of New Holland.

Friday, May the 22d. Strong gales from ESE to SSE, a high sea, and dark dismal night.

Our situation this day was extremely calamitous. We were obliged to take the course of the sea, running right before it, and watching with the utmost care, as the least error in the helm would in a moment have been our destruction. The sea was continually breaking all over us; but, as we suffered not such cold as when wet with the rain, I only served the common allowance of bread and water.

At noon it blew very hard, and the foam of the sea kept running over our stern and quarters; I however got propped up, and made an observation of the latitude, in 14° 17´ S; course N 85° W; distance 130 miles; longitude made 29° 38´ west.

Saturday, May the 23d. Strong gales with very hard squalls, and rain; wind SE, and SSE.

The misery we suffered this day exceeded the preceding. The night was dreadful. The sea flew over us with great force, and kept us baling with horror and anxiety. At dawn of day I found every one in a most distressed condition, and I now began to fear that another such a night would put an end to the lives of several who seemed no longer able to support such sufferings. Every one complained of severe pains in their bones; but these were alleviated, in some degree, by an allowance of two tea-spoonfuls of rum; after drinking which, having wrung our cloaths, and taken our breakfast of bread and water, we became a little refreshed.

Towards noon it became fair weather; but with very little abatement of the gale, and the sea remained equally high. With great difficulty I observed the latitude to be 13° 44´ S; course N 74° W; distance 116 miles since yesterday; longitude made 31° 32´ W from Tofoa.

Sunday, May the 24th. Fresh gales and fine weather; wind SSE and S.

Towards the evening the weather looked much better, which rejoiced all hands, so that they eat their scanty allowance with more satisfaction than for some time past. The night also was fair; but, being always wet with the sea, we suffered much from the cold. A fine morning, I had the pleasure to see, produce some chearful countenances. Towards noon the weather improved, and, the first time for 15 days past, we found a little warmth from the sun. We stripped, and hung our cloaths up to dry, which were by this time become so thread-bare, that they would not keep out either wet or cold.

At noon I observed in latitude 13° 33′ S; longitude, by account, from Tofoa 33° 28′ W; course N 84° W; distance 114 miles. With the usual allowance of bread and water for dinner, I served an ounce of pork to each person.

Monday, May the 25th. Fresh gales and fair weather. Wind SSE.

This afternoon we had many birds about us, which are never seen far from land, such as boobies and noddies.

About three o'clock the sea began to run fair, and we shipped but little water, I therefore determined to know the exact quantity of bread I had left; and on examining found, according to my present issues, sufficient for 29 days allowance. In the course of this time I hoped to be at Timor; but, as that was very uncertain, and perhaps after all we might be obliged to go to Java, I determined to proportion my issues to six weeks. I was apprehensive that this would be ill received, and that it would require my utmost resolution to enforce it; for, small as the quantity was which I intended to take away, for our future good, yet it might appear to my people like robbing them of life, and some, who were less patient than their companions, I expected would very ill brook it. I however represented it so essentially necessary to guard against delays in our voyage by contrary winds, or other causes, promising to enlarge upon the allowance as we got on, that it was readily agreed to. I therefore fixed, that every person should receive one 25th of a pound of bread for breakfast, and one 25th of a pound for dinner; so that by omitting the proportion for supper, I had 43 days allowance.

At noon some noddies came so near to us, that one of them was caught by hand. This bird is about the size of a small pigeon. I divided it, with its entrails, into 18 portions, and by the method of, Who shall have this?* it was distributed with the allowance of bread and water for dinner, and eat up bones and all, with salt water for

*One person turns his back on the object that is to be divided: another then points separately to the portions, at each of them asking aloud, "Who shall have this?" to which the first answers by naming somebody. This impartial method of division gives every man an equal chance of the best share.

sauce. I observed the latitude 13° 32′ S; longitude made 35° 19′ W; and course N 89° W; distance 108 miles.

Tuesday, May the 26th. Fresh gales at SSE, and fine weather.

In the evening we saw several boobies flying so near to us, that we caught one of them by hand. This bird is as large as a good duck; like the noddy, it has received its name from seamen, for suffering itself to be caught on the masts and yards of ships. They are the most presumptive proofs of being in the neighbourhood of land of any seafowl we are acquainted with. I directed the bird to be killed for supper, and the blood to be given to three of the people who were the most distressed for want of food. The body, with the entrails, beak, and feet, I divided into 18 shares, and with an allowance of bread, which I made a merit of granting, we made a good supper, compared with our usual fare.

In the morning we caught another booby, so that Providence seemed to be relieving our wants in a very extraordinary manner. Towards noon we passed a great many pieces of the branches of trees, some of which appeared to have been no long time in the water. I had a good observation for the latitude, and found my situation to be in 13° 41′ S; my longitude, by account, from Tofoa, 37° 13′ W; course S 85° W, 112 miles. Every person was now overjoyed at the addition to their dinner, which I distributed as I had done in the evening; giving the blood to those who were the most in want of food.

To make our bread a little savoury we frequently dipped it in salt water; but for my own part I generally broke mine into small pieces, and eat it in my allowance of water, out of a cocoa-nut shell, with a spoon, economically avoiding to take too large a piece at a time, so that I was as long at dinner as if it had been a much more plentiful meal.

Wednesday, May the 27th. Fresh breezes south-easterly, and fine weather.

The weather was now serene, but unhappily we found ourselves unable to bear the sun's heat; many of us suffering a languor and faintness, which made life indifferent. We were, however, so fortunate as to catch two boobies to-day; their stomachs contained several flying-fish and small cuttlefish, all of which I saved to be divided for dinner.

We passed much drift wood, and saw many birds; I therefore did not hesitate to pronounce that we were near the reefs of New Holland, and assured every one I would make the coast without delay, in the parallel we were in, and range the reef till I found an opening, through which we might get into smooth water, and pick up some supplies. From my recollection of captain Cook's survey of this coast, I considered the direction of it to be NW, and I was therefore satisfied that, with the wind to the southward of E, I could always clear any dangers.

At noon I observed in latitude 13° 26′ S; course since yesterday N 82° W; distance 109 miles; longitude made 39° 4′ W. After writing my account, I divided the two birds with their entrails, and the contents of their maws, into 18 portions, and, as the prize was a very valuable one, it was divided as before, by calling out Who shall have this? so that to-day, with the allowance of a 25th of a pound of bread at breakfast, and another at dinner, with the proportion of water, I was happy to see that every person thought he had feasted.

Thursday, May the 28th. Fresh breezes and fair weather; wind ESE and E.

In the evening we saw a gannet; and the clouds remained so fixed in the west, that I had little doubt of our being near to New Holland; and every person, after taking his allowance of water for supper, began to divert himself with conversing on the probability of what we should find.

At one in the morning the person at the helm heard the sound of breakers, and I no sooner lifted up my head, than I saw them close under our lee, not more than a quarter of a mile distant from us. I immediately hauled on a wind to the NNE, and in ten minutes time we could neither see nor hear them.

I have already mentioned my reason for making New Holland so far to the southward; for I never doubted of numerous openings in the reef, through which I could have access to the shore: and, knowing the inclination of the coast to be to the NW, and the wind mostly to the southward of E, I could with ease range such a barrier of reefs till I should find a passage, which now became absolutely necessary, without a moment's loss of time. The idea of getting into smooth water, and finding refreshments, kept my people's spirits up: their joy was very great after we had got clear of the breakers, to which we had been much nearer than I thought was possible to be before we saw them.

In the morning, at day-light, I bore away again for the reefs, and saw them by nine o'clock. The sea broke furiously over every part, and I had no sooner got near to them, than the wind came at E, so that we could only lie along the line of the breakers, within which we saw the water so smooth, that every person already anticipated the heart-felt satisfaction he would receive, as soon as we could get within them. But I now found we were embayed, for I could not lie clear with my sails, the wind having backed against us, and the sea set in so heavy towards the reef that our situation was become dangerous. We could effect but little with the oars, having scarce strength to pull them; and it was becoming every minute more and more probable that we should be obliged to attempt pushing over the reef, in case we could not pull off. Even this I did not despair of effecting with success, when happily we discovered a break in the reef, about one mile from us, and at the same time an island of a moderate height within it, nearly in the same direction, bearing W$\frac{1}{2}$N. I entered the passage with a strong stream running to the westward, and found it about a quarter of a mile broad, with every appearance of deep water.

On the outside, the reef inclined to the NE for a few miles, and from thence to the NW; on the south side of the entrance, it inclined to the SSW as far as I could see it; and I conjecture that a similar passage to this which we now entered, may be found near the breakers that I first discovered, which are 23 miles S of this channel.

I did not recollect what latitude Providential channel* lies in, but I considered it to be within a few miles of this, which is situate in 12° 51′ S latitude.

Being now happily within the reefs, and in smooth water, I endeavoured to keep near them to try for fish; but the tide set us to the NW; I therefore bore away in that direction, and, having promised to land on the first convenient spot we could find, all our past hardships seemed already to be forgotten.

At noon I had a good observation, by which our latitude was 12° 46′ S, whence the foregoing situations may be considered as determined with some exactness. The island first seen bore WSW five leagues. This, which I have called the island Direction, will in fair weather always shew the channel, from which it bears due W, and may be seen as soon as the reefs, from a ship's mast-head: it lies in the latitude of 12° 51′ S. There, however, are marks too small for a ship

*Providential Channel is in 12° 34′ S, longitude 143° 33′ E.

to hit, unless it can hereafter be ascertained that passages through the reef are numerous along the coast, which I am inclined to think they are, and then there would be little risk if the wind was not directly on the shore.

My longitude, made by dead reckoning, from the island Tofoa to our passage through the reef, is 40° 10′ W. Providential channel, I imagine, must lie very nearly under the same meridian with our passage; by which it appears we had out-run our reckoning 1° 9′.

We now returned God thanks for his gracious protection, and with much content took our miserable allowance of a 25th of a pound of bread, and a quarter of a pint of water, for dinner.

Friday, May the 29th. Moderate breezes and fine weather, wind ESE.

As we advanced within the reefs, the coast began to shew itself very distinctly, with a variety of high and low land; some parts of which were covered with wood. In our way towards the shore we fell in with a point of a reef, which is connected with that towards the sea, and here I came to a grapnel, and tried to catch fish, but had no success. The island Direction now bore S three or four leagues. Two islands lay about four miles to the W by N, and appeared eligible for a resting-place, if nothing more; but on my approach to the first I found it only a heap of stones, and its size too inconsiderable to shelter the boat. I therefore proceeded to the next, which was close to it and towards the main, where, on the NW side, I found a bay and a fine sandy point to land at. Our distance was about a quarter of a mile from a projecting part of the main, bearing from SW by S, to NNW¾W. I now landed to examine if there were any signs of the natives being near us; but though I discovered some old fire-places, I saw nothing to alarm me for our situation during the night. Every one was anxious to find something to eat, and I soon heard that there were oysters on the rocks, for the tide was out; but it was nearly dark, and only a few could be gathered. I determined therefore to wait till the morning, to know how to proceed, and I consented that one half of us should sleep on shore, and the other in the boat. We would gladly have made a fire, but, as we could not accomplish it, we took our rest for the night, which happily was calm and undisturbed.

The dawn of day brought greater strength and spirits to us than I expected; for, notwithstanding every one was very weak, there appeared strength sufficient remaining to make me conceive the most favourable hopes of our being able to surmount the difficulties we might yet have to encounter.

As soon as I saw that there were not any natives immediately near us, I sent out parties in search of supplies, while others were putting the boat in order, that I might be ready to go to sea in case any unforeseen cause might make it necessary. The first object of this work, that demanded our attention, was the rudder: one of the gudgeons had come out, in the course of the night, and was lost. This, if it had happened at sea, would probably have been the cause of our perishing, as the management of the boat could not have been so nicely preserved as these very heavy seas required. I had often expressed my fears of this accident, and, that we might be prepared for it, had taken the precaution to have grummets fixed on each quarter of the boat for oars; but even our utmost readiness in using them, I fear, would not have saved us. It appears, therefore, a providential circumstance, that it happened at this place, and was in our power to remedy the defect; for by great good luck we found a large staple in the boat that answered the purpose.

The parties were now returned, highly rejoiced at having found plenty of oysters and fresh water. I also had made a fire, by help of a small magnifying glass, that I always carried about me, to read off the divisions of my sextants; and, what was still more fortunate, among the few things which had been thrown into the boat and saved, was a piece of brimstone and a tinder-box, so that I secured fire for the future.

One of my people had been so provident as to bring away with him a copper pot: it was by being in possession of this article that I was enabled to make a proper use of the supply we found, for, with a mixture of bread and a little pork, I made a stew that might have been relished by people of more delicate appetites, of which each person received a full pint.

The general complaints of disease among us, were a dizziness in the head, great weakness of the joints, and violent tenesmus, most of us having had no evacuation by stool since we left the ship. I had constantly a severe pain at my stomach; but none of our complaints were alarming; on the contrary, every one retained marks of strength, that, with a mind possessed of any fortitude, could bear more fatigue than I hoped we had to undergo in our voyage to Timor.

As I would not allow the people to expose themselves to the heat of the sun, it being near noon, every one took his allotment of earth, shaded by the bushes, for a short sleep.

The oysters we found grew so fast to the rocks that it was with difficulty they could be broke off, and at last we discovered it to be the most expeditious way to open them where they were found. They were very sizeable, and well tasted, and gave us great relief. To add to this happy circumstance, in the hollow of the land there grew some wire grass, which indicated a moist situation. On forcing a stick, about three feet long, into the ground, we found water, and with little trouble dug a well, which produced as much as we were in need of. It was very good, but I could not determine if it was a spring or not. Our wants made it not necessary to make the well deep, for it flowed as fast as we emptied it; which, as the soil was apparently too loose to retain water from the rains, renders it probable to be a spring. It lies about 200 yards to the SE of a point in the SW part of the island.

I found evident signs of the natives resorting to this island; for, besides fire-places, I saw two miserable wig-wams, having only one side loosely covered. We found a pointed stick, about three feet long, with a slit in the end of it, to sling stones with, the same as the natives of Van Diemen's land use.

The track of some animal was very discernible, and Mr. Nelson agreed with me that it was the Kanguroo; but how these animals can get from the main I know not, unless brought over by the natives to breed, that they may take them with more ease, and render a supply of food certain to them; as on the continent the catching of them may be precarious, or attended with great trouble, in so large an extent of country.

The island may be about two miles in circuit; it is a high lump of rocks and stones covered with wood; but the trees are small, the soil, which is very indifferent and sandy, being barely sufficient to produce them. The trees that came within our knowledge were the man-chineal and a species of purow: also some palm-trees, the tops of which we cut down, and the soft interior part or heart of them was so palatable that it made a good addition to our mess. Mr. Nelson discovered some fern-roots, which I thought might be good roasted, as a substitute for bread, but it proved a very poor one: it however was very good in its natural state to allay thirst, and on that account I directed a quantity to be collected to take into the boat. Many pieces of cocoa-nut shells and husk were found about the shore, but we could find no cocoa-nut trees, neither did I see any like them on the main.

I had cautioned every one not to touch any kind of berry or fruit that they might find; yet they were no sooner out of my sight than they began to make free with three different kinds, that grew all over the island, eating without any reserve. The symptoms of having eaten too much, began at last to frighten some of them; but on questioning others, who had taken a more moderate allowance, their minds were a little quieted. The others, however, became equally alarmed in their turn, dreading that such symptoms would come on, and that they were all poisoned, so that they regarded each other with the strongest marks of apprehension, uncertain what would be the issue of their imprudence. Happily the fruit proved wholesome and good. One sort grew on a small delicate kind of vine; they were the size of a large gooseberry, and very like in substance, but had only a sweet taste; the skin was a pale red, streaked with yellow the long way of the fruit: it was pleasant and agreeable. Another kind grew on bushes, like that which is called the sea-side grape in the West Indies; but the fruit was very different, and more like elder-berries, growing in clusters in the same manner. The third sort was a black berry, not in such plenty as the others, and resembled a bullace, or large kind of sloe, both in size and taste. Seeing these fruits eaten by the birds made me consider them fit for use, and those who had already tried the experiment, not finding any bad effect, made it a certainty that we might eat of them without danger.

Wild pigeons, parrots, and other birds, were about the summit of the island, but, as I had no fire-arms, relief of that kind was not to be expected, unless I met with some unfrequented spot where we might take them with our hands.

On the south side of the island, and about half a mile from the well, a small run of water was found; but, as its source was not traced, I know nothing more of it.

The shore of this island is very rocky, except the part we landed at, and here I picked up many pieces of pumice-stone. On the part of the main next to us were several sandy bays, but at low-water they became an extensive rocky flat. The country had rather a barren appearance, except in a few places where it was covered with wood. A remarkable range of rocks lay a few miles to the SW, or a high peaked hill terminated the coast towards the sea, with other high lands and islands to the southward. A high fair cape showed the direction of the coast to the NW, about seven leagues, and two small isles lay three or four leagues to the northward.

I saw a few bees or wasps, several lizards, and the black-berry bushes were full of ants nests, webbed as a spider's, but so close and compact as not to admit the rain.

A trunk of a tree, about 50 feet long, lay on the beach; from whence I conclude a heavy sea runs in here with the northerly winds.

This being the day of the restoration of king Charles the Second, and the name not being inapplicable to our present situation (for we were restored to fresh life and strength), I named this Restoration Island; for I thought it probable that captain Cook might not have taken notice of it. The other names I have presumed to give the different parts of the coast, will be only to show my route a little more distinctly.

At noon I found the latitude of the island to be 12° 39′ S; our course having been N 66° W; distance 18 miles from yesterday noon.

Saturday, May the 30th. Very fine weather, and ESE winds. This afternoon I sent parties out again to gather oysters, with which and some of the inner part of the palm-top, we made another good stew for supper, each person receiving a full pint and a half; but I refused bread to this meal, for I considered our wants might yet be very great, and as such I represented the necessity of saving our principal support whenever it was in our power.

At night we again divided, and one half of us slept on shore by a good fire. In the morning I discovered a visible alteration in every one for the better, and I sent them away again to gather oysters. I had now only two pounds of pork left. This article, which I could not keep under lock and key as I did the bread, had been pilfered by some inconsiderate person, but every one most solemnly denied it; I therefore resolved to put it out of their power for the future, by sharing what remained for our dinner. While the party was out getting oysters, I got the boat in readiness for sea, and filled all our water vessels, which amounted to nearly 60 gallons.

The party being returned, dinner was soon ready, and every one had as good an allowance as they had for supper; for with the pork I gave an allowance of bread; and I was determined forthwith to push on. As it was not yet noon, I told every one that an exertion should be made to gather as many oysters as possible for a sea store, as I was determined to sail in the afternoon.

At noon I again observed the latitude 12° 39′ S; it was then high-water, the tide had risen three feet, but I could not be certain which way the flood came from. I deduce the time of high-water at full and change to be ten minutes past seven in the morning.

Sunday, May the 31st. Early in the afternoon, the people returned with the few oysters they had time to pick up, and every thing was put into the boat. I then examined the quantity of bread remaining, and found 38 days allowance, according to the last mode of issuing a 25th of a pound at breakfast and at dinner.

Fair weather, and moderate breezes at ESE and SE.

Being all ready for sea, I directed every person to attend prayers, and by four o'clock we were preparing to embark; when twenty na-tives appeared, running and holloaing to us, on the opposite shore. They were armed with a spear or lance, and a short weapon which they carried in their left hand: they made signs for us to come to them. On the top of the hills we saw the heads of many more; whether these were their wives and children, or others who waited for our landing, until which they meant not to show themselves, lest we might be intimidated, I cannot say; but, as I found we were dis-covered to be on the coast, I thought it prudent to make the best of my way, for fear of canoes; though, from the accounts of captain Cook, the chance was that there were very few or none of any conse-quence. I passed these people as near as I could, which was within a quarter of a mile; they were naked, and apparently black, and their hair or wool bushy and short.

I directed my course within two small islands that lie to the north of Restoration Island, passing between them and the main land, to-wards Fair Cape, with a strong tide in my favour; so that I was abreast of it by eight o'clock. The coast I had passed was high and woody. As I could see no land without Fair Cape, I concluded that the coast inclined to the NW and WNW, which was agreeable to my recollection of captain Cook's survey. I therefore steered more to-wards the W; but by eleven o'clock at night I found myself mistaken: for we met with low land, which inclined to the NE; so that at three o'clock in the morning I found we were embayed, which obliged us to stand back to the southward.

At day-break I was exceedingly surprised to find the appearance of the country all changed, as if in the course of the night I had been transported to another part of the world; for we had now a miserable low sandy coast in view, with very little verdure, or any thing to indicate that it was at all habitable to a human being, if I except some patches of small trees or brush-wood.

I had many small islands in view to the NE, about six miles distant. The E part of the main bore N four miles, and Fair Cape SSE five or six leagues. I took the channel between the nearest island and the main land, about one mile apart, leaving all the islands on the starboard side. Some of these were very pretty spots, covered with wood, and well situated for fishing: large shoals of fish were about us, but we could not catch any. As I was passing this strait we saw another party of Indians, seven in number, running towards us, shouting and making signs for us to land. Some of them waved green branches of the bushes which were near them, as a sign of friendship; but there were some of their other motions less friendly. A larger party we saw a little farther off, and coming towards us. I therefore determined not to land, though I wished much to have had some intercourse with these people; for which purpose I beckoned to them to come near to me, and laid the boat close to the rocks; but not one would come within 200 yards of us. They were armed in the same manner as those I had seen from Restoration Island, were stark naked, and appeared to be jet black, with short bushy hair or wool, and in every respect the same people. An island of good height now bore N$\frac{1}{2}$W, four miles from us, at which I resolved to see what could be got, and from thence to take a look at the coast. At this isle I landed about eight o'clock in the morning. The shore was rocky, with some sandy beaches within the rocks: the water, however, was smooth, and I landed without difficulty. I sent two parties out, one to the northward, and the other to the southward, to seek for supplies, and others I ordered to stay by the boat. On this occasion their fatigue and weakness so far got the better of their sense of duty, that some of them began to mutter who had done most, and declared they would rather be without their dinner than go in search of it. One person, in particular, went so far as to tell me, with a mutinous look, he was as good a man as myself. It was not possible for me to judge where this might have an end, if not stopped in time; I therefore determined to strike a final blow at it, and either to preserve my command, or die in the attempt: and, seizing a cutlass, I ordered him to take hold of another and defend himself; on which he called out I was going to kill him, and began to make concessions. I did not allow this to interfere further with the harmony of the boat's crew, and every thing soon became quiet.

The parties continued collecting what could be found, which consisted of some fine oysters and clams, and a few small dog-fish that were caught in the holes of the rocks. We also found about two tons of rain-water in the hollow of the rocks, on the north part of the island, so that of this essential article we were again so happy as not to be in want.

After regulating the mode of proceeding, I set off for the highest part of the island, to see and consider of my route for the night. To my surprise I could see no more of the main than I did from below, it extending only from $S\frac{1}{2}E$, four miles, to W by N, about three leagues, full of sand-hills. Besides the isles to the ESE and south, that I had seen before, I could only discover a small key NW by N. As this was considerably farther from the main than where I was at present, I resolved to get there by night, it being a more secure resting-place; for I was here open to an attack, if the Indians had canoes, as they undoubtedly observed my landing. My mind being made up on this point, I returned, taking a particular look at the spot I was on, which I found only to produce a few bushes and coarse grass, and the extent of the whole not two miles in circuit. On the north side, in a sandy bay, I saw an old canoe, about 33 feet long, lying bottom upwards, and half buried in the beach. It was made of three pieces, the bottom entire, to which the sides were sewed in the common way. It had a sharp projecting prow rudely carved, in resemblance of the head of a fish; the extreme breadth was about three feet, and I imagine it was capable of carrying 20 men.

At noon the parties were all returned, but had found difficulty in gathering the oysters, from their close adherence to the rocks, and the clams were scarce: I therefore saw, that it would be of little use to remain longer in this place, as we should not be able to collect more than we could eat; nor could any tolerable sea-store be expected, unless we fell in with a greater plenty. I named this Sunday Island: it lies N by W$\frac{3}{4}$W from Restoration Island; the latitude, by a good observation, 11° 58′ S.

Monday, June the 1st. Fresh breezes and fair weather, ending with a fresh gale. Wind SE by S.

At two o'clock in the afternoon, we dined; each person having a full pint and a half of stewed oysters and clams, thickened with small beans, which Mr. Nelson informed us were a species of Dolichos. Having eaten heartily, and taken the water we were in want of, I only waited to determine the time of high-water, which I found to be at three o'clock, and the rise of the tide about five feet. According to this it is high-water on the full and change at 19 minutes past 9 in the morning; but here I observed the flood to come from the southward, though at Restoration Island, I thought it came from the northward. I think Captain Cook mentions that he found great irregularity in the set of the flood on this coast.

I now sailed for the key which I had seen in the NW by N, giving the name of Sunday Island to the place I left; we arrived just at dark, but found it so surrounded by a reef of rocks, that I could not land without danger of staving the boat; and on that account I came to a grapnel for the night.

At dawn of day we got on shore, and tracked the boat into shelter; for the wind blowing fresh without, and the ground being rocky, I was afraid to trust her at a grapnel, lest she might be blown to sea: I was, therefore, obliged to let her ground in the course of the ebb. From appearances, I expected that if we remained till night we should meet with turtle, as we had already discovered recent tracks of them. Innumerable birds of the noddy kind made this island their resting-place; so that I had reason to flatter myself with hopes of getting supplies in greater abundance than it had hitherto been in my power. The situation was at least four leagues distant from the main. We were on the north-westernmost of four small keys, which were surrounded by a reef of rocks connected by sand-banks, except between the two northernmost; and there likewise it was dry at low water; the whole forming a lagoon island, into which the tide flowed: at this entrance I kept the boat.

As usual, I sent parties away in search of supplies, but, to our great disappointment, we could only get a few clams and some dolichos: with these, and the oysters we had brought from Sunday Island, I made up a mess for dinner, with an addition of a small quantity of bread.

Towards noon, Mr. Nelson, and his party, who had been to the easternmost key, returned; but himself in such a weak condition, that he was obliged to be supported by two men. His complaint was a violent heat in his bowels, a loss of sight, much drought, and an inability to walk. This I found was occasioned by his being unable to support the heat of the sun, and that, when he was fatigued and faint, instead of retiring into the shade to rest, he had continued to do more than his strength was equal to. It was a great satisfaction to me to find, that he had no fever; and it was now that the little wine, which I had so carefully saved, became of real use. I gave it in very small quantities, with some small pieces of bread soaked in it; and, having pulled off his cloaths, and laid him under some shady bushes, he began to recover. The boatswain and carpenter also were ill, and complained of head-ach, and sickness of the stomach; others, who had not had any evacuation by stool, became shockingly distressed with the tenesmus; so that there were but few without complaints. An idea now prevailed, that their illness was occasioned by eating the dolichos, and some were so much alarmed that they thought themselves poisoned. Myself, however, and some others, who had eaten of them, were yet very well; but the truth was, that all those who were complaining, except Mr. Nelson, had gorged themselves with a large quantity of raw beans, and Mr. Nelson informed me, that they were constantly teazing him, whenever a berry was found, to know if it was good to eat; so that it would not have been surprizing if many of them had been really poisoned.

Our dinner was not so well relished as at Sunday Island, because we had mixed the dolichos with our stew. The oysters and soup, however, were eaten by every one, except Mr. Nelson, whom I fed with a few small pieces of bread soaked in half a glass of wine, and he continued to mend.

In my walk round the island, I found several cocoa-nut shells, the remains of an old wigwam, and the backs of two turtle, but no sign of any quadruped. One of my people found three sea-fowl's eggs.

As is common on such spots, the soil is little other than sand, yet it produced small toa-trees, and some others, that we were not acquainted with. There were fish in the lagoon, but we could not catch any. As our wants, therefore, were not likely to be supplied here, not even with water for our daily expence, I determined to sail in the morning, after trying our success in the night for turtle and birds. A quiet night's rest also, I conceived, would be of essential service to those who were unwell.

From the wigwam and turtle-shell being found, it is certain that the natives sometimes resort to this place, and have canoes: but I did not apprehend that we ran any risk by remaining here. I directed our fire, however, to be made in the thicket, that we might not be discovered in the night.

At noon, I observed the latitude of this island to be 11° 47′ S. The main land extended towards the NW, and was full of white sand-hills: another small island lay within us, bearing W by N$\frac{1}{4}$N, three leagues distant. My situation being very low, I could see nothing of the reef towards the sea.

Tuesday, June the 2d. The first part of this day we had some light showers of rain; the latter part was fair, wind from the SE, blowing fresh.

Rest was now so much wanted, that the afternoon was advantageously spent in sleep. There were, however, a few not disposed to it, and those I employed in dressing some clams to take with us for the next day's dinner; others we cut up in slices to dry, which I knew was the most valuable supply we could find here. But, contrary to our expectation, they were very scarce.

Towards evening, I cautioned every one against making too large a fire, or suffering it after dark to blaze up. Mr. Samuel and Mr. Peckover had the superintendence of this business, while I was strolling about the beach to observe if I thought it could be seen from the main. I was just satisfied that it could not, when on a sudden the island appeared all in a blaze, that might have been seen at a much more considerable distance. I ran to learn the cause, and found it was occasioned by the imprudence and obstinacy of one of the party, who, in my absence, had insisted on having a fire to himself; in making which the flames caught the neighbouring grass and rapidly spread. This misconduct might have produced very serious consequences, by discovering our situation to the natives; for, if they had attacked us, we must inevitably have fallen a sacrifice, as we had neither arms nor strength to oppose an enemy. Thus the relief which I expected from a little sleep was totally lost, and I anxiously waited for the flowing of the tide, that we might proceed to sea.

I found it high-water at half past five this evening, whence I deduce the time, on the full and change of the moon, to be 58′ past 10 in the morning: the rise is nearly five feet. I could not observe the set of the flood; but imagine it comes from the southward, and that I have been mistaken at Restoration Island, as I find the time of high-water gradually later as we advance to the northward.

At Restoration Island, high water, full and change, ... 7° 10´
Sunday Island, ... 9 19
Here, ...10 58

After eight o'clock, Mr. Samuel and Mr. Peckover went out to watch for turtle, and three men went to the east key to endeavour to catch birds. All the others complaining of being sick, took their rest, except Mr. Hayward and Mr. Elphinston, who I directed to keep watch. About midnight the bird party returned, with only twelve noddies, a bird I have already described to be about the size of a pigeon: but if it had not been for the folly and obstinacy of one of the party, who separated from the other two, and disturbed the birds, they might have caught a great number. I was so much provoked at my plans being thus defeated, that I gave the offender* a good beating. I now went in search of the turtling party, who had taken great pains, but without success. This, however, did not surprise me, as it was not to be expected that turtle would come near us after the noise which was made at the beginning of the evening in extinguishing the fire. I therefore desired them to come back, but they requested to stay a little longer, as they still hoped to find some before day-light: they, however, returned by three o'clock, without any reward for their labour.

The birds we half dressed, which, with a few clams, made the whole of the supply procured here. I tied up a few gilt buttons and some pieces of iron to a tree, for any of the natives that might come after us; and, happily finding my invalids much better for their night's rest, I got every one into the boat, and departed by dawn of day. Wind at SE; course to the N by W.

We had scarcely ran two leagues to the northward, when the sea suddenly became rough, which not having experienced since we were within the reefs, I concluded to be occasioned by an open channel to the ocean. Soon afterwards we met with a large shoal, on which were two sandy keys; between these and two others, four miles to the

---

*Robert Lamb.—This man, when he came to Java, acknowledged he had eaten nine birds on the key, after he separated from the other two.

west, I passed on to the northward, the sea still continuing to be rough.

Towards noon, I fell in with six other keys, most of which produced some small trees and brush-wood. These formed a pleasing contrast with the main land we had passed, which was full of sandhills. The country continued hilly, and the northernmost land, the same which we saw from the lagoon island, appeared like downs, sloping towards the sea. To the southward of this is a flat-topped hill, which, on account of its shape, I called Pudding-pan hill, and a little to the northward two other hills, which we called the Paps; and here was a small tract of country without sand, the eastern part of which forms a cape, whence the coast inclines to the NW by N.

At noon I observed in the latitude of 11° 18′ S, the cape bearing W, distant ten miles. Five small keys bore from NE to SE, the nearest of them about two miles distant, and a low sandy key between us and the cape bore W, distant four miles. My course from the Lagoon Island N½W, distant 30 miles.

I am sorry it was not in my power to obtain a sufficient knowledge of the depth of water; for in our situation nothing could be undertaken that might have occasioned delay. It may however be understood, that, to the best of my judgment, from appearances, a ship may pass wherever I have omitted to represent danger.

I divided six birds, and issued one 25th of a pound of bread, with half a pint of water, to each person for dinner, and I gave half a glass of wine to Mr. Nelson, who was now so far recovered as to require no other indulgence.

The gunner, when he left the ship, brought his watch with him, by which we had regulated our time till to-day, when unfortunately it stopped; so that noon, sun-rise, and sun-set, are the only parts of the 24 hours of which I can speak with certainty, as to time.

Wednesday, June the 3d. Fresh gales SSE and SE, and fair weather. As we stood to the N by W this afternoon, we found more sea, which I attributed to our receiving less shelter from the reefs to the eastward: it is probable they do not extend so far to the N as this; at least, it may be concluded that there is not a continued barrier to prevent shipping having access to the shore. I observed that the stream set to the NW, which I considered to be the flood; in some places along the coast, we saw patches of wood. At five o'clock, steering to the NW, we passed a large and fair inlet, into which, I imagine, is a safe and commodious entrance; it lies in latitude 11° S: about three leagues to the northward of this is an island, at which we arrived about sun-set, and took shelter for the night under a sandy point, which was the only part we could land at: I was therefore under the necessity to put up with rather a wild situation, and slept in the boat. Nevertheless I sent a party away to see what could be got, but they returned without any success. They saw a great number of turtle bones and shells, where the natives had been feasting, and their last visit seemed to be of late date. The island was covered with wood, but in other respects a lump of rocks. We lay at a grapnel until daylight, with a very fresh gale and cloudy weather. The main bore from SE by S to NNW½W, three leagues; and a mountainous island, with a flat top, N by W, four or five leagues: several others were between it and the main. The spot we were on, which I call Turtle Island, lies in latitude, by account, 10° 52′ S, and 42 miles W from Restoration Island. Abreast of it the coast has the appearance of a sandy desert, but improves about three leagues farther to the northward, where it terminates in a point, near to which is a number of small islands. I sailed between these islands, where I found no bottom at twelve fathoms; the high mountainous island with a flat top, and four rocks to the SE of it, that I call the Brothers, being on my starboard hand. Soon after, an extensive opening appeared in the main land, with a number of high islands in it. I called this the Bay of Islands. We continued steering to the NW. Several islands and keys lay to the northward. The most northerly island was mountainous, having on it a very high round hill; and a smaller was remarkable for a single peaked hill.

The coast to the northward and westward of the Bay of Islands had a very different appearance from that to the southward. It was high and woody, with many islands close to it, and had a very broken appearance. Among these islands are fine bays, and convenient places for shipping. The northernmost I call Wednesday Island: to the NW of this we fell in with a large reef, which I believe joins a number of keys that were in sight from the NW to the ENE. We now stood to the SW half a league, when it was noon, and I had a good observation of the latitude in 10° 31′ S. Wednesday Island bore E by S five miles; the westernmost land SW two or three leagues; the islands to the northward, from NW by W four or five leagues, to NE six leagues; and the reef from W to NE, distant one mile. I now assured every one that we should be clear of New Holland in the afternoon.

It is impossible for me to say how far this reef may extend. It may be a continuation, or a detached part of the range of shoals that surround the coast: but be that as it may, I consider the mountainous islands as separate from the shoals; and have no doubt that near them may be found good passages for ships. But I rather recommend to those who are to pass this strait from the eastward, to take their direction from the coast of New Guinea: yet, I likewise think that a ship coming from the southward, will find a fair strait in the latitude of 10° S. I much wished to have ascertained this point; but in our distressful situation, any increase of fatigue, or loss of time, might have been attended with the most fatal consequences. I therefore determined to pass on without delay.

As an addition to our dinner of bread and water, I served to each person six oysters.

Thursday, June the 4th. A fresh gale at SE, and fair weather.

At two o'clock, as we were steering to the SW, towards the westernmost part of the land in sight, we fell in with some large sandbanks that run off from the coast. We were therefore obliged to steer to the northward again, and, having got round them, I directed my course to the W.

At four o'clock, the westernmost of the islands to the northward bore N four leagues; Wednesday island E by N five leagues; and Shoal Cape SE by E two leagues. A small island was now seen bearing W, at which I arrived before dark, and found that it was only a rock, where boobies resort, for which reason I called it Booby Island. A small key also lies close to the W part of the coast, which I have called Shoal Cape. Here terminated the rocks and shoals of the N part of New Holland, for, except Booby Island, we could see no land to the westward of S, after three o'clock this afternoon.

I find that Booby Island was seen by Captain Cook, and, by a remarkable coincidence of ideas, received from him the same name; but I cannot with certainty reconcile the situation of many parts of the coast that I have seen, to his survey. I ascribe this to the very different form in which land appears, when seen from the unequal heights of a ship and a boat. The chart I have given, is by no means meant to supersede that made by Captain Cook, who had better opportunities than I had, and was in every respect properly provided for surveying. The intention of mine is chiefly to render the narrative more intelligible, and to shew in what manner the coast appeared to me from an open boat. I have little doubt that the opening, which I named the Bay of Islands, is Endeavour Straits; and that our track was to the northward of Prince of Wales's Isles. Perhaps, by those who shall hereafter navigate these seas, more advantage may be derived from the possession of both our charts, than from either singly.

At eight o'clock in the evening, we once more launched into the open ocean. Miserable as our situation was in every respect, I was secretly surprised to see that it did not appear to affect any one so strongly as myself; on the contrary, it seemed as if they had embarked on a voyage to Timor, in a vessel sufficiently calculated for safety and convenience. So much confidence gave me great pleasure, and I may assert that to this cause their preservation is chiefly to be attributed; for if any one of them had despaired, he would most probably have died before we reached New Holland.

I now gave every one hopes that eight or ten days might bring us to a land of safety; and, after praying to God for a continuance of his most gracious protection, I served an allowance of water for supper, and kept my course to the WSW, to counteract the southerly winds, in case they should blow strong.

We had been just six days on the coast of New Holland, in the course of which we found oysters, a few clams, some birds, and water. But perhaps a benefit nearly equal to this we received from not having fatigue in the boat, and enjoying good rest at night. These advantages certainly preserved our lives; for, small as the supply was, I am very sensible how much it relieved our distresses. About this time nature would have sunk under the extremes of hunger and fatigue. Some would have ceased to struggle for a life that only promised wretchedness and misery; while others, though possessed of more bodily strength, must soon have followed their unfortunate companions. Even in our present situation, we were most wretched spectacles; yet our fortitude and spirit remained; every one being encouraged by the hopes of a speedy termination to his misery.

For my own part, wonderful as it may appear, I felt neither extreme hunger nor thirst. My allowance contented me, knowing I could have no more.

I served one 25th of a pound of bread, and an allowance of water, for breakfast, and the same for dinner, with an addition of six oysters to each person. At noon, latitude observed 10° 48′ S; course since yesterday noon S 81 W; distance 111 miles; longitude, by account, from Shoal Cape 1° 45′ W.

Friday, June the 5th. Fair weather with some showers, and a strong trade wind at ESE.

This day we saw a number of water-snakes, that were ringed yellow and black, and towards noon we passed a great deal of rock-weed. Though the weather was fair, we were constantly shipping water, and two men always employed to bale the boat.

At noon I observed in latitude 10° 45′ S; our course since yesterday W$\frac{1}{4}$N, 108 miles; longitude made 3° 35′ W. Served one 25th of a pound of bread, and a quarter of a pint of water for breakfast; the same for dinner, with an addition of six oysters; for supper water only.

Saturday, June the 6th. Fair weather, with some showers, and a fresh gale at SE and ESE. Constantly shipping water and baling.

In the evening a few boobies came about us, one of which I caught with my hand. The blood was divided among three of the men who were weakest, but the bird I ordered to be kept for our dinner the next day. Served a quarter of a pint of water for supper, and to some, who were most in need, half a pint.

In the course of the night we suffered much cold and shiverings. At day-light, I found that some of the clams, which had been hung up to dry for sea-store, were stolen; but every one most solemnly denied having any knowledge of it. This forenoon we saw a gannet, a sand-lark, and some water-snakes, which in general were from two to three feet long.

Served the usual allowance of bread and water for breakfast, and the same for dinner, with the bird, which I distributed in the usual way, of Who shall have this? I determined to make Timor about the latitude of 9° 30′ S, or 10° S. At noon I observed the latitude to be 10° 19′ S; course N 77° W; distance 117 miles; longitude made from the Shoal Cape, the north part of New Holland, 5° 31′ W.

Sunday, June the 7th. Fresh gales and fair weather till eight in the evening. The remaining part of the 24 hours squally, with much wind at SSE and ESE, and a high sea, so that we were constantly wet and baling.

In the afternoon, I took an opportunity of examining again into our store of bread, and found remaining 19 days allowance, at my

former rate of serving one 25th of a pound three times a day: therefore, as I saw every prospect of a quick passage, I again ventured to
grant an allowance for supper, agreeable to my promise at the time it
was discontinued.

We passed the night miserably wet and cold, and in the morning I
heard heavy complaints of our deplorable situation. The sea was high
and breaking over us. I could only afford the allowance of bread and
water for breakfast; but for dinner I gave out an ounce of dried clams
to each person, which was all that remained.

At noon I altered the course to the WNW, to keep more from
the sea while it blew so strong. Latitude observed 9° 31′ S; course
N 57° W; distance 88 miles; longitude made 6° 46′ W.

Monday, June the 8th. Fresh gales and squally weather, with some
showers of rain. Wind E and ESE.

This day the sea ran very high, and we were continually wet, suffering much cold in the night. I now remarked that Mr. Ledward, the
surgeon, and Lawrence Lebogue, an old hardy seaman, were giving
way very fast. I could only assist them by a tea-spoonful or two of
wine, which I had carefully saved, expecting such a melancholy necessity. Among most of the others I observed more than a common
inclination to sleep, which seemed to indicate that nature was almost
exhausted.

Served the usual allowance of bread and water at supper, breakfast, and dinner. Saw several gannets.

At noon I observed in 8° 45′ S; course WNW¼W, 106 miles; longitude made 8° 23′ W.

Tuesday, June the 9th. Wind SE. The weather being moderate, I
steered W by S.

At four in the afternoon we caught a small dolphin, the first relief
of the kind we obtained. I issued about two ounces to each person,
including the offals, and saved the remainder for dinner the next day.
Towards evening the wind freshened, and it blew strong all night, so
that we shipped much water, and suffered greatly from the wet and
cold. At day-light, as usual, I heard much complaining, which my
own feelings convinced me was too well founded. I gave the surgeon
and Lebogue a little wine, but I could give no farther relief, than assurances that a very few days longer, at our present fine rate of sailing, would bring us to Timor.

Gannets, boobies, men of war and tropic birds, were constantly about us. Served the usual allowance of bread and water, and at noon dined on the remains of the dolphin, which amounted to about an ounce per man. I observed the latitude to be 9° 9′ S; longitude made 10° 8′ W; course since yesterday noon S 76° W; distance 107 miles.

Wednesday, June the 10th. Wind ESE. Fresh gales and fair weather, but a continuance of much sea, which, by breaking almost constantly over the boat, made us miserably wet, and we had much cold to endure in the night.

This afternoon I suffered great sickness from the oily nature of part of the stomach of the fish, which had fallen to my share at dinner. At sun-set I served an allowance of bread and water for supper. In the morning, after a very bad night, I could see an alteration for the worse in more than half my people. The usual allowance was served for breakfast and dinner. At noon I found our situation to be in latitude 9° 16′ S; longitude from the north part of New Holland 12° 1′ W; course since yesterday noon W½S, distance 111 miles.

Thursday, June the 11th. Fresh gales and fair weather. Wind SE and SSE.

Birds and rock-weed showed that we were not far from land; but I expected such signs must be here, as there are many islands between the east part of Timor and New Guinea. I however hoped to fall in with Timor every hour, for I had great apprehensions that some of my people could not hold out. An extreme weakness, swelled legs, hollow and ghastly countenances, great propensity to sleep, with an apparent debility of understanding, seemed to me melancholy presages of their approaching dissolution. The surgeon and Lebogue, in particular, were most miserable objects. I occasionally gave them a few tea-spoonfuls of wine, out of the little I had saved for this dreadful stage, which no doubt greatly helped to support them.

For my own part, a great share of spirits, with the hopes of being able to accomplish the voyage, seemed to be my principal support; but the boatswain very innocently told me, that he really thought I looked worse than any one in the boat. The simplicity with which he uttered such an opinion diverted me, and I had good humour enough to return him a better compliment.

Every one received his 25th of a pound of bread, and quarter of a pint of water, at evening, morning, and noon, and an extra allowance of water was given to those who desired it.

At noon I observed in latitude 9° 41′ S; course S 77° W; distance

109 miles; longitude made 13° 49′ W. I had little doubt of having now passed the meridian of the eastern part of Timor, which is laid down in 128° E. This diffused universal joy and satisfaction.

Friday, June the 12th. Fresh breezes and fine weather, but very hazy. Wind from E to SE.

All the afternoon we had several gannets, and many other birds, about us, that indicated we were near land, and at sun-set we kept a very anxious look-out. In the evening we caught a booby, which I reserved for our dinner the next day.

At three in the morning, with an excess of joy, we discovered Timor bearing from WSW to WNW, and I hauled on a wind to the NNE till day-light, when the land bore from SW by S about two leagues to NE by N seven leagues.

It is not possible for me to describe the pleasure which the blessing of the sight of land diffused among us. It appeared scarce credible, that in an open boat, and so poorly provided, we should have been able to reach the coast of Timor in forty-one days after leaving Tofoa, having in that time run, by our log, a distance of 3618 miles, and that, notwithstanding our extreme distress, no one should have perished in the voyage.

I have already mentioned, that I knew not where the Dutch settlement was situated; but I had a faint idea that it was at the SW part of the island. I therefore, after day-light, bore away along shore to the SSW, and the more readily as the wind would not suffer us to go towards the NE without great loss of time.

The day gave us a most agreeable prospect of the land, which was interspersed with woods and lawns; the interior part mountainous, but the shore low. Towards noon the coast became higher, with some remarkable head-lands. We were greatly delighted with the general look of the country, which exhibited many cultivated spots and beautiful situations; but we could only see a few small huts, whence I concluded no European resided in this part of the island. Much sea ran on the shore, so that landing with a boat was impracticable. At noon I was abreast of a very high head-land; the extremes of the land bore SW½W, and NNE½E; our distance off shore being three miles; latitude, by observation, 9° 59′ S; and my longitude, by dead reckoning, from the north part of New Holland, 15° 6′ W.

With the usual allowance of bread and water for dinner, I divided the bird we had caught the night before, and to the surgeon and Lebogue I gave a little wine.

Saturday, June the 13th. Fresh gales at E, and ESE, with very hazy weather.

During the afternoon, we continued our course along a low woody shore, with innumerable palm-trees, called the Fan Palm from the leaf spreading like a fan; but we had now lost all signs of cultivation, and the country had not so fine an appearance as it had to the eastward. This, however, was only a small tract, for by sun-set it improved again, and I saw several great smokes where the inhabitants were clearing and cultivating their grounds. We had now ran 25 miles to the WSW since noon, and were W five miles from a low point, which in the afternoon I imagined had been the southernmost land, and here the coast formed a deep bend, with low land in the bight that appeared like islands. The west shore was high; but from this part of the coast to the high cape which we were abreast of yesterday noon, the shore is low, and I believe shoal. I particularly remark this situation, because here the very high ridge of mountains, that run from the east end of the island, terminate, and the appearance of the country suddenly changes for the worse, as if it was not the same island in any respect.

That we might not run past any settlement in the night, I determined to preserve my station till the morning, and therefore hove to under a close-reefed fore-sail, with which the boat lay very quiet. We were here in shoal water, our distance from the shore being half a league, the westernmost land in sight bearing WSW½W. Served bread and water for supper, and the boat lying too very well, all but the officer of the watch endeavoured to get a little sleep.

At two in the morning, we wore, and stood in shore till day-light, when I found we had drifted, during the night, about three leagues to the WSW, the southernmost land in sight bearing W. On examining the coast, and not seeing any sign of a settlement, we bore away to the westward, having a strong gale, against a weather current, which occasioned much sea. The shore was high and covered with wood, but we did not run far before low land again formed the coast, the points of which opening at west, I once more fancied we were on the south part of the island; but at ten o'clock we found the coast again inclining towards the south, part of it bearing WSW½W. At the same time high land appeared from SW to SW by W$\frac{1}{2}$W; but the weather was so hazy, that it was doubtful whether the two lands were separated, the opening only extending one point of the compass. I, for this reason, stood towards the outer land, and found it to be the island Roti.

I returned to the shore I had left, and in a sandy bay I brought to a grapnel, that I might more conveniently calculate my situation. In this place we saw several smokes, where the natives were clearing their grounds. During the little time we remained here, the master and carpenter very much importuned me to let them go in search of supplies; to which, at length, I assented; but, finding no one willing to be of their party, they did not choose to quit the boat. I stopped here no longer than for the purpose just mentioned, and we continued steering along shore. We had a view of a beautiful-looking country, as if formed by art into lawns and parks. The coast is low, and covered with woods, in which are innumerable fan palm-trees, that look like cocoa-nut walks. The interior part is high land, but very different from the more eastern parts of the island, where it is exceedingly mountainous, and to appearance the soil better.

At noon, the island Roti bore SW by W seven leagues. I had no observation for the latitude, but, by account, we were in 10° 12′ S; our course since yesterday noon being S 77 W, 54 miles. The usual allowance of bread and water was served for breakfast and dinner, and to the surgeon and Lebogue, I gave a little wine.

Sunday, June the 14th. A strong gale at ESE, with hazy weather, all the afternoon; after which the wind became moderate.

At two o'clock this afternoon, having run through a very dangerous breaking sea, the cause of which I atributed to a strong tide setting to windward, and shoal water, we discovered a spacious bay or sound, with a fair entrance about two or three miles wide. I now conceived hopes that our voyage was nearly at an end, as no place could appear more eligible for shipping, or more likely to be chosen for an European settlement: I therefore came to a grapnel near the east side of the entrance, in a small sandy bay, where we saw a hut, a dog, and some cattle; and I immediately sent the boatswain and gunner away to the hut, to discover the inhabitants.

The SW point of the entrance bore W$\frac{1}{2}$S three miles; the SE point S by W three quarters of a mile; and the island Roti from S by W$\frac{1}{2}$W to SW$\frac{1}{4}$W, about five leagues.

While we lay here I found the ebb came from the northward, and before our departure the falling of the tide discovered to us a reef of rocks, about two cables length from the shore; the whole being covered at high-water, renders it dangerous. On the opposite shore also appeared very high breakers; but there is nevertheless plenty of room, and certainly a safe channel for a first-rate man of war.

The bay or sound within, seemed to be of a considerable extent; the northern part, which I had now in view, being about five leagues distant. Here the land made in moderate risings joined by lower grounds. But the island Roti, which lies to the southward, is the best mark to know this place.

I had just time to make these remarks, when I saw the boatswain and gunner returning with some of the natives: I therefore no longer doubted of our success, and that our most sanguine expectations would be fully gratified. They brought five Indians, and informed me that they had found two families, where the women treated them with European politeness. From these people I learned, that the governor resided at a place called Coupang, which was some distance to the NE. I made signs for one of them to go in the boat, and show me Coupang, intimating that I would pay him for his trouble; the man readily complied, and came into the boat.

These people were of a dark tawny colour, and had long black hair; they chewed a great deal of beetle, and wore a square piece of cloth round their hips, in the folds of which was stuck a large knife. They had a handkerchief wrapped round their heads, and at their shoulders hung another tied by the four corners, which served as a bag for their beetle equipage.

They brought us a few pieces of dried turtle, and some ears of Indian corn. This last was most welcome to us; for the turtle was so hard, that it could not be eaten without being first soaked in hot water. Had I staid they would have brought us something more; but, as the pilot was willing, I was determined to push on. It was about half an hour past four when we sailed.

By direction of the pilot we kept close to the east shore under all our sail; but as night came on, the wind died away, and we were obliged to try at the oars, which I was surprised to see we could use with some effect. However, at ten o'clock, as I found we got but little ahead, I came to a grapnel, and for the first time I issued double allowance of bread and a little wine to each person.

At one o'clock in the morning, after the most happy and sweet sleep that ever men had, we weighed, and continued to keep the east shore on board, in very smooth water; when at last I found we were again open to the sea, the whole of the land to the westward, that we had passed, being an island, which the pilot called Pulo Samow. The northern entrance of this channel is about a mile and a half or two miles wide, and I had no ground at ten fathoms.

Hearing the report of two cannon that were fired, gave new life to every one; and soon after we discovered two square-rigged vessels and a cutter at anchor to the eastward. I endeavoured to work to windward, but we were obliged to take to our oars again, having lost ground on each tack. We kept close to the shore, and continued rowing till four o'clock, when I brought to a grapnel, and gave another allowance of bread and wine to all hands. As soon as we had rested a little, we weighed again, and rowed till near day-light, when I came to a grapnel, off a small fort and town, which the pilot told me was Coupang.

Among the things which the boatswain had thrown into the boat before we left the ship, was a bundle of signal flags that had been made for the boats to show the depth of water in sounding; with these I had, in the course of the passage, made a small jack, which I now hoisted in the main shrouds, as a signal of distress; for I did not choose to land without leave.

Soon after day-break a soldier hailed me to land, which I instantly did, among a croud of Indians, and was agreeably surprised to meet with an English sailor, who belonged to one of the vessels in the road. His captain, he told me, was the second person in the town; I therefore desired to be conducted to him, as I was informed the governor was ill, and could not then be spoken with.

Captain Spikerman received me with great humanity. I informed him of our miserable situation; and requested that care might be taken of those who were with me, without delay. On which he gave directions for their immediate reception at his own house, and went himself to the governor, to know at what time I could be permitted to see him; which was fixed to be at eleven o'clock.

I now desired every one to come on shore, which was as much as some of them could do, being scarce able to walk: they, however, got at last to the house, and found tea with bread and butter provided for their breakfast.

The abilities of a painter, perhaps, could never have been displayed to more advantage than in the delineation of the two groups of figures, which at this time presented themselves. An indifferent spectator would have been at a loss which most to admire; the eyes of famine sparkling at immediate relief, or the horror of their preservers at the sight of so many spectres, whose ghastly countenances, if the cause had been unknown, would rather have excited terror than pity. Our bodies were nothing but skin and bones, our limbs were full of sores, and we were cloathed in rags; in this condition, with the tears of joy and gratitude flowing down our cheeks, the people of Timor beheld us with a mixture of horror, surprise, and pity.

The governor, Mr. William Adrian Van Este, notwithstanding his extreme ill-health, became so anxious about us, that I saw him before the appointed time. He received me with great affection, and gave me the fullest proofs that he was possessed of every feeling of a humane and good man. Sorry as he was, he said, that such a calamity could ever have happened to us, yet he considered it as the greatest blessing of his life that we had fallen under his protection; and, though his infirmity was so great that he could not do the office of a friend himself, he would give such orders as I might be certain would procure me every supply I wanted. In the mean time a house was hired for me, and, till matters could be properly regulated, victuals for every one were ordered to be dressed at his own house. With respect to my people, he said I might have room for them either at the hospital or on board of Captain Spikerman's ship, which lay in the road; and he expressed much uneasiness that Coupang could not afford them better accommodations, the house assigned to me being the only one uninhabited, and the situation of the few families such, that they could not accommodate any one. After this conversation an elegant repast was set before me, more according to the custom of the country, than with design to alleviate my hunger: so that in this instance he happily blended, with common politeness, the greatest favour I could receive.

On returning to my people, I found every kind relief had been given to them. The surgeon had dressed their sores, and the cleaning of their persons had not been less attended to, besides several friendly gifts of apparel.

I now desired to be shewn to the house that was intended for me, and I found it ready, with servants to attend, and a particular one, which the governor had directed to be always about my person. The house consisted of a hall, with a room at each end, and a loft overhead; and was surrounded by a piazza, with an outer apartment in one corner, and a communication from the back part of the house to the street. I therefore determined, instead of separating from my people, to lodge them all with me; and I divided the house as follows: One room I took to myself, the other I allotted to the master, surgeon, Mr. Nelson, and the gunner; the loft to the other officers; and the outer apartment to the men. The hall was common to the officers, and the men had the back piazza. Of this I informed the governor, and he sent down chairs, tables, and benches, with bedding and other necessaries for the use of every one.

The governor, when I took my leave, had desired me to acquaint him with every thing of which I stood in need; but I was now informed it was only at particular times that he had a few moments of ease, or could attend to any thing; being in a dying state, with an incurable disease. On this account, whatever business I had to transact would be with Mr. Timotheus Wanjon, the second of this place, and the governor's son-in-law; who now also was contributing every thing in his power to make our situation comfortable. I had been, therefore, misinformed by the seaman, who told me that Captain Spikerman was the next person to the governor.

At noon a very handsome dinner was brought to the house, which was sufficient to make persons, more accustomed to plenty, eat too much. Cautions, therefore, might be supposed to have had little effect; but I believe few people in such a situation would have observed more moderation. My greatest apprehension was, that they would eat too much fruit.

Having seen every one enjoy this meal of plenty, I dined with Mr. Wanjon; but I found no extraordinary inclination to eat or drink. Rest and quiet, I considered, as more necessary to my doing well, and therefore retired to my room, which I found furnished with every convenience. But, instead of rest, my mind was disposed to reflect on our late sufferings, and on the failure of the expedition; but, above all, on the thanks due to Almighty God, who had given us power to support and bear such heavy calamities, and had enabled me at last to be the means of saving eighteen lives.

In times of difficulty there will generally arise circumstances that bear more particularly hard on a commander. In our late situation, it was not the least of my distresses, to be constantly assailed with the melancholy demands of my people for an increase of allowance, which it grieved me to refuse. The necessity of observing the most rigid oeconomy in the distribution of our provisions was so evident, that I resisted their solicitations, and never deviated from the agreement we made at setting out. The consequence of this care was, that at our arrival we had still remaining sufficient for eleven days, at our scanty allowance: and if we had been so unfortunate as to have missed the Dutch settlement at Timor, we could have proceeded to Java, where I was certain every supply we wanted could be procured.

Another disagreeable circumstance, to which my situation exposed me, was the caprice of ignorant people. Had I been incapable of acting, they would have carried the boat on shore as soon as we made the island of Timor, without considering that landing among the natives, at a distance from the European settlement, might have been as dangerous as among any other Indians.

The quantity of provisions with which we left the ship, was not more than we should have consumed in five days, had there been no necessity for husbanding our stock. The mutineers must naturally have concluded that we could have no other place of refuge than the Friendly Islands; for it was not likely they should imagine, that, so poorly equipped as we were in every respect, there could have been a possibility of our attempting to return homewards: much less will they suspect that the account of their villany has already reached their native country.

When I reflect how providentially our lives were saved at Tofoa, by the Indians delaying their attack, and that, with scarce any thing to support life, we crossed a sea of more than 1200 leagues, without shelter from the inclemency of the weather; when I reflect that in an open boat, with so much stormy weather, we escaped foundering, that not any of us were taken off by disease, that we had the great good fortune to pass the unfriendly natives of other countries without accident, and at last happily to meet with the most friendly and best of people to relieve our distresses; I say, when I reflect on all these wonderful escapes, the remembrance of such great mercies enables me to bear, with resignation and chearfulness, the failure of an expedition, the success of which I had so much at heart, and which was frustrated at a time when I was congratulating myself on the fairest prospect of being able to complete it in a manner that would fully have answered the intention of his Majesty, and the honourable promoters of so benevolent a plan.

With respect to the preservation of our health, during a course of 16 days of heavy and almost continual rain, I would recommend to every one in a similar situation the method we practiced, which is to dip their cloaths in the salt-water, and wring them out, as often as they become filled with rain; it was the only resource we had, and I believe was of the greatest service to us, for it felt more like a change of dry cloaths than could well be imagined. We had occasion to do this so often, that at length all our cloaths were wrung to pieces: for, except the few days we passed on the coast of New Holland, we were continually wet either with rain or sea.

Thus, through the assistance of Divine Providence, we surmounted the difficulties and distresses of a most perilous voyage, and arrived safe in an hospitable port, where every necessary and comfort were administered to us with a most liberal hand.

As, from the great humanity and attention of the governor, and the gentlemen, at Coupang, we received every kind of assistance, we were not long without evident signs of returning health: therefore, to secure my arrival at Batavia, before the October fleet sailed for Europe, on the first of July, I purchased a small schooner, 34 feet long, for which I gave 1000 rix-dollars, and fitted her for sea, under the name of His Majesty's schooner Resource.

On the 20th of July, I had the misfortune to lose Mr. David Nelson: he died of an inflammatory fever. The loss of this honest man I very much lamented: he had accomplished, with great care and diligence, the object for which he was sent, and was always ready to forward every plan I proposed, for the good of the service we were on. He was equally useful in our voyage hither, in the course of which he gave me great satisfaction, by the patience and fortitude with which he conducted himself.

July 21st. This day I was employed attending the funeral of Mr. Nelson. The corpse was carried by twelve soldiers drest in black, preceded by the minister; next followed myself and second governor; then ten gentlemen of the town and the officers of the ships in the harbour; and after them my own officers and people.

After reading our burial-service, the body was interred behind the chapel, in the burying-ground appropriated to the Europeans of the town. I was sorry I could get no tombstone to place over his remains.

This was the second voyage Mr. Nelson had undertaken to the South Seas, having been sent out by Sir Joseph Banks, to collect plants, seeds, &c. in Captain Cook's last voyage. And now, after surmounting so many difficulties, and in the midst of thankfulness for his deliverance, he was called upon to pay the debt of nature, at a time least expected.

August the 20th. After taking an affectionate leave of the hospitable and friendly inhabitants, I embarked, and we sailed from Coupang, exchanging salutes with the fort and shipping as we ran out of the harbour.

I left the governor, Mr. Van Este, at the point of death. To this gentleman our most grateful thanks are due, for the humane and friendly treatment that we have received from him. His ill state of health only prevented him from showing us more particular marks of attention. Unhappily, it is to his memory only that I now pay this tribute. It was a fortunate circumstance for us, that Mr. Wanjon, the next in place to the governor, was equally humane and ready to relieve us. His attention was unremitting, and, when there was a doubt about supplying me with money, on government account, to enable me to purchase a vessel, he chearfully took it upon himself; without which, it was evident, I should have been too late at Batavia to have sailed for Europe with the October fleet. I can only return such services by ever retaining a grateful remembrance of them.

Mr. Max, the town surgeon, likewise behaved to us with the most disinterested humanity: he attended every one with the utmost care; for which I could not prevail on him to receive any payment, or to render me any account, or other answer, than that it was his duty.

Coupang is situated in 10° 12′ S latitude, and 124° 41′ E longitude.

On the 29th of August, I passed by the west end of the Island Flores, through a dangerous strait full of islands and rocks; and, having got into the latitude of 8° S, I steered to the west, passing the islands Sumbawa, Lombock, and Bali, towards Java, which I saw on the 6th of September. I continued my course to the west, through the Straits of Madura.

On the 10th of September, I anchored off Passourwang, in latitude 7° 36′ S, and 1° 44′ W of Cape Sandana, the NE end of Java.

On the 11th I sailed, and on the 13th arrived at Sourabya, latitude 7° 11´ S, 1° 52´ west.

On the 17th of September, sailed from Sourabya, and the same day anchored at Crissey, for about two hours, and from thence I proceeded to Samarang. Latitude of Crissey 7° 9´ S, 1° 55´ west.

On the 22nd of September, anchored at Samarang; latitude 6° 54´ S, 4° 7´ W. And on the 26th I sailed for Batavia, where I arrived on the 1st of October. Latitude 6° 10´ S; 8° 12´ W from the east end of Java.

On the day after my arrival, having gone through some fatigue in adjusting matters to get my people out of the schooner, as she lay in the river, and in an unhealthy situation, I was seized with a violent fever.

On the 7th, I was carried into the country, to the physician-general's house, where, the governor-general informed me, I should be accommodated with every attendance and convenience; and to this only can I attribute my recovery. It was, however, necessary for me to quit Batavia without delay; and the governor, on that account, gave me leave, with two others, to go in a packet that was to sail before the fleet; and assured me, that those who remained should be sent after me by the fleet, which was to sail before the end of the month: that if I remained, which would be highly hazardous, he could not send us all in one ship. My sailing, therefore, was eligible, even if it had not been necessary for my health; and for that reason I embarked in the Vlydt packet, which sailed on the 16th of October.

On the 16th of December, I arrived at the Cape of Good Hope, where I first observed that my usual health was returning; but for a long time I continued very weak and infirm.

I received the greatest attention and politeness from the governor-general, and all the residents on the coast of Java; and particular marks of friendship and regard from the governor, M. Van de Graaf, at the Cape of Good Hope.

On the 2d of January, 1790, we sailed for Europe, and on the 14th of March, I was landed at Portsmouth by an Isle of Wight boat.

F I N I S.

MINUTES

OF THE

PROCEEDINGS

OF THE

COURT-MARTIAL held at PORTSMOUTH,

AUGUST 12, 1792.

ON

TEN PERSONS charged with MUTINY

on Board His Majesty's Ship the BOUNTY.

WITH AN

APPENDIX,

CONTAINING

A full Account of the real Causes and Circumstances of that
unhappy Transaction, the most material of which have
hitherto been withheld from the Public.

———

Advertisement

THE FOLLOWING MINUTES of the Trial of the Mutineers of the
BOUNTY were taken by myself and my Clerks, being employed to
give Assistance before the Court-Martial, to William Musprat, one of
the Prisoners. They were not continued beyond the Evidence for the
Prosecution, nor do they comprize the Whole of the Evidence respecting the Capture of all the different Prisoners at Otaheite. They
were not intended for Publication. Repeated Assurances have been
given that an impartial State of all the Circumstances attending that
unhappy Mutiny, as well as a complete Trial of the Prisoners, would
be published. The anxious Relations of the unfortunate Parties in that
Mutiny, worn out with Expectation of that Publication, have repeatedly solicited my Consent to publish my Minutes, and as such Publication may in some Degree alleviate their Distress, I cannot think
myself justified in withholding such Consent, and hope this will be a
sufficient Apology for my Conduct.

I affirm, that as far as those Minutes go, they contain a just State of
the Evidence given at the Court-Martial.

STEP^{N.} BARNEY

PORTSMOUTH,
May 1st, 1794.

The Trial, &c.

AT A COURT MARTIAL, assembled and holden on the 12th Day of August 1792, on Board His Majesty's Ship *DUKE*, in *Portsmouth Harbour,*

BEFORE

The Right Honourable Lord HOOD, Vice Admiral of the Blue, } President.

CAPTAINS

SIR AND. SNAPE HAMMOND,　JOHN THOMAS DUCKWORTH,
JOHN COLEPOYS,　　　　　JNº NICHOLSON INGOLDFIELD,
GEORGE MONTAGUE,　　　JOHN KNIGHT,
SIR ROGER CURTIS,　　　　RICHARD GOODWIN KEATES,
JOHN BAZELEY,　　　　　　　　　　and
SIR ANDREW DOUGLAS,　　ALBEMARLE BERTIE.

On a Charge of Mutiny on the 28th April 1789, on Board His Majesty's Ship Bounty, for running away with the Ship, and deserting his Majesty's Service;

AGAINST

Joseph Coleman,　*James Morrison,*　*Thomas Ellison,*
Charles Norman,　*John Milward,*　　　and
Thomas McIntosh,　*William Musprat,*　*Michael Byrne.*
Peter Heywood,　　*Thomas Burkitt,*

The following Letter from Captain Bligh to the Lords of the Admiralty was read, as containing the Charge of Mutiny and Desertion:

COUPANG IN TIMOR, AUGUST 18, 1789.

SIR,

I am now unfortunately to request of you to acquaint the Lords Commissioners of the Admiralty, that his Majesty's armed vessel Bounty under my command, was taken from me, by some of the inferior officers and men, on the 28th April 1789, in the following manner:

A little before sunrise, *Fletcher Christian*, who was mate of the ship, and officer of the watch, with the ship's corporal, came into my cabin, while I was asleep, and seizing me, tied my hands with a cord, assisted by others who were also in the cabin, all armed with muskets and bayonets. I was now threatened with instant death if I spoke a word; I however called for assistance and awakened every one; but the officers who were in their cabins were secured by sentinels at their doors, so that no one could come to me. The arms were all secured, and I was forced on deck in my shirt with my hands tied, and secured by a guard abaft the mizen-mast, during which the mutineers expressed much joy that they would soon see Ottaheite. I now demanded of Christian the cause of such a violent act, but no other answer was given but "Hold your tongue, Sir; or you are dead this instant"; and holding me by the cord, which tied my hands, he as often threatened to stab me in the breast with a bayonet he held in his right hand. I however did my utmost to rally the disaffected villains to a sense of their duty, but to no effect. The boatswain was ordered to hoist the launch out, and while I was kept under a guard with Christian at their head abaft the mizen-mast, the officers and men not concerned in the mutiny were ordered into the boat. This being done, I was told by Christian, "Sir, your officers and men are now in the boat, and you must go with them"; and with the guard they carried me across the deck, with their bayonets presented on every side, when attempting to make another effort, one villain said to the others, "Blow his brains out." I was at last forced into the boat, and we were then veered astern, in all, nineteen souls. I was at this time 10 leagues to the S.W. of Tofoa, the North Westernmost of the Friendly Islands, having left Ottaheite the 4th of April with 1015 fine bread-fruit plants and many fruit kind, in all 774 pots, 39 tubs, and 24 boxes. These plants were now in a very flourishing order. I anchored at Annamocha 24th April, and left it on the 26th. The boatswain and carpenter, with some others, while the boat was alongside, collected several necessary things and water, and with some difficulty a compass and quadrant were got, but arms of no kind, or any maps or drawings, of which I had many very valuable *ones*. The boat was very deep and much lumbered, and in this condition we were cast adrift, with about 28 gallons of water, 150 lbs. of pork, six quarts of rum, and six bottles of wine. The day was calm, attended with light breezes, and I got to Tofoa by seven o'clock in the evening, but found no place to land, the land being so steep and rocky. On the 30th I found landing in a cove, on the North West part of the island, and here I remained in search of supplies until the 2d of May; when the natives discovered we had no fire-arms, they made an attack on us with clubs and stones, in the course of which I had the misfortune to lose a very worthy man, John Norton quarter-master, and most of us were hurt, more or less. But getting into our boat was no security, for they followed us in canoes loaded with stones, which they threw with much force and exactness; happily night saved the rest of us. I had determined to go to Amsterdam, in search of Paulchow the king; but taking this transaction as a real sample of their native dispositions, there was little hope to expect much from them; for I considered their good behaviour hitherto owing to a dread of our fire-arms, which now knowing us to have none would not be the case, and that supposing our lives were in safety, our boat and every thing would be taken from us, and thereby I should never be able to return. I was also earnestly solicited by all hands to take them towards home, and when I told them no hopes of relief remained for us but what I might find at New Holland, until I came to Timor, a distance of 1200 leagues, they all agreed to live on one ounce of bread per day and a gill of water. I therefore, after recommending this promise for ever to their memory, bore away for New Holland and Timor, across a sea but little known, and in a small boat deep loaded with 18 souls, without a single map of any kind, and nothing but my own recollection and general knowledge of the situation of places to direct us. Unfortunately we lost part of our provision; our stock therefore only consisted of 20 pounds of pork, three bottles of wine, five quarts of rum, 150 lbs. of bread, and 28 gallons of water. I steered to the W.N.W. with strong gales and bad weather, suffering every calamity and distress. I discovered many islands, and at last, on the 28th May, the coast of New Holland, and entered a break of the reef in latitude about 12° 50′ south, and longitude 145° 00′ east. I kept on in the direction of the coast to the northward, touching at such places as I found convenient, refreshing my people by the best means in my power. These refreshments consisted of oysters and a few clams; we were however greatly benefited by them and a few good nights' rest. On the 4th June, I passed the north part of New Holland and steered for Timor, and made it on the 12th, which was a happy sight to every one, particularly several who perhaps could not have existed a week or a day longer.

I followed the direction of the south side of the island, and on the 14th in the afternoon saw the island Rotty and west part of Timor, round which I got that night, and took a Maloy on board, to shew me Coupang, where he described to me the governor resided. On the next morning before day I anchored under the fort, and about eleven, I saw the governor, who received me with great humanity and kindness. Necessary directions were instantly given for our support, and perhaps more miserable beings were never seen.

Thus happily ended, through the assistance of Divine Providence, without accident, a voyage of the most extraordinary nature that ever happened in the world, let it be taken either in its extent, duration, or so much want of the necessaries of life.

The people who came in the boat were,

John Fryer, ... Master.
William Cole, ... Boatswain.
William Peckover, ... Gunner.
William Purcell, ... Carpenter.
Thomas Ledward, ... Acting Surgeon.
William Elphinstone, ... Master's Mate.
Thomas Hayward, ... Midshipman.
John Hallett, ... Midshipman.
John Samuel, ... Clerk.
Peter Linkletter, ... Quarter Master.
John Norton, ... Ditto, killed at Tofoa.
George Simpson, ... Quarter Master.
Laurence Labogue, ... Sail Maker.
Robert Tinkler, ... Able Seaman.
John Smith, ... Ab.
Thomas Hall, ... Able Seaman.
Robert Lamb, ... Ab.
David Nelson, ... Botanist, since dead.

Total 18.

The people who remained in the ship were,

Fletcher Christian, ... Master's Mate.
George Stewart, ... Acting ditto.
Peter Heywood, ... Midshipman.
Edward Young, ... Ditto.
Charles Churchill, ... Corporal.

James Morrison, ... Boatswain's Mate.

John Mills, ... Gunner's ditto.

Charles Norman, ... Carpenter's ditto,

Thomas McIntosh, ... Ditto Crew,

Joseph Coleman, ... Armourer ,

detained against their consent.

Thomas Burkett, ... Able Seaman.

John Summer, ... Ab.

John Williams, ... Ab.

Matthew Thompson, ... Ab.

Thomas Ellison, ... Ab.

William Mackiehoy, ... Ab.

John Millward, ... Ab.

Richard Skinner, ... Ab.

Matthew Quintal, ... Ab.

Michael Byrn, ... Ab.

Henry Hilbrant, ... Ab.

Isaac Martin, ... , ... Ab.

Alexander Smith, ... Ab.

William Muspratt, ... Ab.

William Brown, ... Botanist's Assistant.

Total 25.

The secrecy of this mutiny was beyond all conception, so that I cannot discover that any who were with me had the least knowledge of it; and the comparative lists will shew the strength of the pirates.

I found three vessels here bound to Batavia, but as their sailing would be late, I considered it to the advantage of His Majesty's Service, to purchase a vessel to take my people to Batavia, before the sailing of the fleet for Europe in October, as no one could be hired but at a price equal to a purchase; I therefore gave public notice of my intent, and assisted by the governor, I got a vessel for 1000 rix dollars, and called her The Resource.

We have not yet our health perfectly established. Four of my people are still ill, and I had the misfortune to lose Mr. Nelson the botanist, whose good conduct in the course of the whole voyage, and manly fortitude in our late disastrous circumstances, deserve this tribute to his memory.

I have given a summary account of my proceedings to the governor, and have requested, in His Majesty's name, that necessary orders and directions may be given to their different settlements, to detain the ship wherever she may be found.

There is but little chance that their Lordships can receive this before I arrive myself; I therefore have not been so particular as I shall be in my letters from Batavia.

I shall sail in the morning without fail, and use my utmost exertions to appear before their Lordships, and answer personally for the loss of His Majesty's ship.

I beg leave to acquaint their Lordships, that the greatest kindness and attention have been shewn to us while here, by the second governor, Timotheus Wanjon, whose zeal to render services to His Majesty's subjects has been unremitting during the sickness of the governor William Adrian Van Este, who is now at the point of death.

The surgeon of the fort, a Mr. Max, has also been ever attentive to my sick people, and has daily and hourly attended them with great care.

I have the honor to be, SIR,
Your most obedient humble Servant,
WILLIAM BLIGH.

To Philip Stephens, Esq.   (A Copy.)

JOHN FRYER, MASTER *of the* BOUNTY, *sworn.*

I had the first watch on the 28th April 1789, Captain Bligh came on deck, and gave orders for the night. I was relieved at twelve o'clock by William Peckover the gunner, and the gunner was relieved at four by Mr. Christian; all was quiet at twelve, when I was relieved; at dawn of day I was alarmed by a noise in the cabin, and as I went to jump up from my bed, Sumner and Quintal laid their hands on my breast, and desired me to lay down, adding, "Sir, you are a prisoner." I attempted to expostulate with them, but they told me to hold my tongue, or I was a dead man; if quiet, no man in the ship would hurt me. I then, by raising myself on the locker, saw Captain Bligh on the ladder going on the quarter-deck in his shirt, with his hands tied behind him, Christian holding him by the cord; Churchill came to my cabin, and took a brace of pistols and a hanger, saying, "I'll take care of these, Mr. Fryer." When I saw Captain Bligh on the ladder, I asked, what they were going to do with him; when Sumner answered, "Damn his eyes, put him into the boat, and let the bugger see if he can live upon three-quarters of a pound of yams per day." I said, For God's sake for what? Sumner and Quintal replied, "Hold your tongue, Mr. Christian is captain of the ship, and recollect, Mr. Bligh brought all this upon himself." I advised them to consider what they were about. Sumner replied, "they knew well what they were about, or they would not persist." I then persuaded them to lay down their arms, and assured them nothing should happen for what they had done. They replied, "Hold your tongue, it is too late now." They said they would put Captain Bligh into the small cutter. I said, her bottom was almost worn out. They said, "Damn his eyes, the boat is too good for him." I said I hoped he was not to be sent by himself. They said, "No; Mr. Samuel, Mr. Heywood, and Mr. Hallet, are going with him." I then requested to go on deck to Captain Bligh, before he went into the boat; they refused to let me. I then prevailed on them to let me call to Christian on the deck, to get permission; I did so, and was permitted to go on deck. When I came on deck, Captain Bligh was standing by the mizen-mast with his hands tied behind him, Christian holding the cord with one hand, and a bayonet in the other. I said to Christian, Consider what you are about; Christian answered, "Hold your tongue, Sir, I've been in hell for weeks past; Captain Bligh has brought all this upon himself." I said, their not agreeing was no reason for taking the ship. Christian replied, "Hold your tongue, Sir, this instant." I then said, You and I have been upon friendly terms during the voyage, give me leave to speak; let Captain Bligh go down to his cabin, I make no doubt all will be friends again in a short time. Christian again said, "Hold your tongue, Sir, it is too late." Being threatened by Christian, I said no more on that head. I then said, Mr. Christian, pray give Captain Bligh a better boat than the cutter, the bottom is almost out, let him have a chance to get on shore. Christian answered, "No; that boat is good enough." I whispered to Captain Bligh to keep up his spirits, for if I stay on board I may find means to follow you. Captain Bligh said aloud, "By all means stay, Mr. Fryer"; and further said, "Isaac Martin" (then under arms) "was a friend"; and likewise said several times, "Knock Christian down." Christian must have heard all this, but took no notice. Sumner and Quintal, who had followed me upon deck, were behind all the time with musquets and bayonets. I tried to pass Christian to speak to Martin, but could not. Christian, putting a bayonet to my breast, said, "If you advance an inch further, I'll run you through"; and ordered me down to my cabin, and Sumner and Quintal conveyed me there. Going down the hatchway, I saw Morrison fixing a tackle to the launch's stern. I said, Morrison, I hope you have no hand in this business; he said, "No, Sir; I do not know a word about it." I said in a low voice, If that is the case be on your guard, there may be an opportunity of rescuing the ship. His answer was, "Go down, Sir, it is too late." I was then confined to my cabin, and Milward was put over me as a third centinel. I then thought Milward friendly, and winked at him to knock Sumner down, who stood next him. Milward immediately cocked his piece and dropped it, pointing to me, saying, "Mr. Fryer, be quiet, no one will hurt you." I said, Milward, your piece is cocked, you had better uncock it, you may shoot some person; then holding up his piece said, "Sir, there is no one means to hurt you." Sumner said, "No, that was our agreement not to commit murder." Mr. Peckover and Nelson continued in the cock-pit, and I persuaded the guards set over me to let me go to them. I found Mr. Nelson and Mr. Peckover in his cabin. Nelson said, "Mr. Fryer, what have we brought on ourselves?" and Mr. Peckover said, "What is best to be done?" I told them, I had spoke to Captain Bligh to keep up his spirits, and if I stay on board, I hope soon to be able to follow him; and that Captain Bligh had desired me to stay by all means. I then said to Mr. Nelson and Mr. Peckover, If you are ordered into the boat, say you will stay on board; and I flatter myself we shall restore the ship in a short time. Mr. Peckover said, "If we stay, we shall all be deemed pirates." I said, No; I would be answerable for any one who would join me. Whilst we were talking, Hilbrant was in the bread room getting bread to put in the boat. I think Hilbrant must have heard our conversation, and went upon deck and told Christian, for I was immediately ordered up into the cabin. I then heard from the centinels Sumner, Quintal, and Milward, that Christian had consented to give Captain Bligh the launch, but not for his sake, but for the safety of those that were going with him. I then asked if they knew who were going with him; they said No, but they believed a great many. Christian then ordered every man a dram that was under arms, and Smith, the Captain's servant, served the drams out. I then hoped I should stay on board, that if the men got drunk, I should be able to take the ship. Mr. Nelson and Peckover were then ordered upon deck, and I soon afterwards. And Christian said to me, Mr. Fryer, go into the boat; I said, I will stay with you, Sir, if you will give me leave; but Christian said, No Sir, go directly. Captain Bligh being on the gangway without the rail, his hands at liberty, said, Mr. Fryer, stay in the ship. Christian said, No, by God, Sir, go into the boat, or I will run you through, pointing the bayonet to my breast. I then went outside the rail to Captain Bligh, and asked Christian to let Mr. Tinkler (my brother-in-law) go with me: Churchill said, No; but after some time Christian permitted it, and upon request let me have his trunk, but ordered nothing else to be taken out of my cabin. I requested my log book and quadrant, but they were denied, as Captain Bligh had a quadrant. I cannot say who went into the boat first, whether Captain Bligh or myself, we were both on the gangway together, and all the time bad language was used towards Captain Bligh, by the people under arms. I begged for muskets, but Churchill refused, saying Captain Bligh was well acquainted where he was going. The boat was then ordered astern, and four cutlasses handed into her, by whom I know not; but the people all this time used very bad language towards the Captain, adding, Shoot the bugger. William Cole, the boatswain, said to Captain Bligh, We had better put off, or they will do us some mischief; which Captain Bligh agreed to, and we rowed astern to get out of the way of the guns. Christian ordered the top gallant sails to be loosened, and the ship steered the same course as Captain Bligh had ordered. From the confusion and great attention we were obliged to pay for our preservation, I had no means or opportunity to make any notes or memorandums until we arrived at Timor. I observed under arms, Christian, Churchill, and Burkitt, that they were in the cabin securing the Captain; Sumner, Quintal, and Milward, were centinels over me, Martin was centinel at the hen coop, and the four persons following wished to go into the boat. Coleman, who called to the witness several times to recollect that he had no hand in the business; McIntosh and Norman were leaning over the rail, and Byrne was along side; all appeared to be crying. Byrne said, If he went into Captain Bligh's boat, the people would leave him when he got on shore, as he could not see to follow them. I did not perceive Heywood upon the deck the time the ship was seized.

COURT. What number of men did you see on the deck at each time you went there?

A. Eight or ten.

Q. How long did you remain there each time?

A. Ten minutes, or a quarter of an hour.

Q. What works were going on each time?

A. When I went first, hoisting out the boats; the last time nothing particular except the centinels over Captain Bligh and myself forcing us into the boat.

Q. Do you think the boats could be hoisted out by eight or ten persons?

A. No.

Q. You have no reason to know who were under arms besides those you have named?

A. No.

Q. When you was on the quarter-deck or gangway, did you see either of the prisoners active in obeying orders given by Christian or Churchill?

A. Burkitt and Milward were under arms as centinels over Captain Bligh and myself on the gangway, which I suppose was by their orders.

Q. You say you saw Morrison the boatswain's mate helping to hoist out the boats, did you see any others of the prisoners employed so, or otherwise?

A. No; my attention was taken up with Captain Bligh—. I did not.

Q. When the dram was served, did you see any of the prisoners partake?

A. One.—Milward.

Q. When the boat in which Captain Bligh and others were put had veered astern, did you observe any one of the prisoners use the bad language which you say passed on that occasion?

A. Not to the best of my recollection.—I saw Milward on the tafferel rail with a musket; there was so much noise in the boat I could not hear one man from another.

Q. You say when the cutlasses were handed into the boat there was much bad language, did any one of the prisoners join on that occasion?

A. Not to my knowledge, it was a general thing.

Q. Did you see Ellison on the day of the mutiny?

A. No.

Q. Did you see Musprat?

A. No.

Q. At the time you were ordered upon the deck after the conversation in the cockpit, how, and by whom were these orders conveyed to you?

A. By the centinels, Milward, Sumner, and Quintal.

Q. When you and Captain Bligh were ordered into the boat, did any person assist Christian, or offer so to do?

A. Yes; Churchill, Sumner, and Quintal, and Burkitt, were under arms on the quarter deck.

Q. You say when the boat was cast off, you rowed astern to get out of the way of the guns: had you seen any preparations made for firing?

A. I meant the small arms they had in their hands, when they said Shoot the bugger.

Q. When you heard Christian order the top gallant sails to be hoisted, was you near enough to know any of the people that went on the yards?

A. I saw only Ellison.

Q. I ask you as Master of his Majesty's ship Bounty, how many men it would require to hoist out the launch?

A. Ten.

Q. Was the remark of your not having seen Heywood on the deck on the 29th of April made at Timor, or since you knew he was apprehended by the Pandora?

A. Since: I frequently told the people in the boat, that I had not seen the Youngsters on deck.

Q. How many men went up to loosen the topsails?

A. Only Ellison.

Q. What reason had you to imagine that Milward was friendly when he was centinel over you?

A. He appeared very uneasy.

Q. You say you obtained permission for Tinkler to go with you: had he been compelled to remain in the ship?

A. He had been told by Churchill that he was to stay on board as his servant; then came crying to me.

Q. Do you think that any of the people who remained in the Bounty were kept against their consent?

A. None but the four.

Q. In what part of the ship was the Youngster's birth?

A. Down the main hatchway on each side.

Q. Did you observe any centinel over the main hatchway?

A. Yes; I omitted to mention Thompson, who was sitting on the arm chest; I wanted to go to my mess-place, but was stopt by Sumner and Quintal.

Q. Was Thompson armed?

A. I believe he was, with a cutlass.

Q. Did you consider him as a centinel over the Youngster's birth?

A. Yes; and a centinel on the arm chest at the same time.

Q. Was any effort made by any person to rescue the ship?

A. Only by what I said to Mr. Peckover and Morrison, Mr. Cole the boatswain came down, and I whispered him to stay in the ship.

Q. What was the distance of time from the first alarm to the time of your being forced into the boat?

A. Two hours and a half, or three hours.

Q. What did you suppose Christian meant, when he said he had been in hell for a fortnight?

A. His frequent quarrels with, and abuses received from, Captain Bligh.

Q. Had there been any recent quarrel?

A. The day before, Captain Bligh had been challenging all the young gentlemen and people with stealing his cocoa nuts.

Q. When you went into the cockpit, were any centinels over Mr. Peckover and Mr. Nelson?

A. No; the same centinels that confined me, kept them below.

N. B. Prisoners were now asked, If they had any questions to ask the witness.

Coleman.—None.

Heywood.—None at present.

Q. *per* BYRNE.—Was you on the deck when the large cutter was hoisted out?

A. No.

Q. *per* MORRISON.—Do you recollect, when you spoke to me, my particular answer; and are you positive it was I who said, "Go down to your cabin?"

A. Yes, I am; "Go down to your cabin, it is too late."

Q. Ditto.—Do you recollect my saying, I will do my endeavours to raise a party and rescue the ship?

A. No.

Q. Ditto.—Did you observe any part of my conduct on any part of that day that leads you to think I was one of the mutineers?

A. I never saw him only at that time, and his appearance gave me reason to speak to him; he appeared friendly, but his answer surprized me; I did not expect it from him; whether he spoke from fear of the others, I know not.

COURT. Might not Morrison speaking to you, telling you to keep below, be from a laudable motive, supposing your assistance at that time might prevent a more advantageous effort?

A. Probably it might; if I had staid in the ship, he would have been one of the first I should have opened my mind to, from his good behaviour.

Q. Did he speak to you in a threatening tone, or address you as advice?

A. As advice.

Q. Did you see any person that appeared to be forcing the prisoner Morrison to put the tackle to the launch?

A. No.

Q. Did you see Morrison employed in any other way than you have related from the time you was first confined, till the boat was cast loose from the ship.

A. No.

Q. Did you consider the hoisting out of that boat as assisting the mutineers, or as giving Captain Bligh a better chance for his life?

A. As assisting Captain Bligh, and giving him a better chance for his life.

Norman.—None.

McIntosh.—None.

Musprat.—None at present.

Q. *per* BURKITT.—If you did not see Captain Bligh before he was going up the ladder, how could you see me seize him in the cabin?

A. I have not said I saw you assist in seizing him, but when Captain Bligh was on the ladder, I saw you and Churchill come out of the cabin armed.

Q. Did you see or hear me swearing or giving any directions, or taking any charge when on the deck, or during the mutiny?

A. No.

Q. Did I not do my duty on the voyage as a seaman?

A. Yes.

Millward.

Q. Did you see me when you spoke to Morrison to rescue the ship?

A. No, you was ordered as an additional centinel over me after-wards.

Q. Had I the arms I held at that time voluntarily, or by force?

A. I cannot tell.

Q. Do you recollect what I said when I came down to the cock-pit?

A. Nothing but what I have said already.

WILLIAM COLE, BOATSWAIN *of the* BOUNTY, *deposed,*

That Quintal, a seaman belonging to the Bounty, but in what part of the ship he knows not, calling to the carpenter (Purcell) said, they had mutinied and taken the ship; that Christian had the command, and the Captain was a prisoner upon the quarter deck; that the witness being thus awaked, jumped out of the cabin, and said to the carpenter, For God's sake I hope you know nothing of this; he said, he did not; that the sail-maker Lawrence Lebogue lying by witness's cabin, witness asked him what he meant to do; Lebogue answered, he did not know, but would do as the witness did; that witness went up the fore hatchway, and looking aft, saw Thompson centinel at the main hatchway, and Heywood leaning over his hammock, in the lar-board birth, and Mr. Young in the starboard birth, Mr. Elphinstone looking likewise over the side of the birth which was boarded up; that witness then went on deck, saw men under arms around the fore hatchway, Churchill, Brown, Alexander Smith, William McKoy, and Williams; that Williams looked aft, saw the Captain's hands tied be-hind him, and Mills, Martin, Ellison, and Burkitt, centinels over him. That witness jumped down the fore hatchway, awaked Morrison, Milward, McIntosh, and Simpson, all lying in the same tier. I in-formed them what happened and hoped to form a party; they denied all knowledge of the mutiny; that Milward said, he was very sorry for it, and said he had a hand in the foolish piece of business before, and was afraid they would make him take a part in that; that Churchill then came forward and called out to Millward to come on deck immediately, for he had a musket for him, or to take a musket; that they all went up as they got their cloaths on; that witness did not see any of the rest at that time have arms. That witness went on deck and asked Christian what he meant to do; that Christian then ordered this witness to hoist out the boat, and threatening him with the bayonet if he did not take care that the boat was hoisted out; and witness asked liberty to go and speak with Mr. Fryer, which was granted; witness went below and asked Mr. Fryer what was best to do, when Mr. Fryer in a low voice told witness by all means to stay; that one of the centinels over Mr. Fryer, (Sumner, as witness believes,) said to Mr. Fryer, "you have a wife and family, but all will be forgot in a little time"; that Mr. Fryer came upon deck and asked Christian what he was about, and told him, "If he did not approve of the Captain's behaviour, to put him under an arrest, and proceed on the voyage"; that Christian then said, "If that's all you have to say, go down to your cabin, for I've been in hell for weeks past"; that they were then intending to send away the Captain and Hayward, Hallet, and Samuel, with him; that the small cutter being stove, they made interest with Christian for the other cutter, which was fitted out; that Christian still threatened the witness, if he carried any thing away, or sprung any yard; that witness then finding the Captain was to be sent from the ship, went aft and asked for the long boat; that Hayward and Hallet were upon deck all this time; that after asking Christian three or four times without an answer, Captain Bligh said, For God's sake, Mr. Cole, do all in your power; that the carpenter said, "I've done nothing I am ashamed or afraid of, I want to see my native country"; that the launch was then granted; that the carpenter and armourer were employed in fitting her; that when the boat was going over the side, Byrne was in the cutter along-side, but how he came there witness don't know; witness says, we were employed in getting the launch out; that Christian ordered a dram to be given to each of the men under arms; that Smith brought some spirits and gave witness some in water; that Christian was continually threatening witness with the bayonet, to take care not to carry any thing away; that witness saw Heywood standing there at the same time, lending a hand to get the fore-stay sail along; that when the boat was hooked, Heywood said something to me, but what it was I do not know, Christian threatening witness at the time; that Heywood then went below, and witness saw no more of him; that witness says, they got the boat out, and Norman, McIntosh, Coleman, and Morrison, who did not go into the boat with others who did, were busy in getting necessary things into the launch; that Churchill and Quintal were walking about, saying Damn them, they have enough; that at this time witness saw William Musprat with a musket in his hand, but don't remember seeing him before; that witness heard Churchill call out, Keep somebody below, but who he knows not; that Churchill and Quintal were forcing the people into the boat; that Coleman was handing a bag into the boat which appeared to contain iron, or it was in the boat before; that Christian ordered it to be stopped; that Norman and McIntosh were then going into the boat, and endeavouring to get in the carpenter's tool chest, when Quintal said, "If you will let them have these things, they will build a vessel in a month"; that the chest was then handed in, some tools first being taken out; that the carpenter got his cloaths chest in; that they were then forcing the people out that were going and not of their side; that witness went then into the boat, and that Peckover, Samuel, Hayward, and Hallet, soon after were put or came into the boat; that Captain Bligh was then brought to the side, and put into the boat, which was then veered astern; that Coleman and Norman were crying on the gangway from the time they were ordered not to go into the boat; that McIntosh was standing by, not crying, but wished to come into the boat; that Byrne was in the cutter all the time crying; that when the launch was dropt astern, some pork, and other provisions and necessaries were handed over; that Burkitt went and got some cloaths from the gunner and threw into the boat; that Sumner demanded the Boatswain's call of witness, and said it would be of no use to him where he was going; that witness asked him in the Indian tongue, if he would give him any thing for it, and sent it up, but got nothing for it; that Norton asked for his jacket when Sumner said, "If I had my will you, bugger, I would blow your brains out"; that witness then told Captain Bligh it would be best to cast off, as the witness thought they might fire upon the boat; that Captain Bligh then called and wished to speak with Christian, but he did not come aft; that Coleman called over, and said "he had no hand in it, and desired if any of them reached England, to remember him to Mr. Green of Greenwich"; that the boat then cast off, being at midships only seven or eight inches out of water; that the last person witness saw was Ellison, loosing the maintop gallant sail, and they sailed directly.

Q. *per* COURT.—How many men did you see under arms?

A. Nine at first on the deck, viz. Churchill, Williams, Mills, Brown, McKoy, Burkitt, A. Smith, Martin, Ellison, and two or three at other parts; Thompson at the main hatchway; Quintal and Sumner over the master's cabin, and at the cock-pit; Hillbrant about the deck; Skinner on the deck, but not at first; Musprat on the deck abaft the fore-hatchway, it was at the latter part of the time I saw him. Millward was ordered to take a musket and had it on the deck, Churchill called out to him, "Damn you, come up, here's a musket ready for you."

Q. What number of men was helping you to hoist the launch out?

A. Fourteen or fifteen; those who had no arms helped out with the boat, but those who had did not quit their arms; the master at arms had a pistol. I was not put under any restraint, but often threatened by Christian.

Q. Did any of the prisoners assist you in getting the launch out?

A. Yes; Coleman, Norman, McIntosh, and Morrison, were forward, Heywood and Hallet aft, I believe.

Q. Had you any conversation with the prisoners respecting the mutiny?

A. No conversation about the mutiny, except with the men mentioned whom I awaked.

Q. What force was used to prevent the people getting into the boat, who were not permitted to go?

A. Nothing but orders; the people stood round them with arms, but they did not attempt to break the order.

Q. Did you see any attempt by any one of the prisoners to prevent the mutiny?

A. None, I saw Heywood handle the forestay tackle fall.

Q. You say you saw Heywood handle the forestay tackle fall, was that voluntarily done?

A. Voluntarily. He was not forced.

Q. You say you saw no one of the prisoners make any attempt to stop the mutiny. Did you see any make any marks of disapprobation at what was going forward?

A. No.

Q. When the drams were ordered, did either of the prisoners partake?

A. Smith the servant served all in general, I did not observe who in particular.

Q. Did you hear any one threaten to shoot into the launch before you cast off?

A. Skinner.

Q. You have said, that Coleman, McIntosh, and Norman, were detained against their will; have you reason to believe that any other of the prisoners were so detained?

A. I believe Heywood. I thought he intended to come away, he had no arms.

Q. Have you any other reason to think that Heywood was detained against his will?

A. I heard Churchill call out to keep *them* below; who he meant I do not know, but I believe Heywood.

Q. You have said you did not see any of the prisoners shew any marks of disapprobation of what was going on. What was the cause of Coleman, Norman and Byrne crying, as you have represented?

A. Coleman and Norman wanted to come into the boat; why Byrne cried I know not, but he was blind.

Q. What was Burkitt's situation when on deck?

A. He was on the starboard side next the wheel, he had his musket shouldered, and was standing there.

Q. When you awoke Morrison, Millward, McIntosh, and Simpson, what did they do, when first on the deck?

A. Millward was ordered to take a musket, and went up, the other three were clearing the boat from yams.

Q. How long was it from the time Heywood quitted the tackle fall and went below, before you was forced into the boat?

A. Twenty minutes, or half an hour.

Q. Did you see any of the prisoners forcing Captain Bligh into the boat, or any under arms at that particular time?

A. I was in the boat alongside, and cannot tell who forced him.

Q. In consequence of Churchill calling to Millward to come upon deck, and take a musket; did Millward make any objection?

A. Not to my knowledge.

Q. You say, that Coleman, Norman, and McIntosh, assisted at the top tackle fall to get out the launch. Did you suppose that they meant to be of use to Captain Bligh and accompany him, or that they were well disposed towards the mutineers, and wished to get quit of their Captain?

A. I think they wished to go with him.

Q. Do you think Heywood assisted from the same motive?

A. I have no reason to think otherwise, we did not converse at all. I did not see him at the tackle fall until the boat went out.

Q. Where was Musprat when under arms?

A. Abaft the hatchway.

Q. Did he appear to be centinel over any place or person?

A. He did not.

Q. Who were the persons that forced Captain Bligh into the boat?

A. I do not remember. I was in the boat, they on the deck.

Q. *per* BYRNE.—When the large cutter was hoisted out, who was the person that threw the fall out of her, to hook on the fore stay tackle?

A. I do not remember.

Q. When the orders were given for hoisting her out, did you not look down the hatchway, and see three or four people abreast in the starboard cable tier?

A. No; I saw Norton (since killed) get out of his hammock, and I believe the cook was there.

Q. Do you remember any one ordering some person to hook on the tackle to the boat?

A. Not in particular.

Q. Did you not call to people below, to come up and hoist out the cutter?

A. I do not know that I did, but I might.

Q. When the cutter was out, did you not order me to stay in her, to keep her from thumping against the ship?

A. I do not remember I did, but I told you to hawl her a-head when the launch was going over the side.

Q. When Purcell and you came out of the cock-pit, on the first alarm, did you perceive any one sitting on the chest on the fore hatchway?

A. I do not remember.

Q. Did any one speak to you or Mr. Purcell on the fore hatchway?

A. They may, but I do not know.

Q. When Mr. Purcell and you came up, did not I say to you, "Sir, the people are in arms, and Captain Bligh is a prisoner"?

A. I do not remember seeing you, but you might be there; but your being blind I should have taken but little notice of you in the confusion.

Morrison.—Do you recollect when I came upon deck, after you called me out of my hammock, I came to you abaft the windlass, and said, Mr. Cole, what's to be done? Your answer was, "By God, James, I don't know, but go and help them out with the cutter."

A. Yes, I do remember it.

Q. Do you remember in consequence of your order, I went about clearing the cutter?

A. Yes.

Q. Do you remember I did hawl a trawl or grapnel from the main hold, and put them into the boat?

A. I remember such things being in the boat, who put them in I know not.

Q. Do you remember calling to me to assist in hoisting a cask of water from the hold, same time threatening Norton the quarter master that he should not go in the boat, if he was not more attentive in getting the things into her?

A. I remember telling Norton that, for he was frightened, and believe that Morrison was employed on that business.

Q. Do you recollect I came to you when you were getting your things (which were tied up in part of your bedding) into the boat, and telling you the boat was then overloaded, and that Captain Bligh had begged no more should go into her, and in consequence I would take my chance in the ship; that you took me by the hand and said, God bless you, my boy, I'll do you justice if ever I get to England?

A. I remember shaking hands with you, and your saying you would take your chance in the ship; I had no reason before but to think you meant to leave the ship.

Q. *per* COURT.—Do you remember saying, If you got to England you would do him justice?

A. I do not remember it, but I have no doubt but I did.

Q. *Morrison.*—Was my conduct on that day such, or during the voyage, as to give you reason to suppose I was concerned in the mutiny?

A. I had no reason to suppose so.

Q. *per* COURT.—Did you hear prisoner Morrison say that Captain Bligh said, that no other men could come into the boat, as she was deeply laden already?

A. I remember taking him by the hand, but the conversation I do not recollect.

Q. Did you at that time believe that prisoner Morrison would have gone with you into the boat, if it had not been apprehended the boat was too deeply laden?

A. From his conduct and behaviour I had no reason but to think so, he did what I ordered him.

Q. What was Morrison doing when you desired him to clear the cutter?

A. To the best of my knowledge standing on the booms doing nothing, just come up.

Q. You said, Morrison assisted in getting out the boat, did you consider all those that assisted in getting out that boat to be of the Captain's party?

A. No. Some were under arms.

Q. Did you consider these not under arms, at that time, to be of the Captain's party?

A. I certainly did think they had no hand in the mutiny.

Q. Do you think all Mr. Christian's party was entrusted with arms?

A. I do not know, for some came on deck with arms, afterwards Mr. Young came upon deck with a musket; and Musprat came afterwards, which was after the first boat was hoisted out.

Q. Did you on that day consider Morrison as a person that was awed by the people under arms, to assist in hoisting the boat out, or as one aiding and assisting them in their design?

A. I do not think he was in awe of the people, nor that he was aiding or assisting them in their design.

Q. Did Morrison express any desire to come into the boat, and was he prevented?

A. He did not make any express desire, nor was he prevented from so doing.

Q. *Ellison.*—Are you certain, when you came upon deck and looked round, whether it was me that was armed, or the man that stood before me, as I stood at the wheel?

A. To the best of my knowledge I think it was you under arms; there were four men then on the quarter-deck under arms; Ellison, Mills, Martin, and Burkitt.

Q. Are you certain it was me, I was only a boy and scarcely able to lift a musket at that time?

A. You stood by Captain Bligh part of the time, he was upon deck with a musket, and I believe a bayonet fixed.

Q. In what position did I stand?

A. I do not know, I cannot answer that question.

Q. *Burkitt.*—When you came aft to get the compass out of the binnacle from the starboard-side of the quarter-deck, did not Quintal come and say, he would be damned if you should have it; you said, Quintal, It is very hard you will not let me have a compass, when there is a plenty more in the store-room; then you looked very hard at me, and I said, Quintal, let Mr. Cole have it, and any thing else that will be of service?

A. Quintal objected to the compass going, but I do not remember that you said what you mention; you might, you were standing there, I do not remember what conversation passed, the confusion was so great.

Q. Did you hear me that morning, during the time you said I was under arms, give any orders or use any bad language?

A. I did not. But when Mr. Peckover asked you for the cloaths, you went and got them, and threw them into the boat.

Q. Do you remember my coming aft and looking over and asking the people in the boat, if they wanted any thing I could get for them? Mr. Peckover told me to get his pocket-book out of his cabin and his cloaths.

A. I do not remember your asking any body if they wanted any thing; I have said you brought Mr. Peckover's cloaths.

Q. *Millward.*—Can you positively say that I took the musket according to Churchill's orders?

A. I don't know if by Churchill's orders, but you had one.

Q. Do you recollect speaking to me as I stood by the windlass, when you came up the fore-hatchway, and asked me what I was doing? I told you, Nothing; you told me to lend a hand and clear the large cutter.

A. No.

Q. *per* COURT.—Were all the people that were called on deck bound and put in the boat, or were they all at liberty?

A. They were not bound, but brought up by centinels at different times, and put into the boat.

Q. Were there no other arms in the ship but in the chest, at the main hatchway?

A. Not to my knowledge.

Q. Was it Burkitt's watch on deck the morning of the mutiny?

A. I think it was.

Q. Was it Musprat's?

A. I do not know he watched at all, he assisted the cook.

Q. Was it Ellison's watch?

A. To the best of my knowledge it was.

Q. Was it Norman's?

A. I do not remember what watch he was in.

Q. Was it Byrne's?

A. I do not think it was.

Q. Was Byrne on deck when you first came up?

A. I do not remember.

Q. Was it Coleman's watch?

A. No.

Q. Was he on deck in the morning early?

A. I did not see him.

Q. What time did day break?

A. About a quarter before five o'clock.

Q. *Byrne.*—When you and all the people were in the boat, did you not hear me speak to some of the people forward in the launch's bow, as I was in the large cutter's stern?

A. I do not remember; you may.

Q. Did you ever hear any of the people in the launch say I had so spoken to them?

A. Yes; Mr. Purcell.

Q. Did you hear any one else?

A. I do not remember.

Q. Did you say yesterday, you did not know how I came in the cutter?

A. I did not know if you was hoisted out in her or not.

Mr. PECKOVER, *the* GUNNER *of the* BOUNTY, *sworn.*

I was awaked from my sleep by a confused noise, and directly afterwards thought I heard the fixing of bayonets; I jumped up, and at the door met Mr. Nelson; he told me the ship was taken from us. I answered, "We were a long way from land, when I came off deck." Mr. Nelson said, "It is by our own people, Christian at their head, or Christian has the command, but we know whose fault it is, or who is to blame." I answered, "Let us go forward and see what's to be done." On going to the hatchway to get up, we were stopped by Sumner and Quintal, by a fixed bayonet down the hatchway, who said, "Peckover you can't come up; we have mutinied, and taken the ship, and Mr. Christian is captain": That in a short while, Mr. Samuel came down, and said "he was going away in the small cutter with Captain Bligh, Hayward, and Hallet." He advised with me what he should take with him, I advised him but a few things, he took only a few shirts and stockings in a bag. That Mr. Fryer came down afterwards, and asked me what I meant to do; I told him I wished to do for the best, and to get home if I could, for staying behind we should be reckoned as pirates if taken. He said he would be answerable for that, and something about Captain Bligh, but what I could not distinguish, as we were about this time ordered on the deck. I was a long while down, before I was ordered on the deck; when I came up, I saw Captain Bligh and Christian alongside of him with a naked bayonet. I saw Burkitt in arms on the quarterdeck, with a cartouch box around him, but whether he had any arms I cannot say. I asked Christian to let me go down forward, to get my things out of my chest; Christian said, you have no things down aft, I said only a few, then stept to the gangway, and went over the side. There was a centinel on the gangway, but who I cannot say. I saw Muspratt forward on the forecastle, he seemed to be doing something about wood, he was not under arms, nor was he splitting wood. I saw three or four more people, I don't recollect their names, nor who they were under arms. I then went into the boat, and a centinel saw me down, I believe there were then in the boat ten or twelve. The cutter was alongside with Byrne in it, and in about four or five minutes the remainder of the people, who went with Captain Bligh came into the boat; and in a short time after we dropt or were veered astern, when lying astern Burkitt asked me if I wanted any thing; I told him I had nothing but what I stood in; he said, if I would send the keys up, he would get me some cloaths; I said I had lost them; he made some answer which I do not remember; he told me he would go and get me some things, and being gone about ten minutes, returned and threw a handkerchief full of different cloaths into the boat. Another person, who I don't know, went and fetched me more cloaths. Coleman called to me over the stern, and begged I would call on his friend at Greenwich and acquaint him of the matter. I think he said he wished to come into the boat. Cole at different times asked Captain Bligh to cast off the boat, fearing the people would fire into the boat, soon after cast adrift.

Q. *per* COURT. Was you upon deck any considerable time before you was put in the boat?

A. Two or three minutes.

Q. Was you carried on the quarterdeck?

A. No.

Q. What part of the ship did you remain in?

A. I believe on the after hatchway.

Q. Did you see Christian, and where was he?

A. Yes, on the starboard side of the quarterdeck.

Q. Could you discover every one on the quarterdeck from the combings of the hatchway on which you stood?

A. By looking round I could, except in the wake of the mizen mast.

Q. Could you see any persons that were not below in any other part of the ship?

A. All, except where the pigs were stowed, on the larboard side of the deck.

Q. What hindered you from seeing the larboard side?

A. The main mast I don't doubt, I looked round but I saw nobody.

Q. Was any centinel over you while you was upon deck?

A. I don't remember any, the two centinels that were over us were at the bottom of the ladder.

Q. Were you placed there by centinels, or were you at liberty to go to any part of the ship?

A. I was not at liberty to go to any part of the ship, Christian ordered me into the boat, and told me the boat was alongside, and Captain Bligh was just going in.

Q. What number of men did you see under arms in any part of the ship?

A. Burkitt, Mills with a cartouch box round him, but whether under arms I cannot say, Christian upon deck with a bayonet, and Sumner and Quintal below.

Q. Are you sure no more?

A. No more.

Q. Name them again.

A. Christian, Burkitt, Sumner, Quintal, and Mills with a cartouch box.

Q. Where are the arms kept?

A. All in the chest upon the main grating.

Q. Was the arm chest usually kept locked?

A. Yes. And the keys in the Master's cabin.

Q. How long was it from that time you first heard of the mutiny to the time you went into the boat?

A. Two hours, or two hours and an half.

Q. How many people did the Bounty's company consist of?

A. Only forty-three at that time.

Q. How many of the people did you consider were concerned in the mutiny?

A. Four or five.

Q. Was it your opinion that four people could take the ship from thirty-nine?

A. By no means.

Q. Give your reasons for thinking so.

A. There must have been more concerned. I saw no more under arms when I came on deck.

Q. What was your reason for submitting when you saw four only under arms?

A. I came naked on the quarterdeck, except my trowsers; I saw Burkitt with a musket and bayonet, Christian alongside Captain Bligh, and the centinel on the gangway, who he was I do not know.

Q. Did you expostulate with Christian?

A. No.

Q. Did you with the centinels over you?

A. I reasoned with these below, but to no purpose.

Q. Was any force used to put you into the boat?

A. The centinel saw me up, and Burkitt being on the quarterdeck as I mentioned, and Christian ordered me into the boat.

Q. Did you on that day see Coleman?

A. Yes.

Q. Did he appear under arms?

A. No.

Q. What was he doing?

A. Looking over the stern.

Q. Did you see Heywood that day?
A. No.
Q. Did you see Byrne?
A. Yes.
Q. At what time?
A. Near eight o'clock.
Q. Was he under arms?
A. No.
Q. What was he doing?
A. In the cutter alongside.
Q. Did you see Morrison?
A. No.
Q. Did you see Norman?
A. Yes.
Q. Was he under arms?
A. No.
Q. What was he doing?
A. Looking over the stern.
Q. Did you consider him as one of the mutineers?
A. No.
Q. Did you see Ellison?
A. No.
Q. Did you see McIntosh?
A. Yes.
Q. What was he doing?
A. Looking over the stern.
Q. Did you consider him as one of the mutineers?
A. No.
Q. Did you see Musprat?
A. Yes.
Q. Was he under arms, or what was he doing?
A. Upon the forecastle.
Q. Did he appear to be obeying the orders of Christian?
A. He was standing on the forecastle not doing any thing.
Q. Did you see Millward?
A. Yes.
Q. Was he under arms?
A. Not to my knowledge.
Q. Did you consider him as a mutineer?

A. I cannot say, he was not under arms.

Q. Was he one that awed you to go into the boat?

A. No.

Q. You saw Coleman looking over the stern, Did you consider him as a mutineer?

A. No.

Q. You saw Byrne in the cutter, did you consider him as a mutineer?

A. No.

Q. You said you was put into the boat by a centinel; Do you know by whom?

A. No.

Q. Was any centinel on the gangway as you went over the ship's side?

A. There was, but I cannot say what his name is, he must have been under arms at the same time, but I cannot upon my oath say whether he was or not.

Q. In what situation was Byrne in the cutter?

A. To the best of my knowledge, standing.

Q. Did he seem to be sorrowful?

A. He did.

Q. Did Norman when he looked over the stern, call to any one in the boat?

A. I don't recollect.

Q. What are your reasons for believing Coleman, Norman, McIntosh, and Byrne, were adverse to the mutiny?

A. I often heard Captain Bligh mention it in the launch.

Q. What were your observations?

A. It is impossible for me to say, they were upon the stern and appeared to wish to come into the boat; I was busy, I do recollect Coleman calling to me.

Q. In conversation with Nelson, he said to you; "You know who's fault it was"; Did you apprehend he alluded to any of the prisoners?

A. No; it was impossible to judge what he meant.

Q. Did either of the thirty-nine people, not of the mutineers, or under arms, offer to relieve Captain Bligh?

A. No.

Q. Of these men who remained in the ship, did you believe them all to be of Christian's party except the four.

A. I had every reason to suppose so.

Q. Do you know if Burkitt had the watch upon deck in the morning?

A. He had.

Q. Was Musprat on that watch?

A. I believe he was not on any watch; he was in the galley.

Q. Was Ellison on that watch?

A. I cannot say.

Q. Was it your watch?

A. No.

Q. In what watch was Norman?

A. I believe in that watch, he was not in mine.

Q. Had Coleman and Byrne that watch?

A. I cannot remember.

Q. Where was Millward when you saw him?

A. Looking over the stern.

Q. In what watch was Heywood?

A. In the first with Mr. Fryer.

Q. *Morrison.*—Do you recollect when you was in the boat astern, I handed over cutlasses, pork, water, spunyarn, &c.?

A. No.

Q. *per* Ditto.—Did you ever observe any thing in my conduct that led you to believe I was concerned in the mutiny?

A. No.

Q. *Burkitt.*—Did you see me when you came upon deck, or did I offer to force you or any body else into the boat? Did I use any bad expressions, or make any game at any one?

A. No farther than standing with musket and bayonet fixed.

Q. Did ever my conduct during the voyage, or the five months I was on shore with you at Otaheite, before the mutiny, give you reason to think I was ringleader in the mutiny?

A. Not in the least.

Observations *per* COURT.—You said it was concluded that each person left on board was concerned in the mutiny, now you say Morrison was not concerned.

Q. Who were Christian's mess-mates?

A. Elphinstone, Young, Hallet, Ledward, and Tinkler.

Q. When he relieved you at four in the morning, did you observe any thing particular in his conduct?

A. No.

Q. Were centinels usually placed on board the Bounty when at sea, in any part of the ship?

A. No.

WILLIAM PURCELL, Carpenter *of the* Bounty, *sworn:*

April the 28th, the morning of the mutiny, Quintal came to my cabin and awaked me, saying, you and Mr. Cole may go on deck and do as you think proper, for we have mutinied and taken the ship; Mr. Christian has the command, Captain Bligh is confined, resistance is in vain, and if you attempt it you are a dead man. I called Mr. Cole, and went up the hatchway, saw Thompson standing centinel armed in the main hatchway, Heywood and Steward were in their births abreast of the main hatchway, on the larboard side, Mr. Elphinstone on the other side. John Williams came down the fore hatchway armed, and accompanied us on deck. I saw Captain Bligh standing on the quarter deck with his hands tied, Christian standing over him with a bayonet. The small cutter was alongside. I asked Alexander Smith what they meant to do; he answered, "To put Captain Bligh, Hayward, Hallet, and Samuel into her, to put Captain Bligh on shore." I then said to Christian, I hope you will not send any body in that boat, the bottom is almost out, and she cannot swim to the shore. An altercation then happened between Christian, Churchill, and others, about another boat; that being determined, Christian ordered me to get the large cutter ready; I hesitated obeying him; he said, Sir, you'll get the boat ready directly; Cole was gone below to turn those in their hammocks on deck. I called McIntosh and Norman to go down to my store room and hand the geer of the cutter to get her ready for hoisting out; they did so, and we in the mean time were clearing the cutter of yams, cocoa nuts, and lumber; when ready, Christian ordered her to be hoisted out; I went to Christian and interceded for the launch, and asked Christian, "If he meant to turn us adrift in the boat, to let us have the launch and not make a sacrifice of us"; Christian then ordered out the launch, but told Cole the Boatswain to carry nothing away. The launch was hoisted out and I went down to my cabin to procure such things as I thought might be useful; I desired McIntosh and Norman to fill a bucket of nails and hand a cross-cut saw out of the store room; I then got my chest upon deck and into the launch, and afterwards got sails and other articles, and asked Christian for my tool chest and a cross-cut saw; the latter he granted, and also my tool chest, after Churchill the master at arms had opposed my having the chest, and taken what he thought proper out of it. Prior to this I had been down to Fryer's cabin, when he desired me to ask Christian to let him come on deck; he came on deck, and had some discourse with Captain Bligh, I could not hear what; Alexander Smith desiring me not to come aft; I then addressed Churchill, on the quarter deck, with Smith, Martin, Mills, Ellison, and Burkitt, desiring them to lay down their arms, asking them what they were about, and advising, "If the Captain had done any thing wrong, to confine him," when Churchill replied, "You ought to have done that months ago," and used other abusive language. Mr. Fryer was then ordered down to his cabin, that Captain Bligh attempted to speak to Christian, who said, "Hold your tongue and I'll not hurt you; it is too late to consider now, I have been in hell for weeks past with you." I then went forward to get what necessaries were handed on the deck, into the boat, and then went into the boat, and stowed my chest and other things. That Martin, one of the mutineers, came into the boat with a bag. I asked him what he did there; he said he was going into the boat; I told him if ever we get to England, I'll endeavour to hang you myself. Quintal and Churchill hearing me, presented their pistols and desired Martin to come out of the boat, which he did. Christian not being determined whether to keep me on board or not, several of the mutineers opposed my going into the boat, saying, that I should be the last suffered to go out, if they had their wills; adding, "They might as well give us the ship as to suffer me to have tools, for we should have another vessel in a month." I then went into the boat to receive a cask of water and other articles that were handing in. Several of the people were in the boat; the rest were then ordered in; we were then veered astern. After much abusive language to the Captain, they threatened to blow his brains out. Cole asked Captain Bligh if he should cast off, as some of the people talked of firing. Captain Bligh consented, and we quitted the ship, keeping right astern to prevent the guns from bearing on us;

we were nineteen in number in the launch, and about seven inches and an half out of water.

Q. *per* COURT.—Who were the people under arms?

Christian,	Churchill,	Sumner,
Quintal,	Mills,	Skinner,
Martin,	A. Smith,	Williams,
Thompson,	McCoy,	Brown,
Ellison,	Burkitt,	Millward,
Young,	Hillbrandt,	

were under arms at different times.

N. B. I forgot to mention a circumstance respecting Millward when Mr. Cole turned the hands up. Millward came up to me and said, Mr. Purcell, I assure you I know nothing of this business, but as I had a hand in the former foolish affair, I suppose they will make me have a hand in this.

Q. When you came on deck, did you see any of the other prisoners?

A. I did.

Q. Did you see Heywood?

A. No.

Q. Had you any conversation with him?

A. Not at that time.

Q. Had you at any other?

A. Yes.

Q. Did you see Heywood standing at the booms?

A. Yes.

Q. Had he a cutlass in his hand?

A. Yes; leaning the flat part of his hand upon it, on the booms. I instantly exclaimed "In the name of God, Peter, what do you do with that?" he instantly dropped it. One or two of the people previous to that had laid down their arms to assist in hoisting out the boats, one or two laid down their cutlasses, but not their pistols.

Q. Did Millward assist in hoisting out the boat?

A. Yes.

Q. What number of men did you see with pistols?

A. About four with pistols and cutlasses, the rest with muskets and bayonets fixt.

Q. Do you recollect seeing any other prisoners upon deck, and having any other conversation with them?

A. I saw all upon deck, but had no other conversation but what I have related.

COURT.—As you was upon deck during the mutiny, recollect what all the prisoners were doing at that time?

A. Coleman assisted in getting the boat ready, and handing things into it after it was hoisted out; he wanted to come in with us, but was prevented by the mutineers, and he desired me to notice that he had no hand in the conspiracy.

Heywood, when I came on deck, was in his birth, I did not see him on deck, until the launch was getting out; then he was standing on the booms resting his hand on a cutlass, I exclaimed, for God's sake, Peter, What do you do with that; he dropped it, and assisted in hoisting out the launch and handing things into it, then went below; I heard Churchill call to Thompson to keep them below, but could not tell who he meant; I did not see Heywood after.

Q. Did Heywood hand any of his own things into the boat?

A. Not to my knowledge.

Byrne was in the large cutter keeping her off from the side, and remained there when we left the ship; he was crying, and said, if he went with us he could be of no service being blind, he was not armed.

Morrison I observed, when Mr. Cole went down to turn the hands up, who were in their hammocks, but I did not observe he was armed; he assisted in hoisting out the launch.

Q. Did you hear any conversation between him and Fryer?

A. I did not.

Q. Did he appear to you at that time to be in league with the mutineers?

A. No.

Norman I called out of his hammock, and ordered him to fetch tools and cloaths, which he did; he gave me every assistance during the whole transaction, was crying when we came away, and desired me to take notice he had no hand in the conspiracy.

Ellison, when I came on the deck, was standing near the gangway, on the larboard-side, armed with a musket and bayonet; in that situation he was during the whole time, to the best of my knowledge, but in different parts of the ship; I had no conversation with him.

COURT.—Relate as to McIntosh.

McIntosh I called out of his hammock, and desired him to go down with Morrison to the store-room to get the gear for the boat;

he did, and gave me every assistance, and desired me to take notice he
had no hand in the mutiny.

Musprat, I cannot charge my memory with any particular circumstances as to him, I do not remember seeing him in arms.

Q. What was he doing?

A. Walking about the ship, handing liquor to the ship's company I
think, and handing the Captain's and Mr. Fryer's things up.

Q. Was that when the dram was ordered?

A. Yes.

Burkitt, when I came upon deck, was standing upon the windlass,
armed with a musket and bayonet; soon after went aft on the quarterdeck, and I believe remained there during the whole transaction
under arms.

Q. Did Burkitt make any answer to the master, when he desired
him and the other men, for God's sake to lay down their arms?

A. Not that I heard.

Milward, when I came upon deck, was in his hammock, Mr. Cole
turned him up, and when he came over the booms, he said, I assure
you, Mr. Purcell, I know nothing of this business; but as I had a hand
in the former foolish affair, I suppose they will force me to take a
part in this; I saw Millward afterwards down the after-ladder by Mr.
Fryer's cabin, armed with a musket, but do not recollect he had a
bayonet fixed, nor seeing him afterwards until we were in the boat;
then I saw him look over the tafferel, but cannot tell if he was armed
then or nor.

Q. When you all went into the boat, was any centry on the gangway?

A. Yes; Quintal and Skinner.

Q. Were they armed?

A. I cannot say they were armed, they were placed as centinels.

Q. Were you forced in the boat suddenly, or did it take some
time?

A. I do not think it was above ten minutes, before every one was
in the boat.

Q. Was it generally known about the ship, that the boat was going
to put off?

A. I think it must, we were a long time collecting our things.

Q. Did you hear any body say he wished to go in the boat, except
those you have named already?

A. I cannot say I did.

Q. Did Norman and McIntosh shew any intentions to regain the ship?

A. They did not.

Q. Did you propose any such thing to them?

A. I did not.

Q. Did any of the prisoners shew any such wish?

A. No.

Q. In what light did you look upon Mr. Heywood at the time you say he dropped the cutlass?

A. I looked upon him as a person confused.

COURT.—You must answer that question.

Witness.—And that he did not know he had the weapon in his hand; his hand being on it, it was not in his hand.

Q. What reason had you to suppose him so confused?

A. By his instantly dropping it, and assisting in hoisting out the boat, convinced me in my own mind, that he had no hand in the conspiracy.

Q. Were any people armed near Heywood at that time?

A. I do not know there were.

Q. After the launch was hoisted out, you say Heywood went below, and you saw no more of him. Did he of your knowledge go below of his own accord, or was he compelled to go by any of the mutineers?

A. I think he went of his own accord, or to get some of the things to put in the boat.

Q. How long was it after the launch was hoisted out, before she went from the ship?

A. Near two hours.

Q. Do you think then that Heywood was so long employed in collecting his things as you before supposed?

A. No; he was assisting me and the rest to get the things into the boat, which I suppose prevented him from collecting any things of his own, until that time.

Q. You have said just now, you saw no more of Heywood after he went below. Did he go below immediately after the boat was hoisted out?

A. No.

Q. How long did the launch remain alongside after Heywood went below?

A. I cannot be positive; ten minutes or a quarter of an hour was the outside.

Q. Were the booms of the Bounty above deck?

A. Yes; off the deck on chocks.

Q. When you represented Heywood leaning his hand upon the cutlass, Was that cutlass leaning against, or supported by any thing else?

A. I cannot be positive.

COURT.—Describe the situation he was standing in with the cutlass. Was it leaning against the booms?

A. I cannot be positive, it might be supported by something.

COURT.—Describe with your own hand, his hand as to the top and handle of the cutlass.

N.B. The Witness then described the cutlass perpendicular on the point, and Mr. Heywood's hand flat on it.

Q. *per* COURT.—Do you, upon the solemn oath you have taken, believe Heywood by being armed with a cutlass, at the time you mentioned, by any thing you could collect, either by gestures, speeches, or any thing else, had any intention of opposing or assisting and joining others, who might endeavour to stop the progress of the mutiny?

A. No.

Q. Except the cutlass upon which you saw Mr. Heywood's hand, did you see any cutlass on the deck, other than those in the mutineers' hands at any time during the mutiny?

A. I cannot say I did; I can't say I did at that time, one man laid one down by him, and assisted in hoisting out the launch.

N. B. The witness said, one man laid one down by him, and took it up, but afterwards recalled his words, "and took it up again," and added while he assisted in hoisting out the launch.

Q. Do you know if any one of the mutineers took notice of Mr. Heywood's having a cutlass?

A. No.

Q. Have you reason to believe that the cutlass you saw in the possession of Heywood was placed upon the booms accidentally, and that he did not furnish himself with it?

A. I have reason to think he did not furnish himself with it.

Q. What is your reason?

A. As Thompson was standing over the arm chest, and Heywood in his birth, had he meant to arm himself, he certainly might have done it before he came on deck.

Q. Was the arm chest near Mr. Heywood's birth?

A. It stood in the center of the main hatchway, between the two births at the after-part.

Q. Did you go on deck before, or after Mr. Heywood?

A. Before him, he was in his birth.

Q. Did you see him leave his birth, and go upon deck?

A. No.

Q. Can you say that he might not have carried the cutlass on deck with him?

A. I have reason to think he did not.

Q. What reason?

A. As Thompson was centry over the arm chest, and knew Mr. Cole and myself were not of the conspiracy, and knew Mr. Heywood was in his birth, and did not attempt to arm himself before we went upon deck, he most certainly suspected Mr. Heywood wanted to procure arms to assist us in retaking the ship.

Q. Do you suppose it possible, that if Mr. Heywood had been inclined to join the mutineers he would have armed himself before you and Cole?

A. I should suppose not, as he might have armed himself before we were called up; Thompson being centinel over the arm chest, and Mr. Heywood in his birth when I went on deck.

Q. From the bulkhead forward, were there any other centinels except Thompson?

A. There were two more when I went upon deck, Quintal, the man who accompanied and called me up, and John Williams; both came to the foot of the lower deck ladder, and followed us up.

Q. Did you see Mr. Heywood as you and Mr. Cole, the boatswain, were going on deck?

A. I saw him in his birth, as I went up the cockpit ladder, whether sitting or leaning I'm not positive; the hammocks were hanging.

Q. Had you any conversation with him?

A. No.

Q. Do you know if at that time he knew of the mutiny?

A. I think he must, as the centinel was upon the arm chest close to his birth.

Q. Was the centinel over the arm chest or their births?

A. I cannot say; he was between both births.

Q. Did the centinel, or any other person, prevent his going on the deck with you and Mr. Cole, had he been inclined so to do?

A. I cannot say.

Q. Did you see any oppose him?

A. I did not.

Q. When Mr. Heywood dropt the cutlass, as you say, did it fall down from his quitting his hand from it, or did he lay it down?

A. I think it fell, for he did not lay it down.

Q. Do you think any of the mutineers noticed Mr. Heywood having the cutlass in his hand?

A. I don't know, as I was busy in getting the boat out, I had no time to make any observation.

Q. Would they have permitted you, or any well-disposed person to the captain, to have touched a cutlass?

A. I cannot tell, as they had pistols I should imagine not.

Q. Did it appear to you, after they had got possession of the ship, that they were careless of their arms?

A. By no means, only in that instance in hoisting out the boat.

Q. In the time Heywood was assisting you to get things into the boat, did he, in any degree whatever, manifest a disposition to assist in the mutiny?

A. No.

Q. Was he, during that time, deliberate or frightened; in what manner did he behave himself?

A. I had not an opportunity to observe every action, being myself, at that time, engaged in getting things into the boat; I was apprehensive the mutineers might have stopt our so doing.

Q. Putting every circumstance together on your going into the boat, declare to the court, upon the oath you have taken, how you consider his behaviour; whether, as a person joined in the mutiny, or wishing well to Captain Bligh?

A. I by no means considered him as a person concerned in the mutiny or conspiracy.

Q. At the time Mr. Heywood was assisting you in getting things into the boat, did he know it was the intention of the mutineers to send the commander of the Bounty, with several of the officers and men, away in the boat?

A. I cannot say.

Q. Did he know that you was going out of the ship?

A. He certainly must think so, seeing me getting my chest and things into the boat.

Q. Did you know Captain Bligh was going in the boat?

A. Yes.

Q. Could it be possible but that every person must have known that Captain Bligh was going to be sent away?

A. I suppose not.

Q. Did Mr. Heywood know what caused you to quit the ship?

A. Every body must have known who was on deck at the time, that I meant to follow my commander.

Q. Did Mr. Heywood express any desire or inclination to follow his commander with you?

A. Not to me.

Q. Was Captain Bligh confined on the quarterdeck, in such a situation as he must have been seen by Mr. Heywood, whilst he was upon deck with you, or when he was assisting in getting out the boats?

A. I think he was in such a situation, that he must have been seen by every one upon deck.

Q. Was any bulkhead round Mr. Heywood's birth?

A. No; it was half boarded, and half canvas.

Q. If the screen was drawn, how could you see Mr. Heywood?

A. The screen was not drawn.

Q. When you saw Mr. Heywood with the cutlass, might it not have been used with advantage?

A. By no means, there being fourteen on the deck armed, the officers confined, and most of the mutineers having cutlasses or pistols.

Q. Were any of the prisoners amongst those who opposed your going into the boat?

A. No.

Q. You say Morrison did not seem to be leagued with the mutineers, did he express to you, any desire to follow the fate of the commander in the boat?

A. No.

Q. Do you know if McIntosh was prevented leaving the Bounty?

A. He desired me to take notice that he was prevented by the mutineers from coming into the boat.

Q. Did you see him prevented?

A. I did not personally see it, but Christian had given orders before, that neither Coleman, Norman, or McIntosh should quit the ship.

Q. How do you know that?

A. I heard him.

Q. *Byrne.*—When you were first alarmed, and came from below with Cole, did you observe any one sitting on the chest on the fore hatchway?

A. I did not.

Q. *per* Ditto.—When you was in the launch, receiving things from some person on board, did I not speak to you from the stern of the large cutter?

A. I don't recollect it, only your desiring every one to take notice, that by your being blind, you could be of no service, and crying.

Q. *per* Ditto.—Before Captain Bligh, Mr. Fryer, and other officers came on the deck, was you not down in the launch?

A. I was several times in her, stowing the things.

Q. *per* Ditto.—Do you recollect my saying, Mr. Purcell, if you live to go home, I hope you will go to my friends, and tell them I know nothing of this transaction, or had any hand in it?

A. No.

————

MR. HAYWARD, *sworn.*

At four o'clock in the morning, of the twenty-eighth day of April 1789, Fletcher Christian relieved the watch as usual, at about five o'clock; after giving orders to prepare for washing the decks, he ordered me to look out, as being master's mate of the watch, whilst he went down to lash his hammock up, a few minutes after I was looking out at a shark, which was at the stern of the ship; when, to my unutterable surprise, I saw Christian, Charles Churchill, Thomas Burkitt, one of the prisoners, John Sumner, Matthew Quintal, William McCoy, Isaac Martin, Henry Hillbrant, and Alexander Smith, coming aft, armed with muskets and bayonets. Going forward to prevent their proceeding, to ask Christian the cause of such an act, he told me to hold my tongue instantly; and left James Martin a centinel upon deck; and proceeded with the rest of his party below to

Captain Bligh's cabin; some men standing with their heads above the deck, Mr. Hallet, myself, Lamb, (Ellison at the helm,) and Mills, being on the deck. Christian being gone below, I asked Mills, If he knew any thing of the mutiny? he said, No. Ellison quitted the helm, and armed himself with a bayonet; the ship's decks now began to throng with men; Young, Millward, Musprat, Williams, Skinner, and Brown on the deck, armed with muskets and bayonets; Heywood, Steward, and Morrison, unarmed on the booms; Christian and his gang had not been down long, before I heard the cry of murder from Captain Bligh; and on the other hand, heard Churchill calling for the rope. It was now I found Mills was of the mutineers' party; contrary to all orders he cut the deep sea line, and carried a piece of it to Christian; soon after, I saw Captain Bligh brought upon the quarter deck, with his hands bound behind him, surrounded by most of those who came last on deck; some of the officers were permitted to come on deck, and Christian ordered us to hoist out the cutter; we remonstrated against it, being too small and unable to contain us. As soon as the launch was out, Christian ordered Mr. Samuel, Mr. Hallet, and me into it; we requested time to collect some things, which was granted; I was going down, but was prevented by Thompson, who was armed with a cutlass, and centinel over the arm chest; he stood aft a part of the main hatchway; he assented, and I went down, and saw Heywood in his birth. I told him to go into the boat, but in my hurry I do not remember receiving an answer. Mr. Hallet and I went down the main hatchway together; after getting a few cloaths, I went up and put them into the launch; then went to Christian and asked him for my instruments and chart, but was refused and hurried into the boat, not before I had seen Captain Bligh brought to the gangway, held by Christian, and surrounded by Mills, Burkitt, Quintal, Sumner, Millward, and McCoy, armed. I do not recollect any more, but Ellison came up in a hurry with a bayonet in his hand, swearing, Damn him, I will be centinel over him. I then went over the gangway. When I was in the launch, I saw Byrne in the cutter, I heard him say he was sorry he could not have leave to come with us. The officers and men being in the boat, Captain Bligh was then forced in, and we were veered astern, the mutineers saying, they would give us a tow towards land. In this situation we prayed much for arms, ammunition, and more provisions, and then (for a watch and boatswain's call) we got four cutlasses and a small addition of pork; a number of mutineers collecting themselves on the taffrail, amongst whom were Skinner, Quintal, Millward, Hillbrant, Ellison, Smith, and Brown, publicly insulting Captain Bligh. Skinner would have shot into the boat, but was prevented by others of the mutineers; Millward jeering, said, Go and see if you can live upon a quarter of a pound of yams per day. Just before casting off, Coleman came to the taffrail, and avowed his innocence and ignorance of the matter. After casting off, I heard orders given for loosing the top gallant sails, and saw Ellison going up the shrouds for that purpose.

Q. COURT.—I think you were sent to apprehend the prisoners gone to Otaheite; inform the court what you know.

A. Before anchoring in Mattavai Bay, in the Pandora, in the island of Otahite, I saw Coleman coming off to the ship; soon after we were at anchor, Steward and Heywood came on board, but I did not see them until they were in Captain Edwards's cabin. They made themselves known to Captain Edwards, saying, they belonged to the Bounty, and were happy they were arrived. On my asking some questions concerning the Bounty, Captain Edwards said, it was unnecessary to ask any questions. I asked how they came to go away with the Bounty? and received for answer from Steward, that when called upon he would answer all particulars. I was prevented from asking any more questions, by Captain Edwards saying again, it was unnecessary. The next day I was dispatched to Papara with a party, in order to receive the mutineers, who were supposed to be in the valley; as soon as I arrived at Papara, I had intelligence that they were not far off, and with a guide marched to find them, but without success. The next morning about eleven o'clock, I had intelligence of them coming down. I drew out my party to receive them; when they came within hearing, I called to them to lay down their arms and go on one side, which they did, and I took them into custody and brought them on board. I wrote to Lieutenant Corner, who was coming to the valley, that I had taken them.

Q. COURT.—I think you say, in the morning of the mutiny you saw eighteen under arms?

A. Yes.

Q. Do you know of any conversation between Captain Bligh and the officers, about launching the cutter?

A. None, but a general clamour.

Q. What number of men was in the boat when you were ordered into it?

A. None; I was the first that was ordered into it.

Q. How long did the boat remain alongside after you was in it?

A. About a quarter of an hour.

Q. Were all the people that went into the boat, ordered in; or did they go voluntarily?

A. I heard no one ordered but Mr. Hallet, Mr. Samuel, and myself.

Q. What number of men were on the deck at the time of hoisting out the boat?

A. I cannot say.

Q. Can you tell if there were any below at that time?

A. None, except those who guarded the officer's cabins in the after part of the ship.

Q. Look at all the prisoners, and relate all you know of them on that day?

A. *Coleman,* I saw nothing of him till he came to the taffrail, and declared his innocence. *Heywood,* I saw on the booms, not doing any thing, and afterwards in his birth below, when I spoke to him, and told him to go into the boat.

Q. Did he make any answer?

A. I believe not.

Q. Did you at any time that day see Mr. Heywood with arms in his hands?

A. I did not.

Q. Did you see him assist in hoisting out the boats?

A. No.

Byrne I saw in the cutter alongside the ship when I was in the launch, I heard him say he was sorry he could not go with us.

Morrison I saw assisting in clearing the yams from the boat, but am doubtful whether he was under arms at first or not.

Q. Did you hear any conversation between him and any officer of the ship?

A. I do not remember any.

Q. Did he at all appear to you by his conduct, to be assisting the mutineers, or in obedience to orders, to get the boats out?

A. If I was to give it as my opinion, I should say he was assisting the mutineers, wishing us away as fast as possible.

Q. Did you at any time that day see him with arms in his hands?

A. I am doubtful if he was under arms at all.

Norman was on deck forward, I neither saw him under arms nor assisting the mutineers, but assisting in getting things into the boat.

Ellison I saw at the helm, and, soon after the people had gone to Captain Bligh's cabin and quitted it, armed himself with a bayonet, and just before my going into the boat saw him as a centinel, with a bayonet in his hand, over Captain Bligh, saying, Damn him, I'll be centinel over him.

McIntosh I did not see under arms, nor did I suppose him one of the mutineers; he assisted to get out the boat.

Musprat I saw on the larboard side with a musket in his hand, supposing him one of the mutineers.

Burkitt I saw come aft, following Christian and Churchill, and saw him descend the after ladder with them armed with a bayonet.

Millward, I don't recollect seeing him at first, but after Captain Bligh was brought on deck, saw him armed as a centinel; after the boat was astern, saw him on the taffrail jeering us, and saying, Go see if you can live upon a quarter of a pound of yams per day, or something to that purpose.

Q. Was you present when Norman, Morrison, and Ellison were taken?

A. No, they had been left there by Lieut. Corner, under the charge of Mr. Saville.

Q. When you fell in with McIntosh, Burkitt, Musprat, and Millward, did they make any resistance?

A. None.

Q. They surrendered themselves upon your demanding them to lay down their arms?

A. They did.

Q. When you went down the main hatchway, who were between decks besides Thompson?

A. Mr. Heywood. Mr. Hallet went with me and Mr. Elphinstone.

Q. Was Thompson centinel?

A. Thompson was the only centinel; but there were armed men round the hatchways on the boom.

Q. Of the ten prisoners, six of whom you describe under arms; do you know of any effort made by those not under arms, or any of them, to restore the ship?

A. No.

Q. Did Norman express any desire to you of going into the boat?

A. To me, none.

Q. Did you hear him to any other person?

A. No.

Q. Did McIntosh?

A. No.

Q. Or any disapprobation of the mutineers' conduct?

A. No.

Q. How long after the mutiny began that you saw Musprat under arms?

A. I beg leave to remind the court that they did not come up together, it might be about ten minutes.

Q. At the time the mutineers went into the cabin, was Burkitt one of them that remained on the hatchway?

A. No.

Q. Have you reason to know that Mr. Heywood would have been prevented from going into the boat at the time you did, after you desired him?

A. No.

Q. How long before your going down in the boat, before you spoke to him?

A. About two or three minutes.

Q. You say, if you were to give your opinion, it is, that Morrison was assisting the mutineers by getting out the boats, and wished to get you away from the ship. You have likewise said, that McIntosh was assisting in getting out the boats, and you did not look upon him in that light; I wish to know the reason of that difference?

A. The difference in the countenances of people may be illgrounded. One looked rejoiced, the other depressed.

Q. You said Norman was employed in putting a tool chest into the boat. Do you know why he did not accompany you?

A. No.

Q. When you spoke to Mr. Heywood in his birth, and admonished him to go into the boat, was he under any restraint as to going on deck?

A. No.

Q. What was he employed about at that time?

A. Nothing but sitting with his arms folded.

Q. Did you by his behaviour, consider him as attached to his duty, or to a part of the mutineers?

A. I rather suppose, after telling him to go into the boat, and not joining us, he was on the part of the mutineers, but that must be only stated as an opinion, as he was not employed during the acting part of it.

Q. Did you observe joy or sorrow in his behaviour?

A. Sorrow.

Q. You have said that McIntosh was unfriendly to the mutineers; you mean he was not attached to them, because he was depressed in his countenance; might not the sorrow in Mr. Heywood arise from the same cause?

A. It might.

Q. *per* Morrison.—You give it from your opinion that I was one of the mutineers, can you declare before God, and this court, that such evidence is not the result of a private pique?

A. It is not: It is an opinion I formed after quitting the ship, from his not coming with us, when he had as good an opportunity as the rest, there being more boats than one.

Q. Ditto.—Are you certain we might have had the large cutter to have accompanied you?

A. My not being present at any conversation with you, I cannot say, but perhaps you might.

Q. Ditto.—Can you deny you were present when Captain Bligh begged, that the long boat might not be overloaded, and said, he would do justice to those who remained?

A. I was present when Captain Bligh did make such declaration, but I understood it respected cloaths and other heavy articles, with which the boat was already too full.

Q. Ditto.—Do you recollect in consequence of such declaration, I told you, I would take my chance in the ship?

A. I do not.

Q. Ditto.—Do you remember when you handed your bag up the main hatchway, and with it your fuzee, that I was the person that received them from you, and Quintal came and seized the fuzee, and swore, Damn his eyes, if you should have it?

A. I do not remember the person who took the bag and fuzee, it might have been you, but I remember Quintal swearing I should not have it, but from whose hands he took it, I cannot say.

Q. Do you remember on any time that day calling on me to assist you in any point of duty, or to give my assistance to retake his Majesty's ship?

A. I have a faint remembrance of a circumstance of that nature.

COURT. Relate it.

A. It is so very faint I can hardly remember it, or who it was.

COURT. Relate it.

A. On seeing Churchill on the booms, I thought if I had a friendly island club, of which there were many on board, had I not been observed, I could have gone forward and knocked him down at the time of handing the bag out, and you might have been the person I called to my assistance.

Q. *per* Morrison. What answer did I give you?

A. I do not know.

Q. Ditto.—Did not I say, "Go it, I'll back you, there are tools enough in the ship"?

A. I cannot remember.

Q. Ditto.—Did you ever observe any thing in my conduct during the voyage, or on that day, to give cause of complaint?

A. None: But on that day I thought he was pleased in preparing the boat for our departure; but, as I said before, I do not know his real intention.

Q. *per* Ditto—Are you sure that there was a continual smile and appearance of joy upon my countenance all the time you observed me, or at the time only when you called upon me for assistance?

A. I cannot say.

Q. *per* Musprat.—In answer to a question just asked by Morrison, you allow Captain Bligh used these words. "Don't let the boat be overloaded, my lads, I'll do you justice"; which you say, alluded to the cloaths and other heavy articles. Do you mean to understand the latter words of "My lads, I'll do you justice," to apply to cloaths or men who he apprehended might go in the boat?

A. If Captain Bligh made use of the words "my lads," it was to the people already in the boat, and not to those in the ship.

Q. COURT.—To whom do you think Captain Bligh alluded, when he said he would do them justice; was it your opinion to the men in the boat with him, or to any person remaining in the ship?

A. To persons remaining in the ship.

Q. Are you of opinion that he meant, he would do them justice on account of remaining in the ship, or that he would cause satisfaction to be given them for any thing they might lose?

A. I rather think it was the few who Captain Bligh knew to be of his party, that were detained contrary to their inclination, that he would do them such justice that should throw aside all doubts of their being true to the service of their country.

Q. Do you know if any were detained contrary to their wish?

A. Coleman and Byrne, which, from the latter's answers, I suppose to be the case.

Q. What authority have you for saying Coleman was detained contrary to his inclination?

A. From hearing amongst the mutineers their intention to detain him, as well as the acting surgeon, who they afterwards let go, saying, they would have little occasion for doctors.

Mr. HALLET's *Evidence.*

On the 28th day of April 1789, at day-break, I had the watch upon deck; I saw Christian, the officer of the watch, come up the fore hatchway armed, and several armed men following him, Burkitt, Churchill, Sumner, and Martin, no more; at first, I attempted to go down the fore hatchway, but was prevented by two fixed bayonets thrust up, and I was ordered to stay where I was; who they were I cannot say, I was then going aft, but before I got on the quarter deck, I heard Captain Bligh sing out "murder"; he was soon after brought on deck in his shirt, with his hands tied behind him, and Christian holding the cord that tied him, and a bayonet in the other hand, and kept in that situation with the guard round him.

COURT. Name the guard.

A. I do not know any more than I before mentioned.—The cutter was ordered by Christian to be hoisted out, and Mr. Samuel and myself ordered into it; but upon the Boatswain's and Carpenter's coming aft, and telling Christian they would prefer going in the boat with the Captain, than staying in the ship, desired to have the launch instead of the cutter; he granted it, and said, he did not wish them or any other to stay against their inclinations, or to go; they then asked for various articles that would be of use; and Mr. Heywood, Mr. Samuel, and myself, then went into the boat and were veered astern,

Christian saying, he would hove us in near the land—We then got a few more things from the ship, and were cast loose.

Q. Did you hear any conversation between Christian and the Officers of the Bounty, about the launch or cutter?

A. The boatswain and carpenter came aft, as I said before, and spoke to Christian about them.

Q. What number of men were in the boat when you went into it?

A. By Christian's order, I was the first in the boat.

Q. How long did the boat remain along side after you was in it?

A. Ten minutes, or a quarter of an hour.

Q. Were all the people ordered in, or did they go voluntarily?

A. I believe the most part went voluntarily.

Q. What number of men assisted in hoisting out the launch?

A. About twenty.

Q. Were all unarmed?

A. One or two gave their arms to others, and assisted, and as soon as done resumed their arms.

Q. What number of men did you see under arms that morning?

A. Ellison, Morrison, Millward, Burkitt, Hillbrant, Sumner, Skinner, Christian, Young, Churchill, Thompson, Alexander Smith, Mills, McKoy, Williams, Brown, Martin, and Quintal.

Q. What time did you make that memorandum?

A. Lately.

Q. Had you any conversation with the officers or men that morning, respecting re-taking the ship?

A. Seeing so many armed men, and no possibility of our procuring any arms ourselves, I believe it was deemed impracticable.

Q. When the mutineers gave their arms to others, whilst they hoisted out the boats, did they give them to their own party?

A. Intirely so.

Q. Did you see Coleman?

A. Yes.

COURT.—Relate his conduct that day.

A. Coleman assisted in getting things into the boat, and when astern, called to the gunner, "Remember, Mr. Peckover, if ever you arrive in England, I had no hand in this."

Q. Did you see Mr. Heywood?

A. I saw him once.

Q. Where?

A. Upon the platform on the larboard side of the deck.

Q. What was he doing?

A. Standing still, looking attentively on Captain Bligh.

Q. Had he any arms at that time?

A. I did not see him under arms at all.

Q. Had you any conversation with him?

A. I do not recollect having spoken to him.

Q. Was he or not prevented from going into the boat?

A. I do not know that he offered to go into it.

Q. Did any person propose to him so to do?

A. I do not know.

Q. Do you know any other particulars of him that day?

A. When he was standing as before related, Captain Bligh said something to him, but what I did not hear; upon which he laughed, turned round, and went away.

Q. Did he appear at liberty, or at any time confined.

A. At liberty.

Q. BYRNE.—Relate what you know of Byrne that day.

A. I remember to have seen him once, keeping the cutter along-side.

Q. MORRISON.—Relate his conduct that day.

A. When I first saw him, he and Millward were talking together unarmed, but he shortly afterwards appeared with a musket.

Q. What part of the ship did you see him in with a musket?

A. I did not see him under arms till the boat was veered astern, then he looked over the taffrail, and jeering, said, "If my friends enquire after me, tell them I am somewhere in the South Seas."

Q. How was he employed at any time, and until you put off?

A. I have related all to the best of my recollection?

Q. NORMAN—Relate all you know of him that day.

A. Norman was employed in getting things out of the carpenter's store-room; just before we came away, he cried, and said, "He wished to go with us, to see his wife and family."

Q. Did you consider him as a mutineer?

A. I considered him as an innocent man, and detained against his inclination.

Q. ELLISON.—Relate all you know of him that day.

A. He appeared early under arms, and came to me insolently, saying, "Mr. Hallet, you need not mind, we are only going to put the

Captain on shore, and then you and the others may return on board," meaning Mr. Hayward and Mr. Samuel, as no others at that time were ordered to quit the ship.

Q. MCINTOSH.—Relate all you know of him.

A. He was employed in getting things from the store-room, and willing to procure things for us that we required.

Q. Did he shew any inclination to come on board?

A. I did not myself observe it.

Q. MUSPRAT.—Relate all you know of him that day.

A. I do not remember to have seen him once.

Q. BURKITT—Relate all you know of him that day.

A. I have related the whole I know.

Q. MILLWARD.—Relate all you know of him that day.

A. As I before said, I saw him and Morrison talking together, and shortly after saw him armed.

Q. Look round, and point out Morrison.

A. This is he; (pointing to Morrison).

Q. Do you know if Coleman, Norman, and McIntosh, were detained against their wills?

A. I have great reason to suppose they were.

Q. Did you speak to Byrne, so as to form an opinion of his mind?

A. He appeared pensive and sorrowful.

Q. Do you believe it proceeded from his disapprobation of the event that had taken place?

A. The cause I am totally ignorant of.

Q. Describe the situation of the commander of the Bounty, when Heywood turned round as you before said.

A. He was standing with his arms tied behind him; Christian holding the cord that bound him with one hand, and a bayonet at his breast with the other hand.

Q. Did you go down the main hatchway with Mr. Heywood that morning?

A. I was below.

Q. Was Mr. Heywood in his birth at that time?

A. I do not remember to have seen him during that morning except at the time already related.

Q. At the time the boats were hoisting out, to whom did the mutineers give their arms?

A. Very few were given; those that were, were to their own party.

Q. When the boat put off from the ship, did you see or hear any person express any dissatisfaction at being left?

A. Yes: Coleman, and Norman.

Q. *per* MORRISON.—You say you saw me under arms at the taffrail, and I did sneeringly say, "Tell my friends, if they inquire, that I am somewhere in the South Seas"; Can you positively declare before God, and this court, that it was me and no other person you saw under arms, and to whom I delivered the said sneering message?

A. I have declared it, but did not remark that the message was said to any particular individual.

Q. Ditto.—Can you deny that I did lower down into the boat from the larboard quarter, two cutlasses, two large jars of water, and five or six and twenty pieces of pork?

A. I remember four cutlasses lowered, and the other things you mention in the boat, but by whom I cannot say.

Q. Do you remember that I personally assisted you to haul your chest up the main hatchway, and if I was armed?

A. Concerning the chest, I do not remember, and have before said, that I did not see you under arms till the boat was veered astern.

JOHN SMITH'S *Evidence:*

Between five and six o'clock, on the 28th of April 1789, Thomas Hall told me I was wanted aft, on the quarter deck; Captain Bligh then stood on the quarter deck in his shirt, Christian holding him in his left hand, and a cutlass in his right. Christian ordered me to bring a bottle of rum, and serve every man under arms; and at the same time to bring up the Captain's cloaths, I did so; and put some cloaths over Captain Bligh's shoulders, and then served the drams.

COURT. Name who you served.

A. Christian first.—I believe McKoy and Williams were on the starboard side.—I served several, but am not positive who; then I went on the quarter deck and served Ellison, no more on the deck; I then went down with the bottle; by that time the Captain was gone over the side; I saw Mr. Samuel in the Captain's cabin, getting his papers and things; there was a centinel below, between the cabin and Mr. Friers; Sumner and Quintal remained below until the Captain was gone over the side; I then came up with wine in my hand, and went across the ship, and put the wine into the boat and we dropt astern.

Q. You say you served the drams by Christian's order?

A. Yes.

Q. Did you give a dram to Coleman?

A. Yes; some in a tin pot.

Q. To Mr. Heywood?

A. No; he refused.

Q. Where was he standing?

A. By the windlass, with his back towards me, and his hands in his pockets.

Q. To Byrne?

A. No.

Q. To Morrison?

A. I don't know.

Q. To Norman?

A. No.

Q. To Ellison?

A. Yes.

Q. To McIntosh?

A. No.

Q. To Musprat?

A. No.

Q. To Burkitt?

A. Yes.

Q. To Millward?

A. Yes.

Q. Did any person go into the boat after you?

A. Not to my knowledge.

Q. How long was the boat alongside after you went into it?

A. It dropt astern directly.

Q. Did Christian order any to go into the boat?

A. No.

Q. Was you ordered to go into it?

A. No.

Q. Did you assist in hoisting out the launch?

A. No.

Q. You did not see her hoisted out?

A. No.

Q. In what station was you?

A. Captain's servant.

Q. Who ordered you to get the Captain's cloaths?

A. Christian—when I went down for the rum.

Q. How long after the mutiny began, before you served the drams?

A. Immediately after putting the Captain's cloaths on. I can't say how long.

Q. When you offered a dram to Coleman, where was he?

A. Forward upon the booms.

Q. Had he arms then?

A. No.

Q. You say when you offered a dram to Mr. Heywood, he had no arms?

A. No; he was neither talking nor doing any thing.

Q. Did you see Morrison?

A. Yes.

Q. Where?

A. I can't tell, I did not offer him a dram.

Q. Had he any arms?

A. No.

Q. Did you see Norman?

A. Yes.

Q. What was he doing?

A. I don't recollect.

Q. What was Ellison doing?

A. Standing with a musket in his hand.

Q. In what part of the ship?

A. Before the mizen mast.

Q. What was McIntosh doing?

A. Standing by the booms, having no arms.

Q. Did you see Musprat?

A. I don't recollect seeing him at all.

Q. Where was Burkitt?

A. On the fore part of the quarter deck.

Q. What was he doing?

A. He was under arms.

Q. What was Millward doing?

A. He stood with a musket in his hand on the after ladder.

Q. *per* MORRISON.—Do you recollect when you came forward with the bottle, that Coleman and I were talking together, and you gave Coleman a glass in a tin pot, and said, "Morrison, you may as well have a drop, though I am ordered to serve none but the centinels"?

A. I do not.

Q. *per* MUSPRAT.—Do you know on that morning, if any one came down abaft, and got a bottle of rum to serve the ship's company besides yourself?

A. Not to my knowledge.

Q. *per* MILLWARD.—Do you recollect any person who took the case from you, and the other necessaries, handing up for the good of those going in the boat?

A. I do not recollect.

CAPTAIN EDWARDS's *Evidence:*

COURT.—Relate all you know concerning the prisoners belonging to the Bounty.

A. Before we came to anchor in Mattavai Bay, Coleman came on board. I was informed that others had sailed in a schooner that had been built by some of the Bounty's people. I likewise heard that one man had been murdered, (the master at arms,) and likewise an account that the Bounty had been twice at Otaheite, in possession of Captain Bligh; the last time, after some people being landed, she went away in the night; and was seen again in the morning in a north west direction. Coleman was ready to give me any information. Steward and Heywood, after we anchored, came on board before any boat was sent on shore. Mr. Larkin brought them to me; "I asked what news?" and Mr. Heywood said, "he supposed I had heard of the affair concerning the Bounty." I cannot recollect all the conversation, but he enquired if Mr. Hayward was on board; I said he was; he desired to see him, and I desired Mr. Hayward to come out of my state room. Mr. Hayward came, and gave them a contemptuous look, and began to enter into a conversation concerning the Bounty. I called people to take the prisoners; some words passed, and Heywood said he should be able to vindicate his conduct. Byrne came on board the third day alone. Ellison, Morrison, and Norman, were sent on board, by parties that were sent after them.

Q. *per* BYRNE—Did you, or any under your command, commissioned, warrant, petty officers, or seamen, bring me on board the Pandora?

A. No; I did not understand it so.

Q. Did you know at what part of the island I was, when the Pandora anchored in Mattavai Bay?

A. Not exactly, but I heard some distance from the place.

Q. *per* BYRNE—Was I not introduced to you by your officers?

A. Probably you was.

Admitted that Byrne voluntarily surrendered himself.

Q. Did Byrne request an interview with you, saying, he came from Papara, a distant part of the island, and that he had walked all night to join the ship?

A. I do not recollect the place, but I believe he did say he had walked all night.

LIEUTENANT LARKIN's *Evidence:*

COURT.—Inform the Court how the prisoners came on board the Pandora.

A. *Coleman* came before we came to anchor voluntarily.

Heywood next, and *Byrne*, both voluntarily.

Norman, Ellison, and Morrison,	Came round in one of our boats from the other side of the island, sent by Mr. Savill (since lost).
McIntosh, Musprat, Millward, and Burkitt,	Brought on board in one of our boats that was sent after them.

LIEUTENANT CORNER's *Evidence:*

COURT.—Inform the court what you know of the prisoners being taken and carried on board the Pandora.

A. *Norman,* | Came to me in company with another person
Morrison, and | named Brown, (who had been left at Otaheite)
Ellison, | at Papara, when I was going in search of the
schooner. I landed about two o'clock in the morning; they were armed with hatchets, and instruments, that Brown had given them to defend themselves from the Indians, I confined them in the boat and went to secure the rest.

Q. Was you sent in pursuit in the Pandora's boat?

A. I was sent in pursuit of the schooner the evening the ship arrived—I got within about a mile of her, when the schooner avoided us; we chased her, but I cannot say who was on board.

Q. Was the schooner in your possession before the prisoners surrendered themselves?

A. No.

Q. Did Norman, Morrison, and Ellison, voluntarily surrender themselves?

A. They made no resistance; they came voluntarily with Brown.

———————

Coleman, Norman, McIntosh, and Byrne were acquitted. Mr. Heywood, Morrison, Musprat, Millward, Burkitt, and Ellison, were found guilty, and sentence of death was pronounced upon them; but the Court at the same time informed Mr. Heywood and Morrison, that they should recommend them to the King for mercy, which his Majesty was afterwards graciously pleased to grant. Musprat having requested that Norman, one of the prisoners, against whom there was no evidence, might be acquitted and examined in his favour, and this being refused by the Court, his sentence was respited till the opinion of the twelve judges could be obtained upon the question. They decided that the evidence ought to have been received, and in consequence Musprat was discharged.

The Sentence of the Court was afterwards executed upon Millward, Burkitt, and Ellison. When they were brought upon the forecastle of the ship in which the execution was ordered, Millward addressed the ships' crews and spectators, in the following words: "Brother Sea-men, You see before you three lusty young fellows about to suffer a shameful death for the dreadful crime of mutiny and desertion. Take warning by our example never to desert your officers, and should they behave ill to you, remember it is not their cause, it is the cause of your country you are bound to support."

THE

APPENDIX

TO STEPHEN BARNEY Esquire, *Portsmouth.*

GRAY'S-INN SQUARE, MAY 15TH, 1794.

SIR,

I Assure you I regard the publication of your Minutes of the Court-martial as a very great favour done to myself, and I am the more sensible of the obligation from being convinced that they were not originally taken with an intent to publish. But they appear to be so full and satisfactory; that, from your further kindness in permitting the extraordinary information which I have collected to be annexed as an Appendix, the Public, I trust, will at length be possessed of a complete knowledge of the real causes and circumstances of that most melancholy event, the Mutiny on board the Bounty. It is unnecessary for me to add, that I alone am responsible for the authenticity, or rather accuracy, of the information contained in the Appendix, as far at least as it has been obtained by me, in the manner and from the persons described therein.

I have the honour to be,

SIR,

Your most obedient,

and obliged Servant,

ED. CHRISTIAN.

THE APPENDIX.

THE CIRCUMSTANCES COMMUNICATED in this Appendix have been collected by a person nearly related to Christian: and it is far from his intention or wish to insinuate a vindication of the crime which has been committed. Justice, as well as policy, requires that mutiny, from whatever causes produced, or with whatever circumstances accompanied, should be punished with inexorable rigour. The publication of the trial, and of these extraordinary facts, it is presumed, will in no degree impede the pursuit of justice, yet it will administer some consolation to the broken hearts, which this melancholy transaction has occasioned. And whilst the innocent families and relations of twenty-one unhappy men are deeply interested in reducing to it's just measure the infamy which this dreadful act has brought upon them; every friend to truth and strict justice must feel his attention awakened to the true causes and circumstances, which have hitherto been concealed or misrepresented, of one of the most remarkable events in the annals of the navy. It is the aim of the writer of this Appendix to state facts as they are, and to refrain, as far as possible, from invective and reproach.

It will naturally be asked from whom, and how have these facts been collected? and why have they been so long suppressed? It may be answered, That the writer of this Appendix, with the other relations of the mutineers, entertained no distrust of the narratives published to the world, or the accounts which they received in private; and as they came from those whose sufferings had unquestionably been extreme, and preservation almost miraculous; and thus carrying with them the stamp of even greater authenticity than the solemn declarations of a death-bed, they precluded all suspicion and enquiries among those who were most concerned in the horrid representation. Their lips were closed, they mourned in silence, and shuddering at the most distant allusion to this melancholy subject, they were of all persons the least likely to discover the real truth of the transaction.

All the circumstances stated here could not be produced at the trial, as the Court confined the witnesses, as much as possible, to the question, Who were actually engaged in the mutiny? for that being a a crime which will admit of no legal justification, the relation of previous circumstances could not be material or legal evidence; yet what passed at the time of the mutiny was so immediately connected with what had happened previously in the ship, that in the testimony of most of the witnesses there will be found an allusion to, or confirmation of, what is here advanced.

Some time after the trial of the mutineers, the writer of this Appendix received such information as surprized him greatly, and in consequence of which, he resolved to make every possible enquiry into this unhappy affair. The following circumstances have been collected from many interviews and conversations, in the presence and hearing of several respectable gentlemen, with Mr. Fryer,* master of the Bounty; Mr. Hayward,† midshipman; Mr. Peckover,‡ gunner; Mr. Purcell,§ carpenter; John Smith,|| cook; Lawrence Lebogue,# sail maker; all these returned in the boat with Captain Bligh: and with Joseph Coleman,** armourer; Thomas McIntosh,†† carpenter's mate; Michael Byrne,‡‡ seaman; these are three of the four, who were tried and honourably acquitted, even with Captain Bligh's testimony in their favour; and with Mr. Heywood, midshipman, who has received his Majesty's pardon; and William Musprat, discharged by the opinion of the judges in his favour, upon a point of evidence: the writer of this has received letters also upon the subject from James Morrison, the boatswain's mate; who was pardoned. Mr. Heywood is now serving again as midshipman, under Lord Howe, in the Queen Charlotte, and is much respected by all who know him; and

*Now of the Inconstant man of war.
†Now Lieutenant in the Diomed, East Indies.
‡Lives at No. 13, Gun Alley, Wapping.
§Now of the Dromedary, West Indies.
||In London, but residence unknown.
#In Greenwich Hospital.
**In Ditto.
††In the merchants' service, his mother keeps a public house at North Shields.
‡‡In Greenwich Hospital.

Morrison and Musprat are also employed again in the king's service; yet the writer of this Appendix thinks it necessary to assure the reader that no material fact here stated stands in need of their testimony or confirmation. The gentlemen who were present at different conversations with the persons just mentioned, are; John Farhill, Esq. No. 38, Mortimer street; Samuel Romilly, Esq. Lincoln's Inn; Mr. Gilpin, No. 432, Strand; the Rev. Dr. Fisher, Canon of Windsor; the Rev. Mr. Cookson, Canon of Windsor; Captain Wordsworth, of the Abergavenny East Indiaman; Rev. Mr. Antrobus, Chaplain to the Bishop of London; John France, Esq. Temple; James Losh, Esq. Temple; Rev. Dr. Frewen, Colchester; and John Atkinson, Esq. Somerset Herald. Each of these gentlemen has heard the declarations of one at the least of the persons before mentioned; some have had an interview with five or six of them at different times, together with the writer of this Appendix, who is confident that every one of these gentlemen will bear testimony that what he has heard is not here exaggerated or misrepresented. There is no contradiction or variance whatever, in the account given by the gentlemen and people of the Bounty, though they could not upon every occasion, be all present together, and therefore cannot all relate exactly the same circumstances.

They declare that Captain Bligh used to call his officers "scoundrels, damned rascals, hounds, hell-hounds, beasts, and infamous wretches"; that he frequently threatened them, that when the ship arrived at Endeavour Straits, "he would kill one half of the people, make the officers jump overboard, and would make them eat grass like cows"; and that Christian, and Stewart, another midshipman, were as much afraid of Endeavour Straits, as any child is of a rod.

Captain Bligh was accustomed to abuse Christian much more frequently and roughly than the rest of the officers, or as one of the persons expressed it, "whatever fault was found, Mr. Christian was sure to bear the brunt of the Captain's anger." In speaking to him in this violent manner, Captain Bligh frequently "shook his fist in Christian's face." But the immediate cause of the melancholy event is attributed to what happened on the 26th and 27th of April, the mutiny broke out on the morning of the 28th of April 1789. The Bounty had stopped at Annamooko, one of the Friendly Islands; on the 26th Christian was sent upon a watering party, with express orders from the Captain, by no means to fire upon the natives; upon their return, the Captain was informed that the natives had stolen the cooper's adze; at this, Captain Bligh was in a great rage, and abused Christian much; saying to him, "G——damn your blood, why did not you fire,—you an officer!" At this island the Captain and ship's company had bought quantities of cocoa nuts, at the rate of 20 for a nail; the Captain's heap lay upon deck, and on the morning of the 27th, Captain Bligh fancied that the number was diminished, but the master, Mr. Fryer, told him he supposed they were pressed closer from being run over by the men in the night. The Captain then ordered the officer of the morning watch, Mr. Christian, to be called; when he came, the Captain accosted him thus, "Damn your blood, you have stolen my cocoa nuts"; Christian answered, "I was dry, I thought it of no consequence, I took one only, and I am sure no one touched another." Captain Bligh then replied, "You lie, you scoundrel, you have stolen one half." Christian appeared much hurt and agitated, and said, "Why do you treat me thus, Captain Bligh?" Captain Bligh then shook his hand in his face and said, "No reply"; and called him "a thief," and other abusive names. He then ordered the quarter masters to go down and bring all the cocoa nuts both from man and officer, and put them upon the quarter deck. They were brought. The Captain then called all hands upon deck, and desired "the people to look after the officers, and the officers to look after the people, for there never were such a set of damned thieving rascals under any man's command in the world before." And he told the men, "You are allowed a pound and a half of yams to-day, but to-morrow I shall reduce you to three quarters of a pound." All declare that the ship's company were before greatly discontented at their short allowance of provisions, and their discontent was increased from the consideration that they had plenty of provisions on board, and that the Captain was his own purser*. About four o'clock on the same day, Captain Bligh abused Christian again. Christian came forward from Captain Bligh, crying, "tears were running fast from his eyes in big drops." Purcell, the Carpenter, said to him, "What is the matter Mr. Christian?" He said, "Can you ask me, and hear the treatment I re-

---

*During the mutiny, Captain Bligh said to Mr. Young, "This is a serious affair Mr. Young" Mr. Young replied, "Yes, it is a serious affair to be starved, I hope this day to get a belly full."

ceive?" Purcell replied, "Do not I receive as bad as you do?" Christian said, "You have something* to protect you, and can speak again; but if I should speak to him as you do, he would probably break me, turn me before the mast, and perhaps flog me; and if he did, it would be the death of us both, for I am sure I should take him in my arms, and jump overboard with him." Purcell said, "Never mind it, it is but for a short time longer." Christian said, "In going through Endeavour Straits, I am sure the ship will be a hell." He was heard by another person to say, when he was crying, "I would rather die ten thousand deaths, than bear this treatment; I always do my duty as an officer and as a man ought to do, yet I receive this scandalous usage." Another person heard him say, "That flesh and blood cannot bear this treatment." This was the only time he ever was seen in tears on board the ship; and one of the seamen being asked, if he had ever observed Christian in tears before, answered, "No, he was no milksop." It is now certainly known, that Christian after this had prepared to leave the ship that night upon a raft; those who came with Captain Bligh, can only know it by circumstances, which they afterwards recollected, and which were the subject of conversation in the boat. He gave away that afternoon all his Otaheite curiosities; he was seen tearing his letters and papers, and throwing them overboard; he applied to the carpenter for nails, who told him to take as many as he pleased out of the locker; and the ship intending to stop at no other island, these could have been of no use to him, but in case of his escape to land. Mr. Tinkler, a young boy, one of Christian's messmates, was hungry in the evening, and went below to get some pig which was left at dinner; this he missed, and after some search, found it packed up with a bread fruit, in a dirty cloaths bag in Christian's cot; when the launch was hoisted out, the two masts were lashed to a plank, which they were obliged to untie. This was the raft or stage upon which he intended to leave the ship. These circumstances are remembered by those who came in the boat, but his design of going off upon the raft was frequently the subject of conversation afterwards in the ship. Norman, one of the four who were honourably acquitted, said to him after the mutiny, "This is a hard case upon me,

*By this he meant his warrant; the warrant-officers can only be punished by suspension and confinement, they cannot be broke and flogged like midshipmen.

Mr. Christian, who have a wife and family in England."* Christian replied, "It is a hard case, Norman, but it never would have happened, if I could have left the ship alone." Christian told them afterwards in the ship, "that he did not expect to reach the shore upon the raft, but he was in hopes of being seen and taken up by some of the natives in their canoes." The reason of his disappointment is said to have been owing to the people being upon deck in greater numbers than usual, looking at a volcano in the island of Tofoa.

All agree that there was no plot or intention to mutiny before Christian went upon his watch, at four in the morning. The mutiny broke out at five o'clock, and all the mutineers were in bed when it began, except those who were in Christian's watch; how soon after four o'clock the conspiracy was entered into, before it was put in execution, does not appear. That there had been some agreement previous to the breaking out of the mutiny is manifest from the evidence of Mr. Fryer, who was told by two of them, "Sir, there is no one means to hurt you; no, that was our agreement, not to commit murder." This statement cannot be reconciled with the testimony of Mr. Hayward and Mr. Hallet, who were both in Christian's watch; if the reader were not apprized of a circumstance which was not mentioned before the court-martial; viz. that these gentlemen who were very young at that time, viz. about fifteen, had both fallen asleep. The circumstance of the rest of the mutineers being in bed when the mutiny began, proves that it had not been preconcerted with them; and it is remarkable that Mr. Young was the only person among Christian's messmates, who was concerned in it, and he was in bed when it broke out. On the 26th, before the ship left Annamooko, Christian and some other officers threw away their beads and trifles among the natives, as articles for which they would have no further occasion.

It appears from the testimony of every witness, that the original intent was to put the Captain on shore, with three other persons only, and if the smallest boat, which was hoisted out for that purpose, had not been leakey, it is probable that this design would have been carried into execution; but by the time that the second cutter or boat was got into the water, a great number desired to leave the ship, and requested the launch. It is agreed by all, that every person who went into the launch, went voluntarily, or might have continued on

*Norman's family live at Portsmouth.

board if he had wished to stay, except the four who were first ordered into the small boat; and afterwards Mr. Fryer, who was commanded to go in consequence of his design to retake the ship being overheard. It is indeed expressly proved by Mr. Hallet, that "the boatswain and carpenters told Christian, they would prefer going in the boat, to staying in the ship; and he said he did not wish them, or any other, to stay against their inclination, or to go; and that the most part went voluntarily." And Mr. Hayward in his evidence has also deposed, "I heard no one ordered to go into the boat, but Mr. Hallet, Mr. Samuel, and myself." Although Mr. Fryer himself wished to stay, from a very laudable motive, viz. that of retaking the ship; yet being obliged to go, he earnestly requested that his brother-in-law, Tinkler, then a young boy, might be permitted to follow him.* In such a dilemma, the alternative was dreadful, yet those who went voluntarily into the launch, were sure of getting to shore, where they expected to live, until an European ship arrived, or until they could raise their boat or build a greater, as one of the mutineers said of the carpenter, "you might as well give him the ship as his tool chest." It is proved by Mr. Hallet, that they were veered astern, in order to be towed towards the land, which was so near, that it is said they might see them reach the shore from the mast head of the ship.

After the mutiny commenced, it was between three and four hours before the launch left the ship, and one reason, besides the number of persons, why she was so deeply laden, was, that almost all Captain Bligh's property in boxes and trunks was put on board. A short time after it had quitted the ship, Christian declared, that "he would readily sacrifice his own life, if the persons in the launch were all safe in the ship again."

At Annamooko, besides the cooper's adze being stolen, the natives, by diving, had cut and carried off a grapnel by which a boat was fastened. Captain Bligh, in order to compel the natives to restore it, had made them believe he would sail away with their chiefs whom he had on board; this was unattended with success, as they assured

---

*It is worthy of notice that Lambe the butcher was a mutineer; but when he saw such a number going off in the launch, he actually laid down his arms and joined them; he afterwards died at Batavia.

Martin, another mutineer, attempted to get into the launch, but was opposed by the carpenter, who said he would get him hanged when they got to England; and he was then ordered back by the people in the ship.

him the grapnel had been carried away in a canoe belonging to another island; but the people of the island, who crowded round the ship to entreat the deliverance of their chiefs, and the chiefs themselves, were greatly frightened and distressed, before they were set at liberty. For Captain Bligh carried them out some distance to sea, and they were followed and taken back in canoes.* This unfortunate circumstance is supposed to have been the cause of the rough reception which the people in the launch met with at Tofoa. For Nageete, one of the chiefs, who had been thus frightened, had come upon a visit from Annamooko, though ten leagues distant, and was one of the first persons they saw at Tofoa. He appeared at the first friendly, yet it is thought that he was glad of having this opportunity of resenting the treatment he had received in the ship at Annamooko.

Those who came in the boat, though they gave vent to no open complaints, yet sometimes made allusions in the hearing of the Captain, to what had passed previous to the mutiny. Captain Bligh was one day observing, that it was surprising that this should have happened after he had been so kind to the people, by making them fine messes of wheat; upon which Mr. Hallet replied, "If it had not been for your fine messes, and fine doings, we should have had the ship for our resource† instead of the boat."

In a misunderstanding about some oysters, between the Captain and the carpenter, Captain Bligh told him, "If I had not taken so much pains with you, you would never have been here"; the carpenter replied, "Yes, if you had not taken so much pains with us, we should never have been here."

In the evidence of Mr. Peckover and Mr. Fryer, it is proved that Mr. Nelson the botanist said, upon hearing the commencement of the mutiny, "We know whose fault this is, or who is to blame; and

---

*When Mr. Nelson told Mr. Peckover, that the ship is taken from us, Mr. Peckover in his evidence says, he answered, "We were a long way from land when I came off deck," (thinking, as he declares, that the people in the canoes had followed and taken the ship); and so it was understood by Mr. Nelson, who replies, "It is by our own people."

†It must be supposed that, after a distance of time, although the ideas and impression are remembered, the exact words will be forgotten; but one person particularly recollects, that Mr. Hallet used the word *resource* upon this occasion, because he afterwards fancied it was thus suggested to Captain Bligh's mind, as the name which he gave to the vessel purchased at Timor.

oh! Mr. Fryer, what have we brought upon ourselves?" In addition to this, it ought to be known that Mr. Nelson, in conversation afterwards with an officer at Timor, who was speaking of returning with Captain Bligh if he got another ship, observed, "I am surprized that you should think of going a second time with one, (using a term of abuse,) who has been the occasion of all our losses."

In Captain Bligh's Narrative no mention is made of the two little boats or cutters, the least boat would not hold more than six, and the larger more than nine persons. But after Captain Bligh relates that he was brought upon deck, he proceeds thus in the two next paragraphs:

"The boatswain was now ordered to hoist out the *launch,* with a threat if he did not do it instantly, to take care of himself.

"The *boat* being out, Mr. Heywood and Mr. Hallet, midshipmen, and Mr. Samuel, were ordered into it." P. 2 [page 6 in this edition].

Every reader must have supposed that the boat mentioned in the latter paragraph, was the same as the launch in the former, and that these four were the first of the nineteen who were ordered into it.

If the small boats had been distinctly mentioned in Captain Bligh's Narrative, it would have been manifest to all the world that the mutiny could not have been the result of a conspiracy of twenty-five of the people, to turn the other nineteen into one or both of them.

Indeed, many readers had the penetration to think that it was incredible, and almost beyond any calculation of probability, that twenty five persons could have been seduced to have concurred in such a horrid plot, without a single one having the virtue to resist the temptation, and to disclose the design to the Captain.

In the Narrative, p. 8 [page 10 in this edition], there is this memorable paragraph:

Notwithstanding the roughness with which I was treated, the remembrance of past kindnesses produced some signs of remorse in Christian. When they were forcing me out of the ship, I asked him, If this treatment was a proper return for the many instances he had received of my friendship? He appeared disturbed at my question, and answered with much emotion, "That, Captain Bligh,—that is the thing; I am in hell—I am in hell."

In Mr. Purcell's evidence before the Court, this conversation is sworn to thus: "Captain Bligh attempted to speak to Christian, who said, 'Hold your tongue, and I'll not hurt you; it is too late to consider now, I have been in hell for weeks past with you.' " But all, who were upon deck and overheard the whole of this conversation, state it thus: "Captain Bligh, addressing himself to Christian, said, 'Consider Mr. Christian, I have a wife and four children in England, and you have danced my children upon your knee.' " Christian replied, "You should have thought of them sooner yourself, Captain Bligh, it is too late to consider now, I have been in hell for weeks past with you." Christian afterwards told the people in the ship, that when Bligh spoke of his wife and children, "my heart melted, and I would then have jumped overboard, if I could have saved you, but as it was too late to do that, I was obliged to proceed." One person, who heard what passed, immediately after Captain Bligh was brought upon deck, says, that Captain Bligh asked Christian, "What is the meaning of all this?" And Christian answered, "Can you ask, Captain Bligh, when you know you have treated us officers, and all these poor fellows, like Turks?"

Captain Bligh in his Narrative asserts, "When we were sent away, Huzza for Otaheite, was frequently heard among the mutineers."— P. 7 [page 10 in this edition]. But every one of those who came in the boat, as well as all who staid in the ship, declare, that they neither heard nor observed any huzzaing whatever in the ship.

In Captain Bligh's Narrative, p. 11 [page 12 in this edition], there is the following paragraph:

> Had their mutiny been occasioned by any grievances, either real or imaginary, I must have discovered symptoms of their discontent, which would have put me upon my guard, but the case was far otherwise. Christian in particular I was on the most friendly terms with; that very day he was engaged to have dined with me; and the preceding night he excused himself from supping with me, on pretence of being unwell, for which I felt concerned, having no suspicions of his integrity and honour.

It is said that the Captain had his officers to dine with him in rotation, and Christian's turn might have fallen on the day of the mutiny; but in consequence of the charge of stealing the cocoa nuts, the gentlemen (or most of them) had resolved not to dine again at the Captain's table. Mr. Fryer had not dined there for a long time before. It is true that Captain Bligh had asked Christian to supper; but it now appears, he excused himself, not to meditate the destruction of his benefactor, but his own flight.

It was proved on the trial, that Christian, during the mutiny, told Mr. Fryer, "You know, Mr. Fryer, I have been in hell on board this ship for weeks past"; and that he said to the Captain, "I have been in hell for weeks past with you": but what particular period Christian referred to, or when the poignancy of his distress had begun to prey upon his mind, does not appear. But instances are mentioned of Christian's being hurt by Captain Bligh's treatment, even at the Cape of Good Hope, in their outward bound voyage. Christian had the command of the tent on shore at Otaheite, where Captain Bligh sometimes entertained the Chiefs of the island, and before all the company used to abuse Christian for some pretended fault or other, and the Chiefs would afterwards take an opportunity of observing to Christian, "Titriano, Brie worrite beha": i.e. "Christian, Bligh is perhaps angry with you." Christian would turn it off by saying, No, no. But he afterwards complained to the officers, of the Captain's cruelty in abusing him before the people of the country, observing, that he would not regard it, if he would only find fault with him in private. There is no country in the world, where the notions of aristocracy and family pride are carried higher than at Otaheite; and it is a remarkable circumstance, that the Chiefs are naturally distinguished by taller persons, and more open and intelligent countenances, than the people of inferior condition; hence these are the principal qualities by which the natives estimate the gentility of strangers; and Christian was so great a favourite with them, that according to the words of one person, "They adored the very ground he trod upon." He was Tyo, or friend, to a Chief of the first rank in the island, whose name, according to the custom of the country, he took in exchange for his own; and whose property he participated. This Chief dined one day with Captain Bligh, and was told by him, That his Tyo Christian, was only his Towtow, or servant. The Chief upbraided Christian with this, who was much mortified at being thus degraded in the opinion of his friend, and endeavoured to recommend himself again to the Chief, by assuring him, that he, Captain Bligh, and all the officers, were Towtows of the King of Bretane.

These circumstances, although comparatively trifling, are such as to be distinctly remembered; but they prove that there could be little harmony, where such painful sensations were so frequently and unnecessarily excited.

A regard to truth obliges the writer of this Appendix to add, That Captain Bligh has told some of Christian's relations, that after they sailed from Otaheite, Christian, when he was upon duty, had put the ship in great danger; from which Captain Bligh supposed that it had been his intention to cripple the ship, that they might be obliged to return to Otaheite to repair. But no such circumstance is remembered by any person besides the Captain.* Captain Bligh has also declared that the persons in the launch "were turned out to certain destruction, because the mutineers had not the courage to embrue their hands in blood." It has already been observed, that it is proved before the court-martial, that most of the persons went into the launch voluntarily. And it is certainly true, that, although the sufferings of the persons in the boat were distressful to the last degree, they were not the occasion of the death of Mr. Nelson at Timor, or of those who died at Batavia; for all recovered from the extremity to which they had been reduced by this unhappy voyage.

It is agreed that Christian was the first to propose the mutiny, and the project of turning the Captain on shore at Tofoa, to the people in his watch; but he declared afterwards in the ship, he never should have thought of it, if it had not been suggested to his mind by an expression of Mr. Stewart, who knowing of his intention of leaving the ship upon the raft, told him, "When you go, Christian, we are ripe for any thing."

The mutiny is ascribed by all who remained in the ship, to this unfortunate expression, which probably proceeded rather from a regard for Christian, than from a mutinous disposition; for all declare that Stewart was an excellent officer, and a severe disciplinarian; severe to

---

*They had sailed from Otaheite twenty-four days, when the mutiny broke out; and as in those seas a constant trade wind blows from east to west; in order to return to Otaheite, they must have been obliged to have gone into a high southern latitude before they could have gained the advantage of the variable winds. Their return to Otaheite would probably have taken up twice or thrice twenty-four days. If the mutiny had been plotted at Otaheite, it is not probable the execution of it would have been so long delayed.

such a degree as to be disliked by the seamen, though much respected for his abilities. Mr. Stewart was in bed when the mutiny broke out, and afterwards was neither in arms, nor active on the side of the mutineers; yet it ought not to be concealed, that during the mutiny he was dancing and clapping his hands in the Otaheite manner, and saying, "It was the happiest day of his life." He was drowned in the wreck of the Pandora. This gentleman is spoken of by all in terms of great praise and respect. He is said to have been the best practical navigator on board, even superior in that character to Captain Bligh and Christian.* Soon after the launch had left the ship, Christian told the people that he had no right to the command, and that he would act in any station they would assign him. But they all declared that he should be their Captain, and after some persuasion from Christian, they permitted Mr. Stewart to be the second in command, though they were desirous, from Stewart's former severity, of preferring Mr. Heywood; but being told by Christian, that as the ship must be at watch and watch, he thought Mr. Heywood, who was then only sixteen, too young and inexperienced for such a charge, with some reluctance they acceded to his recommendation of Mr. Stewart. The other arrangements being settled, instead of insisting upon going back to Otaheite, they told Christian he might carry them wherever he thought proper. Christian advised them to go to an island called Tobooy, which was laid down in the charts by Captain Cook, though no European ship had ever landed there. This lies about seven degrees south of Otaheite, and it was chosen because it was out of the track of European ships.† When they arrived there, and with difficulty had made a landing, although it was full of inhabitants, they found no quadrupeds but a species of small rats, with which the island was completely overrun. They staid there a few days, and then resolved to sail to Otaheite for a ship load of hogs, goats, dogs, cats,

---

*Though all acknowledge Captain Bligh's great skill and abilities in theory and in making observations, yet they all declare, that in the practical management of a ship he was not superior to Stewart or Christian. For the two last are thus classed and compared with the Captain. Captain Bligh was the best artist on board; Stewart the best seaman; and Christian was the best in both characters united. Stewart was several years senior to Christian, both in age and in the service.

†One of the four acquitted, said, "Mr. Christian was a fine scholar, he carried us like a shot to Tobooy, and told us within half an hour when we should make land."

and fowls, to stock the island of Tobooy, which they had fixed upon for their settlement.*

When they had reached Otaheite, in order to acquire what they wanted more expeditiously, Christian told the Chiefs and people, that Captain Bligh had returned to Captain Cook, who had sent Christian back to purchase for him the different articles which they wished to obtain.

This story was the more plausible, as the people of Otaheite had been told by Captain Bligh, that Captain Cook was still living, and that he had sent him for the bread-fruit. Such is still their love and veneration for the memory of Captain Cook, that the natives even contended for the honour of sending their best hogs and animals to Toote. The ship by this artifice being soon filled, they returned with some Otaheite men and women to Tobooy. It was thought that the Otaheite men would be useful in introducing them to the friendship and good offices of the natives. At Tobooy they built a fort,† and having staid there three months, and finding the inhabitants always inhospitable and treacherous, the people of the ship grew discontented; all hands were called up, and it being put to the vote what should be done, sixteen out of the twenty-five voted that they should go back to Otaheite. Christian, thinking that this was the general wish, said, *"Gentlemen, I will carry you, and land you wherever you please; I desire no one to stay with me, but I have one favour to request, that you will grant me the ship, tie the foresail, and give me a few gallons of water, and leave me to run before the wind, and I shall land upon the first island the ship drives to. I have done such an act that I cannot stay at Otaheite. I will never live where I may be carried home to be a disgrace to my family."*

Upon this, Mr. Young, the midshipman, and seven others declared, *"We shall never leave you, Mr. Christian, go where you will."* It was then agreed, that the other sixteen should be landed at Otaheite, and

---

*They prevailed upon the king to give them a bull and a cow, which were kept tied up as royal curiosities; but the voyage back to Tobooy was very tempestuous, and the bull being old could not stand upon his legs, and died in consequence of the bruises from his falls. There is a breed of English cattle, which run wild upon the mountains of Otaheite, but the natives cannot be persuaded to make use either of their flesh or milk.
†Christian having endeavoured to convince them of the necessity of building a fort for their protection, assured them, that he would take his share of the labour; and calling for a pick-axe, was the first who began the operations.

have their share of the arms and other necessary articles; and he proposed to the rest, that they should go and seek an island, not before discovered, where they were not likely to be found, and having run the ship aground, and taken out every thing of value, and scuttled and broke up the ship, they should endeavour to make a settlement. They reached Otaheite on the 27th of September 1789, and came to an anchor in Matavai Bay about eleven o'clock in the forenoon, and the sixteen were disembarked with their portions of the arms and other necessaries. Christian took leave of Mr. Stewart and Mr. Heywood, and told them he should sail that evening; and desired them, if they ever got to England, to inform his friends and country what had been the cause of his committing so desperate an act; but to guard against any obstruction, he concealed the time of his sailing from the rest.

The natives came on board in crouds as usual, and about twelve o'clock at night he cut his cable, and sailed from the Bay. The people on board consisted of nine Englishmen, about twenty-five men, women, boys, and girls, of different ages, from Otaheite, and two men from Tobooy. It does not appear that any selection was made of the Otaheiteans, who are always eager to be carried away in an English ship. The ship was seen standing off the island the next morning, but from that day, for the nineteen months the others lived at Otaheite, they never saw nor heard any thing more of Christian; and upon the arrival of Captain Edwards in the Pandora, they could give him no further account of the Bounty than what is here stated.*

During his short stay at Otaheite, Christian was much pressed to go on shore to visit the King, but he declined it, saying, *"How can I look him in the face, after the lie I told him when I was here last?"* These circumstances concerning the Bounty, subsequent to the

---

*Sixteen were left at Otaheite; one of whom, in a quarrel about their arms, was shot by another Englishman, who was put to death by the natives, as an act of justice; the other fourteen surrendered themselves to Captain Edwards, or were taken by the people of the Pandora; four of these were lost when the Pandora was shipwrecked; four have been honourably acquitted; two have received his Majesty's pardon; one has been discharged by the opinion of the judges in his favour; and the remaining three have suffered death according to the sentence of the court-martial. Millward, one of the three, was in bed when the mutiny broke out; the other two were in Christian's watch; Ellison, one of them, was a young boy at the time. When the others went down to arm themselves, he was left at the helm. He was afterwards active in the mutiny. He had got a musket in his hand, which Christian having observed, said, "You little monkey, what business have you with that?" and ordered it to be taken from him.

mutiny, must necessarily be collected from the seven persons who were left in the ship, and who are now, or were lately, in England. These say, that Christian was always sorrowful and dejected after the mutiny; and before he left them, had become such an altered man in his looks and appearance, as to render it probable that he would not long survive this dreadful catastrophe. Indeed, it is impossible that he should have appeared* otherwise, if he deserved the character which all unite in giving him.

In the Royal Jamaica Gazette, dated February 9, 1793, which announced the arrival of Captain Bligh in the Providence, the following was one of the paragraphs, and it has been copied into all the English newspapers:

> Captain Bligh could gain no intelligence of the mutineer Christian and his accomplices, who were on board the Bounty. When they returned to Otaheite, after executing their infernal project, the natives, suspecting some mischief from the non-appearance of the Commander and the gentlemen with him, laid a plan to seize the vessel and crew; but a *favourite female* of Christian's betrayed the design of her countrymen. He put to sea in the night, and the next morning the ship was nearly out of sight.

It is immaterial to inquire who was the author of this paragraph, yet it cannot but be remarked, that it is totally different from the account which has been given by those who staid at Otaheite, and who can have no possible interest in concealing this circumstance, if in fact it had existed; nor can it be reconciled with probability, or the treatment and protection which the Englishmen experienced from the natives when the ship had left them.

As this paragraph contains an assertion, that Christian had a

---

*Though they say he kept up good discipline in the ship, yet he was generally below, leaning his head upon his hand, and when they came down for orders, he seldom raised his head to answer more than Yes, or No.

One of the seamen being asked, if they never mutinied afterwards in the ship, and told Christian, they had as good a right to the command as he had, said, "No, no man would ever have mutinied against Mr. Christian, no one ever thought of resisting his authority."

One method, it is said, which he adopted to prevent riot and confusion in the ship, was, to draw off secretly the spirituous liquors from the casks, and he then persuaded the people they had drank them to the bottom.

favourite female at Otaheite, it is proper that it should be known, that although Christian was upon shore, and had the command of the tent all the time that Captain Bligh was at Otaheite with the Bounty, yet the officers who were with Christian upon the same duty declare, that he never had a female favourite at Otaheite, nor any attachment or particular connexion among the women. It is true that some had what they call *their girls,* or women with whom they constantly lived all the time they were upon the island, but this was not the case with Christian.

Until this melancholy event, no young officer was ever more affectionately beloved for his amiable qualities, or more highly respected for his abilities and brave and officer-like conduct. The world has been led to suppose, that the associates in his guilt were attached to him only by his seducing and diabolical villany. But all those who came in the boat, whose sufferings and losses on his account have been so severe, not only speak of him without resentment and with forgiveness, but with a degree of rapture and enthusiasm. The following are, word for word, some of the unpremeditated expressions, used by the gentlemen and people of the Bounty, in speaking of this unfortunate mutineer: *"His Majesty might have his equal, but he had not a superior officer in his service."* This probably had a reference to his age, which was about twenty-three. *"He was a gentleman, and a brave man; and every officer and seaman on board the ship would have gone through fire and water to have served him."*—*"He was a good and worthy gentleman, and was dear to all who ever knew him; and before the fatal day, his conduct was in every respect such as became an officer, a gentleman, and a man of honour."*—*"He was adorned with every virtue, and beloved by all."*—*"He was a gentleman every inch of him, and I would still wade up to the arm-pits in blood to serve him."*—*"As much as I have lost and suffered by him, if he could be restored to his country, I should be the first to go without wages in search of him."*—*"He was as good and as generous a man as ever lived."*—*"Mr. Christian was always good-natured, I never heard him say Damn you, to any man on board the ship."*—*"Every body under his command did their duty at a look from Mr. Christian, and I would still go through fire and water for him."* These are respectively the expressions of nine different persons, and it is the language of one and all. Mr. Hayward in his evidence, no doubt with a proper sentiment of the crime of mutiny, has used the words, *"Chris-*

tian, and his gang": yet that gentleman has declared, that, until the desperate act, Christian deserved the character described by the strongest of the above expressions.

Christian, having staid at school longer than young men generally do who enter into the navy, and being allowed by all who knew him to possess extraordinary abilities, is an excellent scholar, and every one acquainted with him from a boy, till he went on board the Bounty, can testify, that no young man was ever more ambitious of all that is esteemed right and honourable among men, or more anxious to acquire distinction and advancement by his good conduct in his profession. He had been an acting Midshipman but a short time in the service, when Captain Courtenay, the late brave Commander of the Boston frigate, entrusted him with the charge of a watch in the Eurydice all the way home from the East Indies. This, no doubt, was extremely flattering to him, and he declared to a relation who met him at Woolwich, "he had been extremely happy under Captain Courtenay's command"; and at the same time observed, that *it was very easy to make one's self beloved and respected on board a ship; one had only to be always ready to obey one's superior officers, and to be kind to the common men, unless there was occasion for severity, and if you are severe when there is a just occasion, they will not like you the worse for it."** This was after the conclusion of the peace, and within a few days the ship was paid off; and being out of employ, he wished to be appointed a Mate of a West-Indiaman, a situation for which he thought himself qualified. Whilst he was in treaty with a merchant in the city to go in that capacity in his ship, Captain Taubman, a relation of Christian's, came to London from the Isle of Man, and suggested to Christian, that it would be very desirable for him to serve under so experienced a navigator as Captain Bligh, who had been Sailing-master to Captain Cook, and who was then in the merchants' service; and as Captain Taubman was acquainted with Captain Bligh, he offered to make an application to him in Christian's favour. The application was made, and Captain Bligh returned a polite answer, that he was sorry he could not take Christian, having

---

*Christian always spoke of Captain Courtenay as an officer and a gentleman, with the greatest affection and gratitude. The gentlemen and people on board the Eurydice, the writer of this Appendix has been assured, declare that Christian was the last person whom they would have expected to have committed such a crime.

then his complement of officers. Upon this, Christian of his own accord observed, that "wages were no object, he only wished to learn his profession, and if Captain Bligh would permit him to mess with the gentlemen, he would readily enter his ship as a Foremast-man, until there was a vacancy among the officers": and at the same time added, *we Midshipmen are gentlemen, we never pull at a rope; I should even be glad to go one voyage in that situation, for there may be occasions, when officers may be called upon to do the duties of a common man.*

To this proposal Captain Bligh had no objection, and in that character he sailed one voyage, and upon his return spoke of Captain Bligh with great respect: he said, that although he had his share of labour with the common men, the Captain had been kind to him in shewing him the use of his charts and instruments; but at the same time he observed, that Captain Bligh was very passionate; yet he seemed to pride himself in knowing how to humour him. In the next voyage, Captain Bligh took him out as his Second Mate, and before his return the Captain was chosen to command the Bounty.* Christian wishing to go upon a voyage where so much service would be seen, in which he would complete his time as a Midshipman, and if it had been successful, he would, no doubt, with little difficulty upon his return have been raised to the rank of Lieutenant, was recommended to the Admiralty by Captain Bligh himself, as one of his officers; and as it was understood that great interest had been made to get Midshipmen sent out in this ship, Christian's friends thought this recommendation, as they do still, a very great obligation. Captain Bligh had no Lieutenants on board, and the ship at the first was divided into two watches, the charge of which was entrusted to the Master and the Gunner: but after they had sailed about a month, the Captain divided the ship into three watches, and gave the charge of one to Christian, on whom Captain Bligh has always declared he had the greatest reliance. Such was his introduction to, and connexion with, Captain Bligh; and every one must sincerely lament, that what

---

*Upon Christian's return from the second voyage to the West Indies with Captain Bligh, he had no opportunity of a personal interview with his friends, and he made no complaint by letter. But a person, who had sailed with Captain Bligh and Christian, both to the West Indies and the South Seas, being asked, if Captain Bligh's treatment of Christian had always been the same? said, "No, it would not long have been born in the merchants service."

in its commencement had been so honourable to both, should in its event and consequences have proved to both so disastrous and fatal.

The writer of this Appendix would think himself an accomplice in the crime which has been committed, if he designedly should give the slightest shade to any word or fact different from its true and just representation; and lest he should be supposed to be actuated by a vindictive spirit, he has studiously forborn to make more comments than were absolutely necessary upon any statement which he has been obliged to bring forward. He has felt it a duty to himself, to the connexions of all the unfortunate men, and to society, to collect and lay before the Public these extraordinary circumstances.

The sufferings of Captain Bligh and his companions in the boat, however severe they may have been, are perhaps but a small portion of the torments occasioned by this dreadful event: and whilst these prove the melancholy and extensive consequences of the crime of Mutiny, the crime itself in this instance may afford an awful lesson to the Navy, and to mankind, that there is a degree of pressure, beyond which the best formed and principled mind must either break or recoil. And though public justice and the public safety can allow no vindication of any species of Mutiny, yet reason and humanity will distinguish the sudden unpremeditated act of desperation and phrenzy, from the foul deliberate contempt of every religious duty and honourable sentiment; and will deplore the uncertainty of human prospects, when they reflect that a young man is condemned to perpetual infamy, who, if he had served on board any other ship, or had perhaps been absent from the Bounty a single day, or one ill-fated hour, might still have been an honour to his country, and a glory and comfort to his friends.

THE END.

AN

ANSWER

TO

CERTAIN ASSERTIONS

CONTAINED IN

THE APPENDIX TO A PAMPHLET,

ENTITLED

Minutes of the Proceedings on the Court-Martial held at
Portsmouth, August 12th, 1792, on Ten Persons charged
with Mutiny on Board his Majesty's Ship the Bounty.

BY CAPTAIN WILLIAM BLIGH.

IT IS WITH NO SMALL DEGREE OF REGRET, that I find myself under the necessity of obtruding my private concerns on the Public. A pamphlet has appeared, under the title of "*Minutes of the Proceedings on the Court-Martial, held at Portsmouth, August 12th, 1792, on Ten Persons charged with Mutiny on Board his Majesty's Ship the Bounty; with an Appendix, containing a full Account of the real Causes, &c. &c.*" This Appendix is the work of Mr. Edward Christian, the brother of Fletcher Christian, who headed the Mutineers of the Bounty; written apparently for the purpose of vindicating his brother's conduct, at my expence.

The respect I owe to that Public in whose service I have spent my life, as well as regard to my character, compel me to reply to such parts of Mr. Christian's Appendix, as might, if unnoticed, obtain credit to my prejudice.

Of the Minutes of the Court-Martial, thus published, it is necessary to observe, that they differ from the Minutes lodged in the Admiralty-office; and in some places materially. One instance of this will appear among the Proofs, which are here submitted to the Public.

The information which furnished Mr. Edward Christian with materials for his Appendix, he states to "have been collected from many interviews and conversations, in the presence and hearing of several respectable gentlemen." He then mentions the names of all the persons with whom these conversations were held, without distinguishing the particular information given by any individual.

The mixing together the names of men, whose assertions merit very different degrees of credit, and blending their evidence into one mass, is liable to two objections: 1st, the impossibility of tracing the author of any particular assertion; and 2dly, the danger, which to a reader is unavoidable, of supposing, that the statements made by those who were actually accomplices in the Mutiny, came from men of respectable character, with whom he has thus associated them.

One of the hardest cases which can befall any man, is to be reduced to the necessity of defending his character by his own assertions only. As such, fortunately, is not my situation, I have rested my defence on the testimony of others; adding only, such of the written orders issued by me in the course of the voyage, as are connected with the matter in question; which orders being issued publicly in writing, may be offered as evidence of unquestionable credit.

These testimonials, without further remark from me, I trust, will be sufficient to do away any evil impression which the public may have imbibed, from reading Mr. Edward Christian's Defence of his brother.

LIST OF PROOFS.

1. Orders issued upon our Arrival at Otaheite, to regulate our Intercourse with the Natives.—October 25th, 1788.
2. Orders respecting the Confinement of three Men, who had deserted from the ship.—Date, January 24th, 1789.
3. Letter from the Deserters beforementioned.—January 26th, 1789.
4. Examination respecting the Loss of his Majesty's Ship the Bounty, by the High Court of Judicature at Batavia.—October 13th, 1789.
5. Descriptive List of the Mutineers.—Dated 28th April, 1789.
6. Orders given to Mr. John Fryer, the Master, on leaving him at Batavia.—October 14th, 1789.
7. Letter from Mr. Peter Heywood, Midshipman, to Mrs. Bligh.—July 14th, 1792.
8. Extract from Mr. Peter Heywood's Defence, on his Trial by a Court-Martial; held August 12th, 1792, at Portsmouth.
9. Letter from Mr. Peter Heywood to Mr. Edward Christian; published in the Cumberland Packet, and Whitehaven Advertiser, November 20th, 1792.

10. Letter published in the Times, July 16th, 1794, from Mr. Edward Harwood, late Surgeon of his Majesty's ship Providence.
11. Affidavit of Joseph Coleman.—July 31, 1794.
12. Affidavit of John Smith.—August 1, 1794.
13. Affidavit of Lawrence Lebogue.—August 2, 1794.
14. Letter from Lieutenant John Hallet.—August 1, 1794.
15. Letter from Mr. Edward Lamb, Commander of the Adventure, in the Jamaica trade.—October 28th, 1794.

NO. I.

Rules to be observed by every Person on Board, or belonging to the Bounty, for the better establishing a Trade for Supplies of Provisions, and good Intercourse with the Natives of the South Sea, wherever the Ship may be at.

1st. At the Society, or Friendly Islands, no person whatever is to intimate that Captain Cook was killed by Indians; or that he is dead.

2d. No person is ever to speak, or give the least hint, that we have come on purpose to get the bread-fruit plant, until I have made my plan known to the chiefs.

3d. Every person is to study to gain the good will and esteem of the natives; to treat them with all kindness; and not to take from them, by violent means, any thing that they may have stolen; and no one is ever to fire, but in defence of his life.

4th. Every person employed on service, is to take care that no arms, or implements of any kind under their charge, are stolen; the value of such thing, being lost, shall be charged against their wages.

5th. No man is to embezzle, or offer to sale, directly, or indirectly, any part of the King's stores, of what nature soever.

6th. A proper person or persons will be appointed to regulate trade, and barter with the natives; and no officer or seaman, or other person belonging to the ship, is to trade for any kind of provisions, or curiosities; but if such officer or seaman wishes to purchase any particular thing, he is to apply to the provider to do it for him. By this means a regular market will be carried on, and all disputes, which otherwise may happen with the natives will be avoided. All boats are to have every thing handed out of them at sun-set.

Given under my hand, on board the Bounty,
    Otaheite, 25th October, 1788.

WM. BLIGH.

NO. II.

All prisoners are to be kept upon deck in fair weather; and the centinel to report their state in the night, every half hour.

The key of their irons is to be taken care of by the master.

The mate of the watch is to be answerable for the prisoners. When they are released for a while, out of necessity, he is to see them again securely confined.

The mate of the watch is to have the charge of a brace of pistols, and one cartouch box, to be kept in the binnacle.

The mate of the watch is to take care the centinels do not lounge, or sit down.

No canoe is to come on board after eight o'clock at night, or any to go under the bows of the ship upon any pretence; but whatever is handed in or out of the ship is to be at the gangways.

All boats, when moored, to have every thing handed out of them at sun-set: and the centinel is to report the state of the prisoners every half hour, after the watch is set.

Given under my hand, in Oparré harbour,
    on board the Bounty, Jan. 24th, 1789.

WM. BLIGH.

NO. III.

Deserters' Letter, dated on Board the Bounty,
at Otaheite, January 26th, 1789.

Sir,
We should think ourselves wholly inexcusable, if we omitted taking this earliest opportunity of returning our thanks for your goodness in delivering us from a trial by Court-Martial, the fatal consequences of which are obvious; and although we cannot possibly lay any claim to so great a favour, yet we humbly beg you will be pleased to remit

any farther punishment; and we trust our future conduct will fully demonstrate our deep sense of your clemency, and our stedfast resolution to behave better hereafter.

We are Sir,
Your most obedient, most humble servants,*
C. CHURCHILL,
To Captain Bligh.   (Copy.)   WM. MUSPRAT,
JOHN MILLWARD.

NO. IV.

Translation of an Examination before a Court of Inquiry, at Batavia, into the Loss of the Bounty.

This day the 13th October, 1789, came before Nicholas Van Bergen Van der Gryp, notary public of the Noble High Regency of Netherland India, residing in the town of Batavia. Present, the hereafter to be named witnesses: John Fryer, master; Thomas Denman Ledward, surgeon; William Cole, boatswain; William Peckover, gunner; William Elphinstone, master's mate; Thomas Hayward and John Hallet, midshipmen; John Samuel, secretary: and the sailors, Robert Tinkler, Peter Linkleter, Lawrence Lebogue, George Simpson, John Smith, and Robert Lamb; all here present declare, with previous knowledge of Mr. Nicholas Englehard, superior Marchand, and Sabandhaar, and Licence Master in this place; and by interpretation of Mr. Peter Aeneas Mackay, Sub Marchand, in the service of the Noble Company.—That the truth is, they have been together, serving on board his Britannic Majesty's ship the Bounty, commanded by the Requirant.

That on the 28th April, 1789, that the greatest number of the ship's company, consisting of twenty-five persons, by the break of day, were mutineers; and before any body had discovered or got notice of it, had already secured the Requirant, binding his hands behind his back, and forcing him to come on deck in his shirt, where he was kept under a guard behind the mizen-mast. That the boatswain and the others were forced by the mutineers to assist in hoisting out

---

*These three persons, who were afterwards Mutineers, had ran away with the large cutter, and a chest of fire-arms; and this is what Millward, on his trial by the Court-Martial, calls "the former foolish affair."

the launch; which being done, they were forced to go into her, and the last of all the Requirant; after which they were veered astern of the ship by a rope, and soon after cast adrift in the wide ocean.

That they were in all nineteen souls in the launch, with a small quantity of bread and water, and no fire-arms.

That it had been impossible to foresee what has happened to them, as they had sailed homewards from the Friendly Islands, with a great cargo of plants, in the best order.

That there was no possibility to retake the ship, or do more for the welfare of the King's service, than what had been done by the Requirant, who had been tied and kept apart from the attestants until he was let down in the launch.

That there were heard at the time several expressions and huzzas in the ship, which makes them believe that the mutineers are returned to Otaheite.

That on the night of the 28th, they arrived at the island of Tofoa, one of the Friendly Islands, and remained there until the 2d of May, 1789, seeking provisions and water. That they were attacked that day by the natives, whereby one man, John Norton, was killed, and they narrowly escaped.

That they, after having suffered all distress and misery, arrived the 14th June following at Coupang, in Timor, and that there David Nelson, gardener, died of a fever.

That they sailed from Coupang on the 20th August following, in a schooner for that purpose purchased, and arrived here at Batavia the 1st of October, 1789, where that vessel has been sold on the 10th of that month; that likewise on the 10th of October died in the hospital, Thomas Hall.

Alleging that all abovementioned to be the truth and verity, offering to confirm this given attestation with solemn oath.

Thus acted and passed in presence of Hermanus Abraham Simonsz, and Francis Abraham Simonsz, clerks, as witnesses.

The minute of this act is in form signed, and put on stamp paper of 12 styvers.

Was signed N. BERGEN V. D. GRYP, Notary.

This day, the 15th October, 1789, are heard by us, Gose Theodore Vermeer, and Jacobus Martinus Balze, Members in the Honourable Court of Eschevans Commissaries, being qualified thereto by that court, assisted by the sworn clerk, Johannis Lohr, all the above attestants named in this act, and under translation of the sworn translator in the English language, Louis Wybrand Van Schellebeck, on the repetition of this their deposition, in which they declare to persist, with demand only, that for more elucidation, the following changes may be made in it.

That the affair has happened in the vicinity of the Friendly Islands, near the island of Tofoa.

That the whole of the ship's company, at the time of the Mutiny, consisted of forty-four persons, of which twenty-five have mutinied.

That, after they were overpowered, they heard the mutineers say, "We shall in a short time return to the Society Islands:"* and that the attestants, by homeward-bound, mean England.

On which, to prove the veracity of this their deposition, they give their oath, in the Protestant form.

Further is, by us Commissaries, in our qualifications, and on request of the Requirant, resolved of this act to give an account *in forma dupla;* of the same tenor and date, and both signed by the deposants, and authenticated by our common signature.

	John Fryer,
(Signed)	*T. D. Ledward,*
G. T. VERMEER,	*Wm. Cole,*
J. BALZEE.	*Wm. Peckover,*
	Wm. Elphinstone,
	Thos. Hayward,
	John Hallet,
	John Samuel,
	Rob. Tinkler,
	Peter Linkleter, x his mark.
	L. Lebogue, + his mark.
	George Simpson,
	John Smith, + his mark.
	Robt. Lamb.

---

*This fact, and the huzzaing mentioned in the preceding page, are denied by Mr. Edward Christian in a very pointed manner (see his Appendix, page 69 [page 142 in this edition]); yet he professes to have received his information from "every one of those who came in the boat," the very persons who had affirmed both circumstances on their oaths in this instrument.

Note. *By desire of the Court I was not present at these examinations. The originals are lodged in the Admiralty-office.*

NO. V.

Description of the Pirates remaining on Board his Majesty's armed Vessel, Bounty, on the 28th April, 1789. Drawn up at Timor. Copies of this List were forwarded from Batavia to Lord Cornwallis, then Governor-General of India, at Calcutta; to Governor Philips, at New South Wales; and one was left at Batavia, with the Governor-General of the Dutch Possessions in India.

Fletcher Christian, master's mate, aged 24 years, five feet nine inches high, blackish, or very dark brown complexion, dark brown hair, strong made; a star tatowed on his left breast, tatowed on his backside; his knees stand a little out, and he may be called rather bow legged. He is subject to violent perspirations, and particularly in his hands, so that he soils any thing he handles.

George Stewart, midshipman, aged 23 years, five feet seven inches high, good complexion, dark hair, slender made, narrow chested, and long neck, small face, and black eyes; tatowed on the left breast with a star, and on the left arm with a heart and darts, is also tatowed on the backside.

Peter Heywood, midshipman, aged 17 years, five feet seven inches high, fair complexion, light brown hair, well proportioned; very much tatowed; and on the right leg is tatowed the three legs of Man, as it is upon that coin. At this time he has not done growing; and speaks with the Manks, or Isle of Man accent.

Edward Young, midshipman, aged 22 years, five feet eight inches high, dark complexion, and rather a bad look; dark brown hair, strong made, has lost several of his fore teeth, and those that remain are all rotten; a small mole on the left side of the throat, and on the right arm is tatowed a heart and dart through it, with E. Y. underneath, and the date of the year 1788 or 1789.

Charles Churchill, ship's corporal, aged 30 years, five feet ten inches high, fair complexion, short light brown hair, top of the head bald, strong made; the fore-finger of his left hand crooked, and his hand shews the marks of a severe scald; tatowed in several places of his body, legs, and arms.

James Morrison, boatswain's mate, aged 28 years, five feet eight inches high, sallow complexion, long black hair, slender made; has lost the use of the upper joint of the fore-finger of the right hand; tatowed with a star under his left breast, and a garter round his left leg, with the motto of *Honi soit qui mal y pense;* and has been wounded in one of his arms with a musket ball.

John Mills, gunner's mate, aged 40 years, five feet ten inches high, fair complexion, light brown hair, strong made, and raw boned; a scar in his right arm-pit, occasioned by an abscess.

John Millward, seaman, aged 22 years, five feet five inches high, brown complexion, dark hair, strong made; very much tatowed in different parts of the body, and under the pit of the stomach, with a taoomy of Otaheite.

Matthew Thompson, seaman, aged 40 years, five feet eight inches high, very dark complexion, short black hair, slender made, and has lost the joint of the great toe of his right foot; and is tatowed in several places of his body.

William Mickoy, seaman, aged 25 years, five feet six inches high, fair complexion, light brown hair, strong made; a scar where he has been stabbed in the belly, and a small scar under his chin; is tatowed in different parts of his body.

Matthew Quintal, seaman, aged 21 years, five feet five inches high, fair complexion, light brown hair, strong made; very much tatowed on the backside, and several other places.

John Sumner, seaman, aged 24 years, five feet eight inches high, fair complexion, brown hair; a scar on the left cheek, and tatowed in several places.

Thomas Burket, seaman, aged 26 years, five feet nine inches high, fair complexion, very much pitted with the small-pox, brown hair, slender made, and very much tatowed.

Isaac Martin, seaman, aged 30 years, five feet eleven inches high, sallow complexion, short brown hair, raw boned; tatowed with a star on his left breast.

William Musprat, seaman, aged 30 years, five feet six inches high, dark complexion, brown hair, slender made, a very strong black beard, with scars under his chin; is tatowed in several places of his body.

Henry Hilbrant, seaman, aged 25 years, five feet seven inches high, fair complexion, sandy hair, strong made; his left arm shorter than the other, having been broke; is an Hanoverian born, and speaks bad English; tatowed in several places.

Alexander Smith, seaman, aged 22 years, five feet five inches high, brown complexion, brown hair, strong made; very much pitted with the small-pox, and very much tatowed on his body, legs, arms, and feet. He has a scar on his right foot, where it has been cut with a wood axe.

John Williams, seaman, aged 25 years, five feet five inches high, dark complexion, black hair, slender made; has a scar on the back part of his head; is tatowed, and a native of Guernsey; speaks French.

Richard Skinner, seaman, aged 22 years, five feet eight inches high, fair complexion, very well made, and has scars on both ankles, and on his right shin; is very much tatowed.

Thomas Ellison, seaman, aged 17 years, five feet three inches high, fair complexion, dark hair, strong made; has got his name tatowed on his right arm, and dated October 25th, 1788.

William Brown, assistant botanist, aged 27 years, five feet eight inches high, fair complexion, dark brown hair, slender made; a remarkable scar on one of his cheeks, which contracts the eye-lid, and runs down to his throat, occasioned by the king's evil; is tatowed.

Michael Byrne, seaman, aged 28 years, five feet six inches high, fair complexion, short fair hair, slender made: is almost blind, and has the mark of an issue on the back of his neck; plays the violin.

Joseph Coleman, armourer, aged 40 years, five feet six inches high, fair complexion, grey hair, strong made; a heart tatowed on one of his arms.

Charles Norman, carpenter's mate, aged 26 years, five feet nine inches high, fair complexion, light brown hair, slender made, is pitted with the small-pox; and has a remarkable motion with his head and eyes.

Thomas McIntosh, carpenter's crew, aged 28 years, five feet six inches high, fair complexion, light brown hair, slender made; is pitted with the small-pox, and is tatowed.

The four last are deserving of mercy, being detained against their inclinations.

WM. BLIGH.

Note. *This description was made out from the recollection of the persons with me, who were best acquainted with their private marks.*

NO. VI.

Orders to Mr. J. Fryer, Master of the Bounty,
on my leaving him at Batavia.

Sir,

Whereas from a representation of the physician-general, it appears that my life is in great danger if I remain here until the fleet for Europe sails; and that only myself and two others can be taken in the packet, which departs on Friday the 16th instant;

I therefore impower you to take the command of the remaining officers and men, and order you to follow me to the Cape of Good Hope by the first ships his Excellency the Governor-general shall permit you to embark in; and as his Excellency has been pleased to order that the people may be taken care of at the convalescent hospital, about four miles from town, where is a good air and the best of treatment; you are hereby required to see that every one remains there.

You are not to permit any of those who remain in town, to be wandering about between the hours of nine in the morning and four in the afternoon.

You are, upon embarkation, or at a proper time, to get a knowledge of what charges are against his Majesty's subjects; and upon fairly and duly considering them, you are to draw bills for the amount on the Commissioners for victualling his Majesty's navy (if it cannot be done as hereafter expressed), giving them a letter of advice, at the same time, certifying that I sailed to the Cape of Good Hope before you, in a packet that could not take any more men; my health being so exceedingly impaired, as to render my existence very doubtful, and that the Governor-general could not give us all a passage in one ship.

I have agreed with the Sabandhaar, that all debts on the government account, incurred for victualling or passage money, shall be presented to him; that then on your certifying the justness of it, and another signing officer, such account shall stand over until presented to government in England—that of all such accounts you are to secure copies, and to send them, by different opportunities, to me in England, signed as beforementioned, to the care of Messrs. Marsh and Creed, agents, Norfolk-street, Strand. You are, for further security, to send one to your agent.

That before the departure of the people, you are to allow each seaman one month's pay to buy warm clothing to pass the Cape of Good Hope with, and you may also give the officers one month's pay for the same use, except yourself and Doctor.

I shall leave with you the money I received on the sale of the schooner—177 ducatoons, or 295 rix dollars, for the expenditure of which you must produce regular vouchers; but you are to pay no account without consulting the Sabandhaar, that such account is at a moderate price.

The board and lodging for yourself and Doctor, you may consider to be paid at one rix dollar per day; and for the boatswain, gunner, Mr. Elphinstone, Mr. Hayward, and Mr. Hallet, one rupee per day; and the charges for the seamen in the hospital, from the 13th October, you must pay as demanded, allowing for your brother, Robert Tinkler, at the same rate, to be put into the general account.

Should it be demanded of you to pay the passage money for every individual before you sail, you are to draw bills on the Treasurer of his Majesty's navy for the amount.

Before the ships are ready for sea, you are from time to time to apply to the Sabandhaar, Mr. Englehard, who will assist you for the good of his Majesty's service; and through him, or as circumstances may point out, you are to make all necessary application to the Governor-general.

The remaining men and officers you are to take according to the ships they are put into, not separating Mr. Hayward and Mr. Hallet. The carpenter you must apply for to come with you, and is to be considered a prisoner at large in the ship.

On embarkation, you are to see that both officers and men conduct themselves with propriety and regularity.

On your arrival at the Cape of Good Hope, you are forthwith to join me; but should I not be there before the ship you sail in departs for Europe, you are to make the best of your way, in the same ship, and give an account of your transactions to the Admiralty.

While you remain here, you are to examine into the situation of the people in the hospital twice a week; and if they are not properly treated, you must represent the same to the Sabandhaar.

The carpenter having applied to me for clothes, you are to supply him with a month's pay to purchase the necessary articles he is in want of, and to see he is not ill-treated.

Given under my hand, at Batavia, 14th Oct. 1789.
To Mr. J. Fryer, Master in his   WM. BLIGH.
     Majesty's navy.

NO. VII.

HIS MAJESTY'S SHIP HECTOR, PORTSMOUTH, JULY 14, 1792.

DEAR MADAM,

As I make no doubt you have already heard of my arrival here as a prisoner, to answer for my conduct done, on the day that unfortunate Mutiny happened, which deprived Captain Bligh of his ship, and, I then feared, of life; but, thank God, it is otherwise: and I sincerely congratulate you, Madam, upon his safe, but miraculous, arrival in England; I hope, ere this, you have heard of the cause of my determination to remain in the ship; which being unknown to Captain Bligh, who, unable to conjecture the reason, did, as I have had reason to fear, (I must say naturally) conclude, or rather suspect me to have likewise been a coadjutor in that unhappy affair; but God only knows, how little I merited so unjust a suspicion (if such a suspicion ever entered his breast); but yet my thorough consciousness of not having ever merited it, makes me sometimes flatter myself that he could scarcely be so cruel; and, ere long, let me hope I shall have an equitable tribunal to plead at; before which (through God's assistance) I shall have it in my power to proclaim my innocence, and clear up my long injured character before the world. I hear he is gone out again; if so, may he have all the success he can wish.—Alas, Madam! I yesterday heard the melancholy news of the death of your best of parents; I heartily condole with you for his loss; for in him I lost the most kind friend and advocate; whose memory I shall for ever revere with the highest veneration.

I have one request to ask of you, Madam, which is, that you will be so obliging as to inquire whether Mrs. Duncan, in Little Hermitage-street, hath in her possession the clothes (which, if you remember) I left with her in 1787, and gave you an order, by which you might at any time get them from her: so that if they are still there, you will be so good as to send them down here, directing them *(for me, on board his Majesty's ship Hector, to the care of Serjeant William Clayfield, marines, Ports-mouth, or elsewhere):* but if you can hear no tidings of them or her, you will honour with a few lines your much obliged,

obedient humble servant,
P. HEYWOOD.

NO. VIII.

Extract from Mr. P. Heywood's Defence, on his Trial by a Court-Martial; held August 12th, 1792, at Portsmouth. Copied from the Minutes of the Court-Martial, lodged in the Admiralty-office. *

"Captain Bligh, in his Narrative, acknowledges, that he had left some friends on board the Bounty; and no part of my conduct could have induced him to believe that I ought not to be reckoned of the number. Indeed, from his attention to, and very kind treatment of me, personally, I should have been a monster of depravity to have betrayed him. The idea alone is sufficient to disturb a mind, where humanity and gratitude have, I hope, ever been noticed as its characteristic features."

*This part of Mr. Heywood's defence does not appear in the Minutes of the Court-Martial published, or in Mr. Edward Christian's Appendix.

NO. IX.

The following Letter, signed P. Heywood, with the Remarks, appeared in the Cumberland Packet, or Ware's Whitehaven Advertiser, November 20th, 1792, about three Months after the Court-Martial.

We have the following important Information from the most unquestionable Authority.

The late most interesting trial at Portsmouth, of the unfortunate Mutineers of the *Bounty*, will be shortly published by a gentleman of respectability, who was employed before the Court-Martial. That publication will astonish the world; and the public will then correct the erroneous opinions, which, from certain false narratives, they have long entertained; and will be enabled to distinguish between the audacious and hardened depravity of the heart, which no suffering can soften, and the desperation of an ingenuous mind, torn and agonized by unprovoked and incessant abuse and disgrace.

Though there may be certain actions, which even the torture and extremity of provocation cannot justify, yet a sudden act of frenzy, so circumstanced, is far removed, in reason and mercy, from the foul, deliberate contempt of every religious and virtuous sentiment and obligation, excited by selfish and base gratifications.*

For the honour of this county, we are happy to assure our readers, That one of its natives, FLETCHER CHRISTIAN, is not that detestable and horrid monster of wickedness, which with extreme, and perhaps unexampled, injustice and barbarity to him and his relations, he has long been represented: but a character for whom every feeling heart must now sincerely grieve and lament.

When Mr. Heywood, the midshipman, had received his Majesty's free pardon, he felt it his duty to write to Mr. Christian's brother the following letter:

---

*The great resemblance between the last page of Mr. Edward Christian's Appendix and this paragraph is very remarkable, if they were written by different persons.

GREAT RUSSEL-STREET, 5 NOV. 1792.

SIR,

I am sorry to say, I have been informed you were inclined to judge too harshly of your truly unfortunate brother; and to think of him in such a manner, as I am conscious, from the knowledge I had of his most worthy disposition and character (both public and private), he merits not, in the slightest degree: therefore I think it my duty to undeceive you, and to rekindle the flame of brotherly love (or *pity* now) towards him, which I fear the false reports of slander, and vile suspicion, may have nearly extinguished.

Excuse my freedom, Sir:—If it would not be disagreeable to you, I will do myself the pleasure of waiting upon you, and endeavour to prove, that your brother was not that vile wretch, void of all gratitude, which the world had the unkindness to think him: but, on the contrary, a most worthy character; ruined only by having the misfortune, if it can be so called, of being a young man of strict honour, and adorned with every virtue; and beloved by all (except one, whose ill report is his greatest praise) who had the pleasure of his acquaintance.

I am, Sir, with esteem,
          Your most obedient humble servant,

P. HEYWOOD.

This character, every officer and seaman, except one, on board the Bounty, who has yet arrived in England, now unites in bestowing upon him. The mystery of this transaction will soon be unravelled, and then the shame and infamy of it will be distributed, in the just proportions in which they are, and have been, deserved.

NO. X.

Taken from the Times, July 16th, 1794

TO THE CONDUCTOR OF THE TIMES.

SIR,

A publication has lately made its appearance, intitled, "Minutes of the Proceedings of the Court-Martial, held at Portsmouth, August 12, 1792, on Ten Persons charged with Mutiny on Board his Majesty's Ship Bounty; with an Appendix, containing a full Account of the real Causes and Circumstances of that unhappy Transaction, the most material of which have hitherto been withheld from the Public; written by *Edward Christian.*" The obvious tendency of which is to palliate the conduct of Fletcher Christian, his brother, and ultimately to asperse the character of Captain Bligh. As if any thing could be advanced in extenuation of a crime, at the bare recital of which humanity shudders; a crime, marked by such circumstances as to be unexampled in the annals of nautical history. This publication, Mr. Editor, is disgraced by gross misrepresentations, and low malevolence, of which innumerable instances could be adduced, were long details admissible in a newspaper. The shafts of envy are ever levelled against conspicuous merit, but they recoil with redoubled force on the impotent adversary. Captain Bligh's general conduct during the late expedition, which was crowned with the most ample success, his affability to his officers, and humane attention to his men, gained him their high esteem and admiration, and must eventually dissipate any unfavourable opinion, hastily adopted in his absence. I trust that this imbecile and highly illiberal attack, directed by the brother of the Arch-mutineer, will be received by the world with that indignation and contempt it so justly deserves.

I remain, Sir, your humble servant,
ED. HARWOOD,
Late Surgeon of his Majesty's ship Providence,
Captain Bligh.

NO. XI.

Affidavit of Joseph Coleman.

I Joseph Coleman, late belonging to his Majesty's armed vessel Bounty, William Bligh, Esq. Commander, voluntarily do make oath,

That Mr. Edward Christian sent for me, and asked me concerning the Mutiny in the Bounty, and about Captain Bligh; and I said, I knew nothing of him, but that he was a very good man to me.

I told Mr. Christian, that I never heard Captain Bligh say, he would make his officers jump over board, and eat grass like cows.

I told him, that after the ship was taken, I heard the Mutineers say, he swore and damned them; but not that I heard him do it myself. I said, I could never agree with the Mutineers.

I never saw Captain Bligh shake his hand in Christian's face; or heard him damn him for not firing at the Indians.

I do not remember any thing about the heap of cocoa-nuts being taken away, but by hearsay from the Mutineers, after the ship was taken, and we came home.

I never heard, or told Mr. Edward Christian, about his brother's expression, that "he had been in hell for weeks past with you."

I never knew or heard that Captain Bligh and Fletcher Christian had any words at the Cape, or before the Mutiny.

I never told, or heard, of Captain Bligh telling the chiefs at Otaheite, that Christian was a towtow (or servant).

I never knew any thing of Christian intending to make a raft, to quit the ship.

I never told Mr. Christian, that Stewart clapped his hands, and said, it was the happiest day of his life.

I remember Christian having a girl, and of her going with him to the island Tobooy, and lived with him.

I said, I never could be easy with the Mutineers, because they knew I was kept against my will.—Morrison threatened to blow my brains out.

I remember that Musprat, Churchill, and Millward, deserted with the cutter and arms, while at Otaheite, and that they said many others intended to remain among the islands.

I remember that one of our cables was almost cut through at Otaheite, and that afterwards the Captain had always a centinel on the bowsprit.

I know the Captain never suffered any man to hurt the Indians, or insult them.

I know we were at short allowance of bread, and that we were at two-thirds allowance of that article; but I remember, that by the consent of every one, we had only grog every other day while at Otaheite, and that was, that we might not be in want in case we could not get through Endeavour Straits, and we did not want it so much at Otaheite, because we had plenty of cocoa-nut milk.

I never said more to Mr. Christian, than that his brother behaved

very well to me after the Mutiny, and that I knew no harm of him before the Mutiny.

I never said, that Christian, or Stewart, was equal to Captain Bligh
in abilities, I never thought of such a thing.

his
JOSEPH x COLEMAN,
mark.

Sworn before me, at the Public
Office in Great Marlborough-
street, this 31st day of July, 1794.   (A copy.)
      JOHN SCOTT.

NO. XII.

John Smith's Affidavit.

I John Smith late belonging to his Majesty's armed vessel the Bounty,
William Bligh, Esq. Commander, maketh oath, that Mr. Edward
Christian sent for me, and asked me how his brother (who was the
Mutineer in the Bounty) had behaved in the ship.

I said his brother was well liked in the ship, as far as I knew, by
the people.

I never knew Christian and Captain Bligh have any words particular.

On the day before the mutiny happened, I was sent by the
Captain to ask Christian to dine with him; but he said, I am so ill I
cannot wait on the Captain: and I was sent again in the evening to ask
Christian to supper, and he said he was so ill that he could not come.

When in working the ship, and things had been neglected to have
been done at other times that the Captain had ordered, I have known
the Captain to be angry and damn the people, as is common; but the
Captain immediately afterwards always behaved to the people as if
nothing had happened.

I never heard the Captain damn the officers, and call them
names, and threaten to make them jump over board, kill half of
them, and make them eat grass like cows. I never heard any such a
thing.

I never saw the Captain shake his hand in Christian's face, and I never heard of it even, that he did; or in any of their faces.

I never heard that the Captain damned Christian for not firing at the Indians for stealing an adz.

I did not hear Christian say to the Captain, I am in hell, I am in hell, because I was below; but I never understood but that he did say so. The Captain said so in the boat, and had it in his Narrative, which I never heard any one deny.

I never told Mr. Edward Christian any thing about the cocoa-nuts, or did I know any thing about it, any more than that the Captain found fault at a heap of cocoa-nuts being taken away; and I never knew or heard that such a thing could be the cause of the Mutiny.

I never knew or heard of any words that the Captain had with Christian at the Cape of Good Hope; but I always understood he was on good terms with the Captain, and remember he used to dine with him every third day, and did so until the day of the Mutiny, and frequently supped with the Captain besides.

I never heard, or told Mr. Edward Christian, that Captain Bligh told the people of Otaheite, that his brother was a towtow (or servant), or ever heard of such a thing.

I never knew any thing that Christian intended to make a raft, or ever heard of it until the Mutineers arrived in the Pandora, and I never told Mr. Edward Christian about it.

I never told Mr. Edward Christian that his brother never kept a girl; for I remember he had a girl, and she was called Tittriano's girl, which was the name Christian went by.

I never told Mr. Edward Christian that his brother, or Stewart, was equal to Captain Bligh in abilities, nobody could say such a thing as that—I always saw Captain Bligh instructing him.

I never said to Mr. Edward Christian any thing about his brother's abilities, or any thing respecting his qualifications, or the praises which he, in his Appendix, says were repeated by one and the other.

I remember that Christian always had leave to have grog out of Captain Bligh's case whenever he wanted it; and I always gave it him, and Mr. Nelson the gardener, when they chose to ask for it.

I know that we were never at short allowance of provisions except bread, and that was one-third short; but I remember that at Otaheite, all hands, by their own consent, had their grog but every other day, on account of the danger of going through Endeavour Straits, where we might lose our passage; and the want of grog at Otaheite we did not mind, because we had plenty of fine cocoa-nut milk, and the finest fresh pork, bread-fruit, and other things of the country.

Mr. Edward Christian asked me how Captain Bligh was liked in the Providence, and if nothing had happened; and I told him nothing had happened, and all was well, and the Captain very much liked.

I know the Captain was always very kind to the Indians, and would not suffer any man to hurt or insult them.

This is all that I said to Mr. Christian, the brother of Christian the Mutineer on board the Bounty; and Mr. Christian had no right to make use of my name in the manner he has done in his late publication.

I know that three of the Mutineers, Musprat, Churchill, and Millward, while at Otaheite, run away with the cutter and arms.

I remember our cable being cut nearly through at Otaheite, in a stormy night, and that Captain Bligh afterwards ordered a centinel on the bowsprit.

Sworn before me at Guildhall, London,   JOHN SMITH.
    this 1st August, 1794.
        WATKIN LEWES.
                (A Copy.)

NO. XIII.

Lawrence Lebogue's Affidavit.

I Lawrence Lebogue, late sail-maker on board his Majesty's armed vessel Bounty, William Bligh, Esq. Commander, do voluntarily make oath,

That I was sent for by Mr. Edward Christian to a public-house, and asked whether Captain Bligh did flog his people, and why he kept them at short allowance; but the most of his questions were about Captain Bligh's behaviour to the officers of the Providence, and how he behaved to them, and if I thought they liked him.

I told him that Captain Bligh made no distinction, every officer was obliged to do his duty, and he showed no more favour to one man than another. I was sure every person in the Providence would speak well of Captain Bligh—he was a father to every person.

I said I knew Captain Bligh was a very great friend to Christian the Mutineer; he was always permitted to use the Captain's cabin, where I have seen the Captain teaching him navigation and drawing. He was permitted to use the Captain's liquor when he wanted it, and I have many times gone down at night to get him grog out of the Captain's case.

I have heard the Captain damn the people, like many other captains; but he was never angry with a man the next minute; and I never heard of their disliking him.

I never heard of the Captain abusing his officers; nor ever said to Mr. Edward Christian, that he threatened to make them jump over board; or eat grass like cows; or shake his hand in their faces.

I said, Captain Bligh was not a person fond of flogging his men; and some of them deserved hanging, who had only a dozen.

I said we were never at short allowance but in bread, and that we were at two-thirds, because we did not know how long it would be before we got a supply, as we had to go through a terrible passage near New Guinea. And for fear of being in want of spirits, the ship's company had agreed, while at Otaheite, to have their grog but every other day, because they had plenty of fine cocoa-nut milk, and all they cared about.

I remember that a heap of cocoa-nuts, which the Captain had ordered to be saved as a rarity until we got to sea, for a day or two, when we should enjoy them, was taken away; and that the Captain told the officers they had neglected their duty, and disobeyed his orders; and that all the cocoa-nuts, on that account, were brought upon deck; and the matter ended with their being divided.

I never heard nor told Mr. Edward Christian any thing about—I have been in hell, which he speaks of.

I never knew, or heard, that Christian was ever found fault with by Captain Bligh at the Cape of Good Hope; and I always thought they were very good friends, until the Mutiny.

I remember very well, that the Captain came on deck one night and found fault with Christian, because in a squall he had not taken care of the sails. It was after we left Whytootackee.*

I never knew that Christian intended to go away on a raft; or could he have made one without its being known by every person.

*Mr. Edward Christian declares no one ever knew of this circumstance.

I remember Christian had a girl, who was always with him.

I never heard any thing at Otaheite that Captain Bligh had told the chiefs, Christian was a towtow; I know the chiefs did not think so of any of the officers.

I never knew Captain Bligh find fault with Christian for not firing at the Indians at Anamoka.

I was the only person mentioned, who sailed with Captain Bligh to the West Indies, and to the South Sea, as Christian did; and I never told Mr. Edward Christian that his brother could not have borne Captain Bligh's conduct to him much longer, because I knew Captain Bligh was always a friend to Christian, when he sailed with him to the West Indies, as well as afterwards.

I know that three of the Mutineers deserted with one of the boats and an arm chest with arms at Otaheite, because they wished to stay among the islands. Musprat, Churchill, and Millward were the three, and they said many others intended to do it.

I remember one of our cables being almost cut through in a dark stormy night, which we thought was to let the ship go on shore; and that after that, the Captain ordered a centinel on the bowsprit. This was at Otaheite.

Mr. Christian asked me if I thought Captain Bligh could hurt his brother, if he ever came home. I said Captain Bligh had such a forgiving temper, that I did not think he would, unless the law of his country would hurt him. I said Captain Bligh was the best friend Christian ever had.

I remember that Christian was drinking with the carpenter, William Purcell, at 12 o'clock at night, although Christian was to be up at four o'clock in the morning to keep his watch, and that when the Mutiny broke out that morning, I saw a musket at Purcell, the carpenter's cabin door.

Sworn to the truth of the   The mark of
foregoing Narrative 2d day   x
August, 1794, at Guildhall, London   LAWRENCE LEBOGUE.
           WATKIN LEWES.

NO. XIV.

From Lieutenant John Hallet to Captain Bligh.

DEAR SIR,

I have just read a publication, by Mr. Edward Christian, respecting the Mutiny on board the Bounty, and have made a few remarks thereon, which I have transmitted to you, and beg that you will make any use of them you please.

I am, dear Sir,
Your obedient humble servant,
JOHN HALLET, Junior.

Having been long confined by a severe illness, and having consequently not mixed with the world since my arrival, in February last, from Jamaica; it was but lately that the Minutes of the Court-Martial, held in 1792, on Ten Persons charged with Mutiny on board the Bounty; together with an Appendix to those Minutes, published by Mr. Edward Christian, reached my hands. As I was on board the Bounty at the time of the Mutiny, and as my name is not wholly unimplicated in the Appendix, I cannot but consider myself bound, in justice to my own character, as well as to that of Captain Bligh, to advance my mite towards the confutation of the very malevolent assertions and insinuations conveyed to the public through the medium of that Appendix. I will by no means affirm, that I never heard Captain Bligh express himself in warm or hasty language, when the conduct of his officers or people has displeased him; but every seafaring gentleman must be convinced, that situations frequently occur in a ship when the most mild officer will be driven, by the circumstances of the moment, to utter expressions which the strict standard of politeness will not warrant: and I can safely assert, that I never remember to have heard Captain Bligh make use of such illiberal epithets and menaces as the Appendix attributes to him. I must likewise declare, that I always considered Captain Bligh as being a friend to Christian; and I have frequently heard Fletcher Christian assert that he had conducted himself as such. I remember a complaint of some cocoa-nuts having been stolen, but I did not hear that Captain Bligh accused any individual of the theft.

As to the insinuation of the people being at short allowance of provisions, I remember being at two-thirds allowance of bread; but at and from Otaheite, there was full allowance, and fresh pork was thrown over board, because it could not be eaten while it was good; and during our stay there, we were at half allowance of grog. Whether the Mutiny was preconcerted or not, is a question which can be solved only by those who were concerned in it; because any officer or man apprized of the circumstances, and not being a party in it, must have been compelled, if not by his duty, at least by the desire of self-preservation, to have counteracted the plot by his information and exertions.

Much stress is laid on the most part having gone voluntarily into the boat; in answer to which, I would only ask any person, endued with a proper sense of honour, if he would not rather commit himself to the evident danger of the boat, than incur the risk of an ignominious death, or the stigma of being arraigned as a pirate?

The Appendix charges Mr. Hayward and myself with the imputation of being asleep in our watch. With regard to myself, I deny the accusation; and with regard to Mr. Hayward (who is now absent on service), I have reason to believe it is equally false, as I had conversed with him a few minutes before. Besides what immediately belonged to Captain Bligh, every person in the boat had some useful articles; and many general necessaries were included.

I am likewise accused of uttering some dissatisfaction to Captain Bligh in the boat, to which Mr. Edward Christian seems desirous of attaching much criminality. I can only say, that I do not remember to have used such words imputed to me; and even if I had uttered them, they are such as would bear an interpretation diametrically opposite to that put upon them. And it is worthy of observation, that by the kind addition of a note, my whole offence is concentered in the innocent word *resource*.

As to Mr. Christian's ability as an artist, or a seaman, I never considered them to bear any competition with those of Captain Bligh: and he certainly could not be called a fine scholar; as he did not appear to have received any portion of classical education, and was ignorant of all but his native language.

My situation in the Bounty, together with a proper regard to truth, and the introduction of my name in the Appendix, has compelled me to advance so much, uninfluenced by any personal animosity to Mr. Fletcher Christian, whose memory I wish had been quietly committed to oblivion; as I am convinced that the stain will be deeper impressed on his name, by the endeavours which his friends have exerted in vindication of his character.

JOHN HALLET, Junior.

Manchester Buildings,
Aug. 1st, 1794.

NO. XV.

*Letter from Mr. Edward Lamb, Commander of the Adventure,
in the Jamaica Trade, to Captain Bligh.*

ST. GEORGE'S PLACE, ST. GEORGE'S IN THE EAST, OCT. 28,
1794.

DEAR SIR,

Upon my arrival from Jamaica, I saw a pamphlet, published by Mr. Edward Christian, who, in order to lessen the guilt of his brother, Mr. Fletcher Christian, wishes to make the public believe that the Mutiny on board his Majesty's ship the Bounty, proceeded from your treatment of his brother, and the other Mutineers. I was much surprised at what Mr. Edward Christian has introduced in page 78 [page 151 in this edition] in the Appendix, as he insinuates that your bad behaviour to Mr. Fletcher Christian commenced during his last voyage with you to Jamaica, in the ship Britannia, when I was chief mate, and eye witness to every thing that passed. Mr. Edward Christian must have been misinformed, and known very little either of his brother's situation, abilities, or the manner in which he conducted himself during that voyage. He mentions his being second mate with you, when, in fact, he was no officer. I recollect your putting him upon the articles as gunner, telling me, at the same time, you wished him to be thought an officer; and desired I would endeavour to make the people look upon him as such.

When we got to sea, and I saw your partiality for the young man, I gave him every advice and information in my power, though he went about every point of duty with a degree of indifference, that to me was truly unpleasant; but you were blind to his faults, and had him to dine and sup every other day in the cabin, and treated him like a brother, in giving him every information. In the Appendix it is said, that Mr. Fletcher Christian had no attachment amongst the women at Otaheite; if that was the case, he must have been much altered since he was with you in the Britannia; he was then one of the most foolish young men I ever knew in regard to the sex. You will excuse the liberty I have taken in addressing you upon so unpleasant a subject; but I could not pass over many assertions in the Appendix, without feeling for a man, whose kind and uniform behaviour to me, through the whole voyage to Jamaica, was such as to lay me under an everlasting obligation; and I shall still think myself fortunate in having engaged with such an attentive officer, and able navigator as yourself.

I have no pique at Mr. Fletcher Christian; but finding Captain Bligh's character suffering in the opinion of the public, I think it my duty to offer my services in the vindication of it, so far as comes within my knowledge; therefore, can I render him any service, he may command me.

I remain, Sir,
Your most obliged and humble servant,

To Captain William Bligh.   EDWARD LAMB.

I submit these evidences to the judgment of the Public, without offering any comment. My only intention in this publication, is to clear my character from the effect of censures which I am conscious I have not merited: I have therefore avoided troubling the Public with more than what is necessary to that end; and have refrained from remark, lest I might have been led beyond my purpose, which I have wished to limit solely to defence.

WILLIAM BLIGH.

Dec. 3, 1794.

A

SHORT REPLY

TO

Capt. *WILLIAM BLIGH's*

ANSWER.

———

A Short Reply, &c.

IF CAPTAIN WILLIAM BLIGH'S ANSWER had been confined to endeavours to refute the imputations upon his conduct, contained in the Minutes of the Proceedings of the Court-Martial, or in the Appendix annexed to it, I should have been glad to have left him in possession of any benefit or success which those endeavours might have been attended with. But as almost all the material parts of what are called proofs are little more than insinuations that the statements, which I thought it my duty to lay before the public, have been unfairly obtained, or unfairly represented, I feel myself called upon to make a few observations in vindication of my own conduct and character. The first intimation which I received, that the dreadful mutiny on board the Bounty originated from motives, and was attended with circumstances, different from those which had been represented to the world, was in consequence of the following letter from Mr. Heywood, and which is printed in Captain Bligh's Answer, p. 16 [page 170 in this edition].

GREAT RUSSEL-STREET, 5TH NOV. 1792.

SIR,

I am sorry to say I have been informed you were inclined to judge too harshly of your truly unfortunate brother; and to think of him in such a manner as I am conscious, from the knowledge I had of his most worthy disposition and character, (both public and private,) he merits not in the slightest degree: therefore I think it my duty to undeceive you, and to rekindle the flame of brotherly love (or *pity* now) towards him, which, I fear, the false reports of slander and vile suspicion may have nearly extinguished.

Excuse my freedom, Sir:—If it would not be disagreeable to you, I will do myself the pleasure of waiting upon you; and endeavour to prove that your brother was not that vile wretch, void of all gratitude, which the world had the unkindness to think him; but, on the contrary, a most worthy character, ruined only by having the misfortune (if it can be so called) of being a young man of strict honour, and adorned with every virtue; and beloved by all (except one, whose ill report is his greatest praise) who had the pleasure of his acquaintance.

I am, SIR, with esteem,

Your most obedient humble servant,

P. HEYWOOD.

Having had an interview with Mr. Heywood, I immediately communicated the information I had received to a confidential friend of mine, Mr. Romilly, a Barrister of Lincoln's Inn; and, by his advice, I afterwards waited upon a gentleman, then high in the profession of the law, who has since been advanced to the Bench, and who now presides in one of the Courts in Westminster-hall. The object of that visit was to inquire of him what credit was due to the account I had heard, as it had been mentioned in the newspapers that he was present at the trial. His Lordship received me with that politeness and benevolence which have ever distinguished his character. It might be thought indelicate in me to relate any conversation that passed between his Lordship and me; and I trust he will have the goodness to forgive the liberty I have taken in referring to this interview with his Lordship, as a strong proof of the caution with which I wished to proceed in this inquiry. Although it is true that I received the first intimation of the circumstances related in the Appendix from Mr. Heywood, yet, before I saw that gentleman, Mr. Fryer (the master of the Bounty) had communicated the same circumstances to Mr. Joseph Christian of the Strand, No. 10, which were made known to me soon after the conversation I had with Mr. Heywood. He is a distant relation of mine; his name had induced Mr. Fryer to call upon him, and give him the information. From that time I was determined to investigate the subject fully; and I had the precaution upon every occasion, (except when I called upon Mr. Hayward of Hackney,) when I expected to see any of the people of the Bounty, to have some gentlemen in company with me. By the favour of these gentlemen I have published their names and places of residence, that any person interested in the subject might have an opportunity of making inquiries of them, whether the information I received in their company has or has not been fairly represented by me.

It is unnecessary for me to declare that the list is filled with the names of gentlemen, who may be justly said to be the most honourable characters in society; and I may be truly proud in calling them my friends. If I could have entertained a thought of misrepresenting the testimony, to the prejudice of Captain Bligh, I ought to be considered the most infamous of mankind; and if in fact I have misrepresented it, I must have forfeited the esteem of the most valuable part of my acquaintance, and must have incurred a punishment almost equivalent to banishment from society. But I still hope that I shall continue, whilst I live, to enjoy their good opinion and their friendship. Captain Bligh has published Mr. Heywood's letter as one of his proofs, p. 16 [page 170 in this edition]. I presume, with intent to prove the inconsistency between that letter and a passage taken from Mr. Heywood's defence, in which he speaks strongly of Captain Bligh's attention and kind treatment to him personally, p. 15 [page 168 in this edition]. A note is subjoined, that "this part of Mr. Heywood's defence does not appear in the Minutes of the Court-Martial published, or in Mr. Edward Christian's Appendix." As far as this is an insinuation of a wilful omission on my part, I need only answer that Mr. Barney has declared, in his prefatory letter, that his minutes did not extend beyond the evidence for the prosecution. This passage was therefore not contained in those minutes, nor was it in any copy which I could command. I anxiously solicited (as all my friends know) another gentleman to publish, or to permit me to publish, his copy of the minutes, which contained the several defences of the prisoners. Being unable to prevail upon him, I waited upon one of the Lords of the Admiralty to request the copy transmitted to the Board. He politely informed me that it could not be granted to any individual in a private situation. I shall therefore, I trust, stand acquitted of any imputation of having industriously suppressed this testimonial in Captain Bligh's favour. It may be also observed that Mr. Heywood's letter complains of no ill treatment received by him personally from Captain Bligh, and that the defence was drawn up by his counsel when he was tried for his life, charged with an act which can admit of no justification; and I have the authority of one of his counsel to declare that his defence was left entirely to their discretion. Captain Bligh has inserted among his proofs, p. 18 [pages 170–171 in this edition], a letter signed by Ed. Harwood, late surgeon of his Majesty's ship Providence. This letter is a certificate by the surgeon, and by the surgeon only, of Captain Bligh's good conduct in the Providence; but, as Mr. Harwood never belonged to the Bounty, it is difficult to say how it can be considered as a proof of any circumstance which ever occurred on board that ship. Indeed, if abuse and scurrility can be regarded as evidence, it is true that no proof can be stronger. When it was published in the newspaper the Times, I was advised to treat it with silent contempt; and I should have thought myself degraded in the opinion of every man of sense and honour if I had condescended to have taken notice of so illiberal and indecent a letter. With regard to the affidavits made by Joseph Coleman, who is a pensioner in Chelsea Hospital, and by John Smith, who was Captain Bligh's servant, and I am told is now living in his house, I have not much to object to them. Most of the paragraphs begin with "I never told Mr. Ed. Christian, &c." These two persons might easily be induced, without much (or any) violence to their consciences, to swear thus in negatives. Coleman has the appearance of a decent and honest man, but he is old and dull; and I never saw him but in the company of other persons belonging to the Bounty, who took the lead in conversation; but to their information he certainly in every instance assented by his silence, or without making any contradiction. The only observation I ever remember him to have made was, that "Mr. Christian was a fine young man, or a fine young officer"; and throughout the whole of the Appendix there is not a single word used by me as referable to his evidence. John Smith, the Captain's servant, I never saw but once: he came of his own accord to my chambers. He spoke of Mr. Christian in the highest terms of praise and affection; and the sentence in p. 76 [page 149 in this edition] in the Appendix was spoken by him, viz. "Mr. Christian was always good-natured; I never heard him say Damn you to any man on board the ship." He said, that "during the mutiny he ran backward and forward to put all the Captain's things on board the launch; that he was not ordered to leave the ship, but that he went of his own accord, thinking it his duty to follow his master: That there was no huzzaing on board."

Being then asked what could be the cause of the mutiny, and if there had been any previous misunderstanding between Christian and the Captain; he said he could not speak to that, as his duty as cook and Captain's servant confined him below, and he could not say what might have passed upon deck. I told him he spoke like an honest man, and that I should not trouble him with any more questions. It was very fortunate that Mr. Gilpin in the Strand, No. 432, happened to be in my chambers at the time. Mr. Gilpin had an opportunity of seeing several more persons belonging to the Bounty. He can bear witness that this man's information was perfectly consistent, as far as it went, with the account which he heard from the others. Mr. Gilpin, and every gentleman whose name I have used, I am confident will always do me the justice to declare, that what they have heard I have represented fairly, and without the slightest exaggeration. I may add too, that they have all a numerous and honourable acquaintance, who must be perfectly convinced that they would each of them reprobate, with an honest indignation, an attempt to give authenticity by their names to a statement which was inconsistent with their notions of the purest honour and the strictest justice; and which at the same time must necessarily wound the feelings or lessen the reputation of any individual.

Though I have said I have little objection to make to the two first affidavits, yet I am obliged to declare that the third, which is made by Lawrence Lebogue, is the most wicked and perjured affidavit that ever was sworn before a magistrate, or published to the world; and it is perhaps a defect in the law that these voluntary affidavits are permitted to be made; or that, when they are false, the authors of them are subject to no punishment. For if Lawrence Lebogue had made the same affidavit in a court of justice, he would most probably, upon the united evidence of three gentlemen, have been convicted of the grossest and foulest perjury. John Atkinson, Esq. Somerset Herald, and James Losh, Esq. Barrister of the Temple, went with me to dine at the Crown and Scepter at Greenwich. After dinner we sent to the Hospital for Joseph Coleman, Michael Byrne, and Lawrence Lebogue, three of the pensioners, who had belonged to the Bounty. Coleman and Byrne were at home, and came immediately; Lebogue could not then be found. After much conversation with Coleman and Byrne, in which Byrne took the lead, Lebogue came into the room; and without any hesitation, (at which we were much surprised, as he had sailed a second time with Captain Bligh in the Providence,) he gave a full detail, in clear and strong language, of all the material circumstances recited in the Appendix, and which we had just before heard from Byrne. Mr. Atkinson and Mr. Losh have given me permission to publish the following certificate from them:

We were present with Mr. Edward Christian at the Crown and Scepter at Greenwich, and had much conversation with Michael Byrne, Joseph Coleman, and Lawrence Lebogue, and upon another day a long conversation with Mr. Peckover, respecting the unfortunate mutiny on board the Bounty; in which conversations we observed no contradiction or inconsistency: and we hereby declare, that we think that the result of these conversations is faithfully and without exaggeration represented by Mr. Edward Christian, in the Appendix to the Minutes of the Court Martial: and we also declare, that we were much astonished at reading Lebogue's affidavit in Captain Bligh's Answer; as we believe that all the material paragraphs in that affidavit respecting the conversation we had with him at Greenwich are directly the reverse of the truth; and this we should be ready to make oath of, if it were necessary. We also declare, that Mr. Peckover asserted in our company that he was upon shore with Mr. Christian all the time the ship was at Otaheite, and that Mr. Christian had no favourite or particular connection among the women.

JOHN ATKINSON, Heralds' College.
JAMES LOSH, Temple.

Some of the questions, indeed, attributed to me in that affidavit, must have proceeded from such extreme weakness and folly, that I cannot but flatter myself that those who know me will think that they carry with them internal evidence of misrepresentation. Though this man has not only retracted all that he told us, but has had the audacity to swear to the direct contrary, I shall appeal to every candid reader which are most to be credited—his simple declarations made without any solicitation, and which corresponded with the accounts given by several others at different times; or an affidavit made to serve his captain, directly the reverse of what he himself declared, and an affidavit for which in this world he is subject to no punishment whatever.

As to Mr. Hallet's letter to Captain Bligh, I have only to observe upon it, that Mr. Hallet was not in England before the Appendix was published, and this letter is now published after his death. If I had had an opportunity of seeing Mr. Hallet, I certainly should have thought myself much obliged to him if he would have corrected any misrepresentation which I had received from others. But he certainly is mistaken when he thinks so unkindly of me as to suppose I meant any *malevolent* or *false accusations* against him.

Nor would it, I conceive, have been a very heinous offence, if what I had been told was true, that two young men, *viz.* himself and Mr. Hayward, then about 15 or 16 years of age, had fallen asleep in their watch after four o'clock in the morning: and if the mutiny had not been preconcerted, (and Mr. Hallet himself admits there was no proof that it was so,) and if these two young gentlemen were not asleep, it will appear to have been more sudden in its commencement, as it must have been proposed and resolved upon whilst they were upon deck, but out of hearing. I am sorry that Mr. Hallet has ventured to assert that "Christian did not appear to have received any portion of classical learning, and was ignorant of all but his mother tongue." It is very probable that a young midshipman may be unacquainted with the extent of the learning of any other officer on board; but Mr. Hallet's assertion that Christian was absolutely ignorant has been made either with too little caution or too much zeal. Christian was educated by the Reverend Mr. Scott, at St. Bees school in Cumberland, where the young men of the best families in that country receive their education, and from which many are sent to the universities; and I am confident that Mr. Scott, his school-fellows, and all who knew him well, will testify that "Christian was an excellent scholar, and possessed extraordinary abilities." This is a point which a great number of gentlemen in the most respectable situations in life must be acquainted with; and I shall leave it to them to determine, whether Mr. Hallet or I, in this instance, be most deserving of credit. I was sorry also to see in the letter written by Mr. Lamb, who had once been a mate to Captain Bligh in the merchant's service, an attempt to degrade Christian's character, by stating, "that he went about every point of duty with a degree of indifference, that to him (Mr. Lamb) was truly unpleasant." This representation is certainly different from the character which Captain Bligh himself has always given of Christian; it is contrary to the opinion that the gallant Capt. Courtenay had entertained of him, who had immediately before this given him the charge of a watch in the Eurydice throughout the voyage from the East Indies; and it cannot be reconciled with Christian's conduct, which Major Taubman, of the Nunnery in the Isle of Man, can testify, *viz.* that, from his recommendation of Captain Bligh as a navigator, Christian voluntarily preferred sailing with Captain Bligh as a common man in a West India ship, till there was a vacancy among the officers, to the immediate appointment to the rank of a mate in another ship.

Since the publication of the Appendix I have only had an opportunity of seeing two persons belonging to the Bounty—Mr. Peckover, the gunner, who lives at No. 13, Gun-alley, Wapping; and Mr. Purcell, the carpenter, who has since sailed to the West Indies. Mr. Purcell declared, in the hearing of James Losh, Esq. of the Temple, that he had read the Appendix, and that every part of it within his knowledge was correctly stated: and Mr. Peckover also declared once before John France, Esq. of the Temple, and at another time before John Caley, Esq. of the Augmentation-office, that he had read the Appendix, and that every part of it within his knowledge was correctly stated; except that he thought too much praise had been bestowed upon Mr. Stewart, though he thought highly of him before the mutiny as a deserving officer. Mr. Peckover lives constantly in London, and has the appearance of a cautious, discreet man, and a steady, manly officer; yet no application has been made to him by Captain Bligh respecting the publications. Lebogue begins his affidavit by stating that I sent for him to a public house; from which the reader would be induced to infer, that I had attempted to seduce these sailors in a corner of a common alehouse falsely to accuse their captain: but as I have already observed, I not only had the precaution to have some gentleman of honour and character in my company, but I also requested several gentlemen to examine the witnesses when I was not present. Mr. Purcell having accidentally mentioned that he was recommended to the Bounty by Sir Joseph Banks, and expressing a wish to call upon him, I immediately wrote a note to introduce him to Sir Joseph Banks, and to request Sir Joseph to examine him respecting the causes and circumstances of the mutiny. Having never had an opportunity of seeing Mackintosh (the carpenter's mate) but once, and for a short time, I desired Mr. Fearon, a Barrister, resident at Newcastle, to inquire for him at Shields, where his mother lived, and to examine him fully upon the subject. Mr. Fearon went over to Shields with the Reverend Mr. How, of Workington, for that purpose. At the first, Mackintosh was very unwilling to give them any information, saying, that "he had like to have got into trouble for what he had told Mr. Christian in London": but I am authorized to say by these gentlemen, that upon further conversation he confirmed every material circumstance related in the Appendix. Though it may be suspected that I might have an interest or a wish to obtain improper evidence in an improper manner from the witnesses, yet all the gentlemen I have named could only be actuated in their conduct by the purest regard for truth and justice.

Captain Bligh complains that I have not appropriated to each individual the precise and actual information I received from him. If I had requested them to give it in the manner of depositions, they probably would have been deterred from telling any thing, as Mackintosh declared he had been threatened for what he had mentioned. I made the first inquiries only for my own satisfaction, as I was assured by another gentleman that he would publish the trial with the information which he had collected; and it was only when he had declined to proceed in it that I was obliged to undertake the painful task myself. But if what I have ventured to communicate to the world in the Appendix is false, it is the grossest libel that ever was published; for which every Judge would be compelled to declare that no punishment could be too severe, or no damages too excessive. Many gentlemen, besides myself, suppose, that if any answer could be given, it would be attempted in a court of justice by some judicial proceeding. Indeed the bookseller would not have dared to have sold the Appendix if I had not undertaken to stand between him and danger, and to indemnify him as far as was in my power from the consequences of legal prosecutions. It would scarcely then have been prudent to have disclosed the testimony of each witness, by which I was to defend so hazardous a publication; some of whom, as seafaring men, might easily have been sent into a distant part of the world, and others might perhaps have been induced, like Lebogue, to reverse every thing that they had said. But I assert again, and I solemnly appeal to all the gentlemen whose names I have mentioned, that in the accounts we received there was no material (if any) contradiction or inconsistency.

The statement in the Appendix has been insidiously called a defence and vindication. God forbid that any connection or consideration should ever induce me to vindicate the crime of mutiny! But though it is a crime which will admit of no defence, yet with respect to its motives and circumstances it is capable of great exaggeration.

I bear no malice to Captain Bligh; and I trust neither love nor fear will ever impel me to shrink from that which I conceive I owe to myself and to society. I solicit no favour; I supplicate no mercy. It is to austere and rigorous justice I have made the appeal, which will protect from unmerited obloquy the object of its severest vengeance. Great crimes demand great examples. I will not under any circumstances deprecate, or endeavour to intercept, the stroke of justice. Mine has been a painful duty to discharge; I am happy in knowing that I have discharged it with the approbation of some wise and good men; but I am still happier in feeling that I have discharged it with the approbation of my own heart and conscience.

EDWARD CHRISTIAN.

APPENDIXES

APPENDIX A: BLIGH'S ORDERS AND A DESCRIPTION
OF THE BREADFRUIT.

*The following passages are excerpted from the full account Bligh
published as* A Voyage to the South Sea Undertaken by Command
of His Majesty for the Purpose of Conveying the Bread-Fruit Tree
to the West Indies, in His Majesty's Ship the Bounty, Commanded
by Lieutenant William Bligh *(London: George Nicol, 1792), 5–13, 109.*

The object of all the former voyages to the South Seas, undertaken by
the command of his present majesty, has been the advancement of
science, and the increase of knowledge. This voyage may be reckoned
the first, the intention of which has been to derive benefit from those
distant discoveries. For the more fully comprehending the nature and
plan of the expedition, and that the reader may be possessed of every
information necessary for entering on the following sheets, I shall
here lay before him a copy of the instructions I received from the admiralty, and likewise a short description of the bread-fruit.

*By the Commissioners for executing the office of Lord High Admiral
of Great Britain and Ireland, &c.*

WHEREAS the king, upon a representation from the merchants and
planters interested in his majesty's West India possessions that the
introduction of the bread-fruit tree into the islands of those seas, to
constitute an article of food, would be of very essential benefit to the
inhabitants, hath, in order to promote the interests of so respectable a
body of his subjects (especially in an instance which promises general
advantage) thought fit that measures should be taken for the procuring some of those trees, and conveying them to the said West India
islands: And whereas the vessel under your command hath, in consequence thereof, been stored and victualled for that service, and fitted
with proper conveniences and necessaries for the preservation of as
many of the said trees as, from her size, can be taken on board her;

and you have been directed to receive on board her the two gardeners named in the margin [David Nelson, William Brown.], who, from
their knowledge of trees and plants, have been hired for the purpose
of selecting such as shall appear to be of a proper species and size:

You are, therefore, in pursuance of his majesty's pleasure, signi-
fied to us by Lord Sydney, one of his principal secretaries of state,
hereby required and directed to put to sea in the vessel you command, the first favourable opportunity of wind and weather, and
proceed with her, as expeditiously as possible, round Cape Horn, to
the Society Islands, situate in the Southern ocean, in the latitude of
about eighteen degrees South, and longitude of about two hundred
and ten degrees East from Greenwich, where, according to the accounts given by the late Capt. Cook, and persons who accompanied
him during his voyages, the bread-fruit tree is to be found in the
most luxuriant state.

Having arrived at the above-mentioned islands, and taken on
board as many trees and plants as may be thought necessary (the better to enable you to do which, you have already been furnished with
such articles of merchandize and trinkets as it is supposed will
be wanted to satisfy the natives) you are to proceed from thence
through Endeavour Streights (which separate New Holland from
New Guinea) to Prince's Island, in the Streights of Sunda, or, if it
should happen to be more convenient, to pass on the eastern side of
Java to some port on the north side of that island, where any bread-
fruit trees which may have been injured, or have died, may be re-
placed by mangosteens, duriens, jacks, nancas, lansas, and other fine
fruit trees of that quarter, as well as the rice plant which grows upon
dry land; all of which species (or such of them as shall be judged
most eligible) you are to purchase on the best terms you can from the
inhabitants of that island, with the ducats with which you have also
been furnished for that purpose; taking care, however, if the rice
plants above-mentioned cannot be procured at Java, to touch at
Prince's Island for them, where they are regularly cultivated.

From Prince's Island, or the Island of Java, you are to proceed
round the Cape of Good Hope to the West Indies (calling on your
way thither at any places which may be thought necessary) and de-
posit one half of such of the above-mentioned trees and plants as may
be then alive at his majesty's botanical garden at St. Vincent, for the
benefit of the Windward Islands, and then go on to Jamaica: and,

having delivered the remainder to Mr. East, or such person or persons as may be authorized by the governor and council of that island to receive them; refreshed your people, and received on board such provisions and stores as may be necessary for the voyage, make the best of your way back to England; repairing to Spithead, and sending to our secretary an account of your arrival and proceedings.

And whereas you will receive herewith a copy of the instructions which have been given to the above-mentioned gardeners for their guidance, as well in procuring the said trees and plants, and the management of them after they shall be put on board, as for bringing to England a small sample of each species, and such others as may be prepared by the superintendant of the botanical garden at St. Vincent's, and by the said Mr. East, or others, for his majesty's garden at Kew; you are hereby required and directed to afford, and to give directions to your officers and company to afford, the said gardeners every possible aid and assistance, not only in the collecting of the said trees and plants at the places before-mentioned, but for their preservation during their conveyance to the places of their destination.

Given under our hands the 20th November 1787.

> HOWE,
> CHAS BRETT,
> RD HOPKINS,
> J. LEVESON GOWER.

To Lieut. Wm Bligh, commanding
his majesty's armed vessel the
Bounty, at Spithead.

By command of their Lordships,
P. STEPHENS.

In the foregoing orders it is to be observed, that I was particularly directed to proceed round Cape Horn; but, as the season was so far advanced, and we were so long detained by contrary winds, I made application to the Admiralty for discretional orders on that point; to which I received the following answer:

By the Commissioners for executing the office of Lord High Admiral
of Great Britain and Ireland, &c. &c.

THE season of the year being now so far advanced as to render it probable, that your arrival, with the vessel you command, on the sourthern coast of America, will be too late for your passing round Cape Horn without much difficulty and hazard; you are, in that case, at liberty (notwithstanding former orders) to proceed in her to Otaheite, round the Cape of Good Hope.

Given under our hands the 18th December 1787.

HOWE,
CHA^S BRETT,
BAYHAM.

To Lieut. Wm Bligh, commanding
his majesty's armed vessel
Bounty, Spithead.

By command of their Lordships,
P. STEPHENS.

THE BREAD-FRUIT is so well known and described, that to attempt a new account of it would be unnecessary and useless. However, as it may contribute to the convenience of the reader, I have given the following extracts respecting it, with the plate annexed.

Extract from the account of Dampier's Voyage
round the world, performed in 1688.

THE bread-fruit (as we call it) grows on a large tree, as big and high as our largest apple-trees: It hath a spreading head, full of branches and dark leaves. The fruit grows on the boughs like apples; it is as big as a penny-loaf when wheat is at five shillings the bushel; it is of a round shape, and hath a thick tough rind. When the fruit is ripe, it is yellow and soft, and the taste is sweet and pleasant. The natives of Guam use it for bread. They gather it, when full-grown, while it is green and hard; then they bake it in an oven, which scorcheth the rind and makes it black; but they scrape off the outside black crust, and there remains a tender thin crust; and the inside is soft, tender, and white like the crumb of a penny-loaf. There is *neither seed nor stone* in the inside, but all is of a pure substance, like bread. It must be eaten new; for, if it is kept above twenty-four hours, it grows harsh and choaky; but it is very pleasant before it is too stale. This fruit lasts in season *eight months* in the year, during which the natives eat *no other sort of food of bread kind.* I did never see of this fruit any where but here. The natives told us, that there is plenty of this fruit

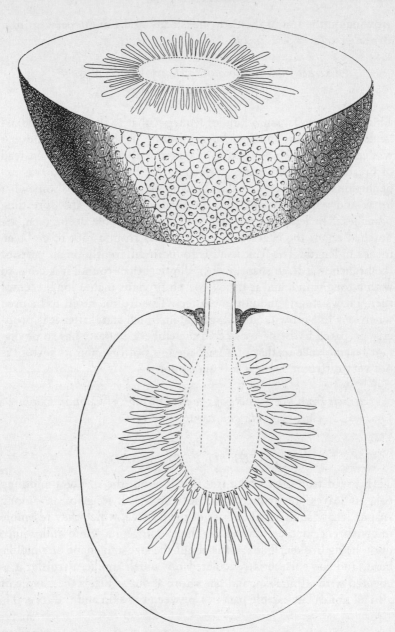

Sections of the Bread Fruit

growing on the rest of the Ladrone islands: and I *did never hear of it any where else.* Vol. I. p. 296.

Extract from the account of Lord Anson's Voyage,
published by Mr. Walter.

THERE was, at Tinian, a kind of fruit, peculiar to these (Ladrone) islands, called by the Indians *rhymay,* but by us the *bread-fruit;* for it was constantly eaten by us, during our stay upon the island,* instead of bread; and so *universally preferred,* that no ship's bread was expended in that whole interval. It grew upon a tree which is somewhat lofty, and which towards the top divides into large and spreading branches. The leaves of this tree are of a remarkable deep green, are notched about the edges, and are generally from a foot to eighteen inches in length. The fruit itself is found indifferently on all parts of the branches; it is, in shape, rather elliptical than round; it is covered with a tough rind, and is usually seven or eight inches long; each of them grows singly, and not in clusters. This fruit is fittest to be used when it is full-grown, but still green; in which state, after it is properly prepared by being roasted in the embers, its taste has some distant resemblance to that of an artichoke's bottom, and its texture is not very different, for it is soft and spungy.

Extracts from the account of the first Voyage of Captain Cook.
Hawkesworth, Vol. II.

IN THE SOCIETY ISLANDS.

THE bread-fruit grows on a tree that is about the size of a middling oak; its leaves are frequently a foot and a half long, of an oblong shape, deeply sinuated like those of the fig-tree, which they resemble in consistence and colour, and in the exuding of a white milky juice upon being broken. The fruit is about the size and shape of a child's head, and the surface is reticulated not much unlike a truffle: it is covered with a thin skin, and has a core about as big as the handle of a small knife. The eatable part lies between the skin and the core; it is

---

*About two months; viz. from the latter end of August to the latter end of October, 1742.

as white as snow, and somewhat of the consistence of new bread: it must be roasted before it is eaten, being first divided into three or four parts. Its taste is insipid, with a slight sweetness somewhat resembling that of the crumb of wheaten bread mixed with a Jerusalem artichoke. P. 80, 81. See also the plate there and at p. 232.

OF the many vegetables that have been mentioned already as serving them for food, the principal is the bread-fruit, to procure which costs them no trouble or labour but climbing a tree. The tree which produces it does not indeed shoot up spontaneously; but, if a man plants ten of them in his life-time, which he may do in about an hour, he will as completely fulfil his duty to his own and future generations as the native of our less temperate climate can do by ploughing in the cold winter, and reaping in the summer's heat, as often as these seasons return; even if, after he has procured bread for his present household, he should convert a surplus into money, and lay it up for his children.

It is true, indeed, that the bread-fruit is not always in season; but cocoa-nuts, bananas, plantains, and a great variety of other fruits, supply the deficiency. P. 197.

Extract from the account of Captain Cook's last Voyage.

IN THE SOCIETY ISLANDS.

I (Captain Cook) have inquired very carefully into their manner of cultivating the bread-fruit tree at Otaheite; but was always answered, that they never planted it. This, indeed, must be evident to every one who will examine the places where the young trees come up. It will be always observed, that they spring from the roots of the old ones, which run along near the surface of the ground. So that the bread-fruit trees may be reckoned those that would naturally cover the plains, even supposing that the island was not inhabited; in the same manner that the white-barked trees, found at Van Diemen's Land, constitute the forests there. And from this we may observe, that the inhabitant of Otaheite, instead of being obliged to plant his bread, will *rather* be under the necessity of preventing its progress; which, I suppose, is sometimes done, to give room for trees of another sort, to afford him some variety in his food. Vol. II. p. 145.

IN THE SANDWICH ISLANDS.

THE bread-fruit trees are planted, and flourish with great luxuriance, on rising grounds.—Where the hills rise almost perpendicularly in a great variety of peaked forms, their steep sides and the deep chasms between them are covered with trees, amongst which those of the bread-fruit were observed particularly to abound. Vol. III. p. 105 and 114, containing Captain King's Narrative.

THE climate of the Sandwich Islands differs very little from that of the West India Islands; which lie *in the same latitude.* Upon the whole, perhaps, it may be rather more temperate. Captain King, ib. p. 116.

THE bread-fruit trees thrive in these islands, not in such abundance, but produce double the quantity of fruit they do on the rich plains of Otaheite. The trees are nearly of the same height, but the branches begin to strike out from the trunk much lower, and with greater luxuriance. Capt. King, ib. p. 120.

The natives reckon eight kinds of the bread-fruit tree, each of which they distinguish by a different name. 1. *Patteah.* 2. *Eroroo.* 3. *Awanna.* 4. *Mi-re.* 5. *Oree.* 6. *Powerro.* 7. *Appeere.* 8. *Rowdeeah.* In the first, fourth, and eighth class, the leaf differs from the rest; the fourth is more sinuated; the eighth has a large broad leaf, not at all sinuated. The difference of the fruit is principally in the first and eighth class. In the first, the fruit is rather larger and more of an oblong form: in the eighth, it is round and not above half the size of the others. I enquired if plants could be produced from the seed, and was told they could not, but that they must be taken from the root. The plants are best collected after wet weather, at which time the earth balls round the roots, and they are not liable to suffer by being moved.

APPENDIX B: LADY BELCHER'S ACCOUNT
OF THE *PANDORA* (1870)

*Lady Diana Belcher drew on the journal of James Morrison to
amplify the account of the sinking of the* Pandora *in her* Mutineers
of the Bounty and their Descendants in Pitcairn and Norfolk
Islands (London: John Murray, 1870), 77–87.

At an early hour [of March 23rd, 1791], a vessel was observed round-
ing the point, and standing in to Maatavaye Bay. She proved to be
H.M.S. *Pandora*, commanded by Captain Edward Edwards, R.N.
Before she had anchored, Coleman was the first to present himself on
board, and was nearly drowned in the attempt, the canoe having been
upset, and he with difficulty rescued. Stewart and Peter Heywood
followed in a large double canoe, and gave themselves up to Captain
Edwards, informing him who they were; but, without further en-
quiry, he ordered them to be taken below, and placed in irons, together with three others, who had successively arrived, and were all
manacled.

Meanwhile, Morrison, Ellison, and Norman, were in the schooner
proceeding round the island, and the hapless prisoners could only indicate the direction their companions had taken. The launch was then
manned and armed, with orders to search for these men, and for the
others resident in the interior of the island. The pilot, being a friend
of Morrison, sent people forward to warn him of the arrival of the
Pandora, and that the launch was despatched in pursuit of him and
his companions, and to secure the schooner. When the messenger
reached the party, the *Resolution* was lying at anchor in a small bay.
Without delay or hesitation, the three left her, took a canoe which
conveyed them a considerable distance, and to expedite their movements, landed and walked fourteen miles across the country to the
harbour where the launch was anchored, which they reached at four
o'clock in the morning. They found Lieutenant Corner, the second
Lieutenant of the *Pandora*, in command, and gave themselves up to

him. He received them courteously, but placed them under guard; at
the same time ordering refreshments, which they much needed. In a
few hours the pinnace of the *Pandora*, also armed, joined the launch,
and Lieutenant Corner* placed the three prisoners in charge of the
third Lieutenant to convey them on board, while he in the launch
proceeded to seize the schooner and the remainder of the people,
who were at the other side of the island. The prisoners found themselves in charge of their former shipmate Hayward, one of the midshipmen of the *Bounty*, who had been promoted to the rank of third
Lieutenant of the *Pandora*. He took little notice of them, beyond en-
quiring about the *Bounty*, and who had remained in her; informing
them how Stewart, Heywood and their companions had been received on board, and the treatment they also might expect. As a
preparation, he ordered fetters to be put on their ankles in order to
prevent escape.

It was with difficulty that, with such obstacles, they mounted the
side of the ship, and on gaining the deck Captain Edwards ordered
them instantly below, to be heavily chained, like their unfortunate
shipmates. Sentinels were placed over them, with orders to shoot the
first man who should speak, especially should they address each
other in the Tahitian language, or speak to the natives who crowded
on board. They had plenty of provisions, and as their friends on
shore were allowed to supply them daily with fresh cocoa-nuts, they
did not care for the forbidden luxury of grog. The unfortunate prisoners remained between decks several days, and some dirty hammocks were supplied to them to lie upon, but these being full of
vermin, they requested they might be removed, as they preferred the
bare deck. They were also unable to make use of the changes of linen
ordered for them by the captain, their irons being clinched so tight
that it was impossible for them to rise or use their arms. Although
the heat between decks was excessive, yet that situation was preferable to the kind of poop or round-house which they had heard was
preparing on the quarterdeck for their reception. The boards of this
prison were so roughly put together as scarcely to shelter them from
the heat of the sun, or from the rain, which frequently fell in torrents.

---

*This officer was always kind to the prisoners, and through life Captain Heywood
continued on friendly terms with him. In after years, Mr. Corner became superinten-
dent of Marine Police at Malta.

On the 9th April the schooner *Resolution* reached the ship, and brought on board the remaining six prisoners, transferring them to the dreaded "*Pandora*'s box," through the scuttle at the top, about 18 inches square. This "box" was fastened by bolts through the combings of a hatchway. There were two scuttles of 9 inches square in the bulk-head of the box, to admit air to the prisoners. The scuttles or apertures were also secured against escape by iron gratings, and even the stern-ports of the ship were barred inside and out. The length of this "box" was 11 feet at the deck, and the width 18 feet at the bulk-head.* In this contracted space fourteen prisoners were confined; two sentries were placed on the top of it, and a midshipman paced up and down across the bulk-head. No one was allowed to hold any communication with the prisoners, except the master-at-arms, and he only on the subject of their provisions. Their condition in this dreadful confinement became daily more pitiable, owing to the extreme heat, and Morrison quaintly records "that their prison-house was only washed out once a week, they were washed with it; and this was the only ablution allowed them!" Such was a picture of the treatment of prisoners by the British Royal Navy, in the year 1791! Each officer of the ship, as he was relieved from his watch of this prison, examined the state of the shackles, and McIntosh's limbs being slight, he contrived to liberate one leg at night, which was a great relief. This circumstance being reported to Captain Edwards,

---

*Peter Heywood, while there a prisoner, and suffering the most cruel hardships from his treatment on board H.M.S. *Pandora*, composed the following lines—the results of experience:—

> Lest I should bend beneath this weighty load,
> And ne'er enjoy thy promised blest abode,
> Attend, thou Hope, on me, and be my guide,
> Thro' all my sorrows, walking by my side:
> Keep in my eyes that distant happy spot
> Where sweet content shall be my future lot,
> Free from ambition or desire of gain,
> Living in peace, exempt from mental pain;
> My food, the fruits with my own culture grown,
> "The world forgetting, by the world unknown":
> There tasting pleasure void of care's alloy,
> Crowning afflictions past with present joy!

March, 1791.   PETER HEYWOOD.

the First Lieutenant, Mr. Larkin, was instructed to make a general inspection of the irons. The leg-irons were immediately reduced in size to fit close, and, writes Morrison, "Mr. Larkin, in trying the handcuffs, placed his foot against our breasts, and hauling them over our hands with all his strength, in several cases took off the skin with them. All that could be handed off in this manner were reduced, and fitted so close there was no possibility of turning the hand in them. When our wrists began to swell, he told us the handcuffs were not intended to fit like gloves."

Sickness soon appeared among the prisoners, and their limbs became galled from the tightness of their irons. One or two of the greatest sufferers were released from their handcuffs, but their legs were still kept fastened to the two iron bars which ran across the deck.

During the whole period of their stay at Tahiti, the ship was daily surrounded by canoes, not only with supplies, but with the numerous friends of the prisoners, full of sorrow and lamentations for their misfortunes. Few were allowed to come on board to see them, but among the few was the young girl Stewart had married, and named Peggy. She came with her infant in her arms, and, seeing her husband lying on the deck among the others heavily ironed, her grief knew no bounds; even the hard-hearted Captain and his Lieutenant were touched by her sorrow, and she was admitted into the prison-house. With reiterated cries, she clung to Stewart, and the scene becoming too painful, it was necessary to remove her by force. Stewart was so completely unnerved by this interview, that he entreated she might not be allowed to see him again. Poor Peggy, however, was not to be deterred from remaining on the beach, where she could at all events see the vessel, from the earliest dawn to midnight. Her father and friends were seen endeavouring to persuade her to take food and rest, but in vain; she was daily at her post, and within a few weeks after the departure of the *Pandora*, the broken-hearted girl sank into an early grave, leaving her infant to the care of her sister, who took a mother's interest in the welfare of the little orphan.*

The necessary supply of water and provisions being completed, and the *Resolution* fitted with sails, Captain Edwards ordered a mid-

---

*In after years this account was brought to England by the Missionaries; by whom the little girl had been educated.

shipman and four men on board to navigate her, with instructions to keep the *Pandora* in sight. On the 19th May, 1791, they sailed from Tahiti, and stood to the north-west, with the intention of prosecuting a strict search among the islands for the remainder of the *Bounty*'s crew, in which service the little schooner proved most useful, as her small draught of water enabled her to lie close to the extensive reefs.

As they approached Chatham Island, the schooner was missed, and, although the *Pandora* cruised about for several days in search of her, she could nowhere be seen, and was given up for lost. (This seemed a second disaster, as previously the jolly-boat had been blown from the land when going off to her, and a midshipman and four men on board never heard of again.) The *Pandora*, having cruised about the different groups of islands for three months, seeking the *Bounty* and her people, Captain Edwards was obliged to relinquish the search, and sailed from the Friendly Islands in the middle of August for the Island of Timor.

The sufferings of the prisoners during this cruise had been intolerable. They had no means of steadying themselves when the ship lurched, and being thrown together, unavoidably wounded themselves and each other with their irons. At the request of Lieutenant Corner, who always evinced much kindness and consideration towards them, Captain Edwards allowed short pieces of plank to be secured to the deck, to remedy these frequent collisions, and consequent suffering. We shall now recur again to Morrison's journal:—

"On the 22nd of August, 1791, we approached Endeavour Strait, and narrowly escaped running on a reef in it, obliging us to be working to windward for some days without finding any opening. On Sunday, the 28th, the Second Lieutenant was sent with the yawl to make a closer examination, while the ship was hove to. At 7 P.M. on Sunday, the 28th August, the current running strongly on the reef, the ship was forced on it in the midst of a heavy surf, at the moment the returning yawl had come within hail, and was warning the people of the danger, but in vain. The ship was forced farther on the reef with violent and repeated shocks, and we expected every surge that the masts would go by the board. Seeing her in this situation, we judged she would not hold long together. As we were in danger at every shock of killing each other with our irons, we broke them, that we might be ready to assist ourselves, and informed the officers of what we had done. When Mr. Corner was acquainted with it he came aft, and we told him we should attempt nothing further, as we only wanted a chance for our lives, which he promised we should have, telling us not to fear.

"In the mean time, the ship lost her rudder, and with it part of the stern-post, and having beat over the reef between 11 and 12 P.M., she was brought up in 15 fathom water with both anchors, and the first news was, 'nine feet of water in the hold!' Coleman, Norman, and McIntosh were ordered out of the box to the pumps, and the boats were got out. As soon as Captain Edwards was informed that we had broken our irons, he ordered us to be handcuffed and leg-ironed again with all the irons that could be mustered, though we begged for mercy, and desired leave to go to the pumps, but to no purpose. His orders were put into execution, though the water in the hold had increased to 11 feet, and one of the chain-pumps was broken. The master-at-arms and corporal were now armed with a brace of pistols each, and placed as additional sentinels over us, with orders to fire among us if we made any motion. The master-at-arms told us that the Captain had said he would either shoot or hang to the yard-arm those who should make any further attempt to break the irons. There was no remedy but prayer, as we expected never to see daylight, and having recommended ourselves to Almighty protection, we lay down, and seemed for a while to forget our miserable situation. We could hear the officers busy getting their things into the boats, which were hauled under the stern for that purpose, and heard some of the men on deck say, 'They shall not go without us.' This made some of us start, and, moving the irons, the master-at-arms said, 'Fire upon the rascals.' As he was just then over the scuttle I spoke to him, and said, 'For God's sake don't fire; what is the matter? there is no one here moving.' In a few minutes after, one of the boats broke adrift, and having but two men in her, she could not reach the ship again till another was sent with hands to bring her back. And now we began to think they would set off together, as it was but natural to suppose that every one would first think of saving his own life. However, they returned, and were secured with better warps.

"We learnt that the boom, being cut loose for the purpose of making a raft, one of the top-masts fell into the waist, and killed a man, who was busy heaving the guns overboard; and everything seemed to be in great confusion. At daylight, August 29th, the boats were hauled up, and most of the officers being aft on the top of the 'box,' we observed that they were armed, and preparing to go into the boats by the stern ladders. We begged that we might not be forgotten, when, by Captain Edwards' order, Joseph Hodges, the armourer's mate, was sent down to take the irons off Muspratt and Skinner, and send them and Byrne (who was then out of irons) up; but Skinner, being too eager to get out, was hauled up with his handcuffs on, and the other two following him close, the scuttle was shut and barred before Hodges could get to it, and he in the mean time knocked off my hand-irons and Stewart's. I begged of the master-at-arms to leave the scuttle open, when he answered, 'Never fear, my boys, we will all go down together.' The words were scarcely out of his mouth when the ship took a sally, and a general cry of 'There she goes' was heard. The master-at-arms and corporal, with the sentinels rolled over-board, and at the same instant we saw through the stern-port Captain Edwards swimming to the pinnace, which was some distance astern, as were all the boats which had pushed off on the first appearance of a motion in the ship. Birkett and Heildbrandt were yet handcuffed, and the ship under water as far as the mainmast. It was now begin-ning to flow in upon us, when Divine Providence directed James Moulter (boatswain's mate) to the place. He was scrambling up on the 'box,' and, hearing our cries, said, 'he would either set us free, or go to the bottom with us,' and took out the bolts, throwing them and the scuttle overboard, such was his presence of mind, though he was forced to follow instantly, as he was nearly drowning.

"So we all got out except Heildbrandt, and were rejoiced even in this trying scene to think that we had escaped from our prison, though it was full as much as I could do to clear myself of the driver-boom before the ship sank. The boats were now so far off that we could not distinguish one from the other; however, observing one of the gangways come up, I swam to it, and had scarcely reached it, be-fore I perceived Muspratt on the other end, whom it had brought up; but it having fallen on the heads of several others, sent them to the bottom. Here I began to get ready for swimming, and the top of our prison having floated, I observed on it Mr. P. Heywood (who had been the last but three to jump overboard), Birkett, Coleman, and the first lieutenant of the ship; and, seeing Mr. Heywood take a short plank and set off to one of the boats,* I resolved to follow him, which I did by means of another short plank. After having been about an hour and a half in the water, I reached the blue yawl, and was taken up by Mr. Bowling, master's mate, who had also taken up Mr. Heywood. After rescuing several others, we were landed on a small sandy quay on the reef, about two and a half or three miles from the ship. Here we soon found that four of our fellow prisoners were drowned, Skinner and Heildbrandt, who had their handcuffs on, and Stewart and Summer, who were struck by the gangway. Birkett being landed with his handcuffs on, the captain ordered them to be taken off. We also heard that thirty-one of the *Pandora*'s ship's company were lost, among whom were the master-at-arms and ship's corporal, but all the officers were saved."

*The only thing he preserved on this occasion was his prayerbook, the last gift of his mother, which he carried between his teeth.

APPENDIX C: THE *QUARTERLY REVIEW* ON
THE *BOUNTY* (1810)

The following brief notice was included in the review of Voyage de Dentrecasteaux *in the* Quarterly Review 3 *(1810), 23–24.*

The following relation was transmitted officially to the Admiralty from Rio de Janeiro by Sir Sidney Smith:

Captain Folger, of the American Ship Topaz of Boston, relates that, upon landing on Pitcairn's island (Incarnation of Quiros) in lat. 25° 2′ S. long. 130° 0′ W. he found there an Englishman of the name of Alexander Smith, the only person remaining of nine that escaped in his Majesty's late ship Bounty, Captain W. Bligh. Smith relates, that after putting Captain Bligh in the boat, Christian the leader of the mutiny, took command of the ship and went to Otaheité, where great part of the crew left her, except Christian, Smith and seven others, who each took wives, and six Otaheitean men servants, and shortly after arrived at the said island, where they ran the ship on shore, and broke her up; this event took place in the year 1790.

About four years after their arrival (a great jealousy existing) the Otaheiteans secretly revolted and killed every Englishman except himself, whom they severely wounded in the neck with a pistol ball. The same night the widows of the deceased Englishmen arose and put to death the whole of the Otaheiteans, leaving Smith the only man alive upon the island, with eight or nine women and several small children. On his recovery he applied himself to tilling the ground, so that it now produces plenty of yams, cocoa nuts, bananas and plantains; hogs and poultry in abundance. There are now some grown up men and women, children of the mutineers, on the island, the whole population amounting to about thirty five, who acknowledge Smith as father and commander of them all; they all speak English, and have been educated by him, (Captain Folger represents) in a religious and moral way.

The second mate of the Topaz asserts that Christian the ringleader became insane shortly after their arrival on the island, and threw himself off the rocks into the sea; another died of a fever before the massacre of the remaining six took place. The island is badly supplied with water, sufficient only for the present inhabitants, and no anchorage.

Smith gave to Captain Folger a chronometer made by Kendall, which was taken from him by the Governor of Juan Fernandez.

Extracted from the log book 29th Sept. 1808.

                              (Signed)   William Fitzmaurice, Lieut.

If this interesting relation rested solely on the faith that is due to Americans, with whom, we say it with regret, truth is not always considered as a moral obligation, we should hesitate in giving it this publicity. The narrative, however, states two facts on which the credibility of the story must stand or fall—the name of the mutineer and the maker of the time-piece; we have taken the trouble to ascertain the truth of both of these facts. Alexander Smith appears on the books of the Bounty as follows: "Entered 7th Sep. 1787 Ab. Born in London. Aged 20. Run 28th April 1789. One of the mutineers": and it appears also that the Bounty was actually supplied with a time-piece made by Kendall.

This more elaborate article concludes the review of Porter's Journal
of a Cruize *in the* Quarterly Review *13 (1815), 374–383.*

To atone for the uniform dulness of Captain Porter's "Journal," and
to relieve, in some measure, the harassed feelings of our readers, we
shall make no apology for laying before them the history of an interesting race of men which this "Cruize" has been the means of making
us better acquainted with; the two frigates above-mentioned having,
by mere accident, fallen in with them. We give this little narrative the
more readily, on account of the awful example it holds forth of the
certain punishment which awaits the guilty, and which no time, nor
distance, nor concealment in unfrequented corners of the world, can
avert. Of the discovery of the descendants of the mutineers of the
Bounty we took occasion, in an early Number, to give some account—we are now enabled to complete their history, and to describe their present condition.

It is well known that in the year 1789 his Majesty's armed vessel
the Bounty, while employed in conveying the bread-fruit tree from
Otaheite to the British colonies in the West Indies, was taken from
her commander, Lieutenant William Bligh, by a part of the crew,
who, headed by Fletcher Christian, a master's mate, mutinied off the
island of Tofoa, put the lieutenant, with the remainder of the crew,
consisting of eighteen persons, into the launch, which, after a passage
of 1200 leagues, providentially arrived at a Dutch settlement on the
island of Timor. The mutineers, twenty-five in number, were supposed, from some expressions which escaped them, when the launch
was turned adrift, to have made sail towards Otaheite. As soon as this
circumstance was known to the Admiralty, Captain Edwards was ordered to proceed in the Pandora to that island, and endeavour to discover and bring to England the Bounty, with such of the crew as he
might be able to secure. On his arrival in March, 1791, at Matavai

bay, in Otaheite, four of the mutineers came voluntarily on board the Pandora to surrender themselves;* and from information given by them, ten others† (the whole number alive upon the island) were, in the course of a few days, taken; and with the exception of four, who perished in the wreck of the Pandora near Endeavour Strait,‡ conveyed to England for trial before a court-martial, which adjudged six of them to suffer death§ and acquitted the other four.||

From the accounts given by these men, as well as from some documents that were preserved, it appeared that as soon as Lieutenant Bligh had been driven from the ship, the twenty-five mutineers proceeded with her to Toobouai, where they proposed to settle; but the place being found to hold out little encouragement, they returned to Otaheite, and having there laid in a large supply of stock, they once

---

*Namely—Peter Heywood, Midshipman.
   Geo. Stewart, Ditto.
   Joseph Coleman, Armourer.
   Richard Skinner, Seaman.
†Namely—James Morrison, Boatswain's Mate.
   Charles Norman, Carpenter's Mate.
   Thomas McIntosh, Carpenter's Crew.
   Thomas Ellison,
   Henry Hilbrant,
   Thomas Burkitt,
   John Millward, } Seamen.
   John Sumner,
   William Muspratt,
   Michael Byrn,
‡Drowned—George Stewart.
   Richard Skinner.
   Henry Hilbrant.
   John Sumner.
§Namely—Peter Heywood.
   James Morrison.
   Thomas Ellison.
   Thomas Burkitt.
   John Millward.
   William Muspratt.
To the first two of these his Majesty's royal mercy was extended at the earnest recommendation of the Court, and the last was respited and afterwards pardoned.
||Namely—Charles Norman.
   Joseph Coleman.
   Thomas McIntosh.
   Michael Byrn.

more took their departure for Toobouai, carrying with them eight men, nine women, and seven boys, natives of Otaheite. They commenced, on their second arrival, the building of a fort, but by divisions among themselves and quarrels with the natives, the design was abandoned. Christian, the leader, also very soon discovered that his authority over his accomplices was at an end; he therefore proposed that they should return to Otaheite; that as many as chose it should be put on shore at that island, and that the rest should proceed in the ship to any other place they might think proper. Accordingly they once more put to sea, and reached Matavai on the 20th September, 1789.

Here sixteen of the five-and-twenty desired to be landed, fourteen of whom, as already mentioned, were taken on board the Pandora; of the other two,* as reported by Coleman, (the first who surrendered himself to Captain Edwards,) one had been made a chief, killed his companion, and was shortly afterwards murdered himself by the natives.

Christian, with the remaining eight of the mutineers, having taken on board several of the natives of Otaheite, the greater part women, put to sea on the night between the 21st and 22d September, 1789; in the morning the ship was discovered from Point Venus, steering in a north-westerly direction; and here terminate the accounts given by the mutineers who were either taken or surrendered themselves at Matavai bay. They stated, however, that Christian, on the night of his departure, was heard to declare that he should seek for some uninhabited island, and having established his party, break up the ship; but all endeavours of Captain Edwards to gain intelligence either of the ship or her crew at any of the numerous islands visited by the Pandora, failed.

From this period, no information respecting Christian or his companions reached England for twenty years; when, about the beginning of the year 1809, Sir Sidney Smith, then commander-in-chief on the Brazil station, transmitted to the Admiralty a paper which he had received from Lieutenant Fitzmaurice, purporting to be an "Extract from the log-book of Captain Folger of the American ship Topaz," and dated "Valparaiso, 10th October, 1808." This we partly verified in our Review of Dentrecasteaux's Voyage, by ascertaining that the

*Churchill and Thompson.

Bounty had on board a chronometer made by Kendal, and that there was on board her a man of the name of Alexander Smith, a native of London.

About the commencement of the present year, Rear Admiral Hotham, when cruizing off new London, received a letter addressed to the Lords of the Admiralty, of which the following is a copy, together with the azimuth compass to which it refers:

Nantucket, 1st March, 1813.

MY LORDS,

THE remarkable circumstance which look place on my last voyage in the Pacific Ocean, will, I trust, plead my apology for addressing your Lordships at this time. In February, 1808, I touched at Pitcairn's island, in latitude 25° 02′ S. longitude 130° W. from Greenwich. My principal object was to procure seal skins for the China market; and from the account given of the island, in Captain Carteret's voyage, I supposed it was uninhabited; but, on approaching the shore in my boat, I was met by three young men in a double canoe, with a present, consisting of some fruit and a hog. They spoke to me in the English language, and informed me that they were born on the island, and their father was an Englishman, who had sailed with Captain Bligh.

After discoursing with them a short time, I landed with them, and found an Englishman of the name of Alexander Smith, who informed me that he was one of the Bounty's crew, and that after putting Captain Bligh in the boat, with half the ship's company, they returned to Otaheite, where part of their crew chose to tarry; but Mr. Christian, with eight others, including himself, preferred going to a more remote place; and, after making a short stay at Otaheite, where they took wives and six men servants, they proceeded to Pitcairn's island, where they destroyed the ship, after taking every thing out of her which they thought would be useful to them. About six years after they landed at this place, their servants attacked and killed all the English, excepting the informant, and he was severely wounded. The same night the Otaheitan widows arose and murdered all their countrymen, leaving Smith with the widows and children, where he had resided ever since without being resisted.

I remained but a short time on the island, and on leaving it, Smith presented me a time-piece, and an azimuth compass, which he told me belonged to the Bounty. The timekeeper was taken from me by the governor of the island of Juan Fernandez, after I had had it in my posession about six weeks. The compass I put in repair on board my ship, and made use of it on my homeward passage, since which a new card has been put to it by an instrument maker in Boston. I now forward it to your Lordships, thinking there will be a kind of satisfaction in receiving it, merely from the extraordinary circumstances attending it.

(Signed)   MAYHEW FOLGER.

Nearly about the same time a further account of these interesting people was received from Vice-admiral Dixon, in a letter addressed to him by Sir Thomas Staines, of his Majesty's ship Briton, of which the following is a copy:

Briton, Valparaiso, 18th Oct. 1814.

SIR,

I HAVE the honour to inform you that on my passage from the Marquesas islands to this port, on the morning of the 17th September, I fell in with an island where none is laid down in the Admiralty, or other charts, according to the several chronometers of the Briton and Tagus. I therefore hove to, until day-light, and then closed to ascertain whether it was inhabited, which I soon discovered it to be, and, to my great astonishment, found that every individual on the island (forty in number) spoke very good English. They prove to be the descendants of the deluded crew of the Bounty, which, from Otaheite, proceeded to the abovementioned island, where the ship was burnt.

Christian appeared to have been the leader and sole cause of the mutiny in that ship. A venerable old man, named John Adams,* is the only surviving Englishman of those who last quitted Otaheite in her, and whose exemplary conduct, and fatherly care of the whole of the little colony, could not but command admiration. The pious manner in which all those born on the island have been reared, the correct sense of religion which has been instilled into their young minds by this old man, has given him the pre-eminence over the

---

*There was no such name in the Bounty's crew; he must have assumed it in lieu of his real name, Alexander Smith.

whole of them, to whom they look up as the father of the whole and one family.

A son of Christian's was the first born on the island, now about twenty-five years of age, (named Thursday October Christian;) the elder Christian fell a sacrifice to the jealousy of an Otaheitan man, within three or four years after their arrival on the island. They were accompanied thither by six Otaheitan men, and twelve women: the former were all swept away by desperate contentions between them and the Englishmen, and five of the latter have died at different periods, leaving at present only one man and seven women of the original settlers.

The island must undoubtedly be that called Pitcairn's, although erroneously laid down in the charts. We had the meridian sun, close to it, which gave us 25° 4′ S. latitude, and 100° 25′ W. longitude, by chronometers of the Briton and Tagus.

It is abundant in yams, plantains, hogs, goats and fowls, but affords no shelter for a ship or vessel of any description; neither could a ship water there without great difficulty.

I cannot, however, refrain from offering my opinion that it is well worthy the attention of our laudable religious societies, particularly that for Propagating the Christian Religion, the whole of the inhabitants speaking the Otaheitan tongue as well as English.

During the whole of the time they have been on the island, only one ship has ever communicated with them, which took place about six years since by an American ship called the Topaz, of Boston, Mayhew Folger, master.

The island is completely iron bound, with rocky shores, and landing in boats at all times difficult, although safe to approach within a short distance in a ship.

(Signed)   T. STAINES.

We have been favoured with some further particulars on this singular society which, we doubt not, will interest our readers as much as they have ourselves. As the real position of the island was ascertained to be so far distant from that in which it is usually laid down in the charts, and as the captains of the Briton and Tagus seem to have still considered it as uninhabited, they were not a little surprized, on approaching its shores, to behold plantations regularly laid out, and huts or houses more neatly constructed than those on the Marquesas islands. When about two miles from the shore, some natives were observed bringing down their canoes on their shoulders, dashing through a heavy surf, and paddling off to the ships; but their astonishment was unbounded on hearing one of them, on approaching the ship, call out in the English language, "Won't you heave us a rope, now?"

The first man who got on board the Briton soon proved who they were. His name, he said, was Thursday October Christian, the first born on the island. He was then about five and twenty years of age, and is described as a fine young man about six feet high; his hair deep black; his countenance open and interesting; of a brownish cast, but free from that mixture of a reddish tint which prevails on the Pacific islands; his only dress was a piece of cloth round his loins, and a straw hat ornamented with the black feathers of the domestic fowl. "With a great share of good humour," says Captain Pipon, "we were glad to trace in his benevolent countenance all the features of an honest English face."—"I must confess," he continues, "I could not survey this interesting person without feelings of tenderness and compassion." His companion was named George Young, a fine youth of seventeen or eighteen years of age.

If the astonishment of the Captains was great on hearing their first salutation in English, their surprize and interest were not a little increased on Sir Thomas Staines taking the youths below and setting before them something to eat, when one of them rose up, and placing his hands together in a posture of devotion, distinctly repeated, and in a pleasing tone and manner, "For what we are going to receive, the Lord make us truly thankful."

They expressed great surprize on seeing a cow on board the Briton, and were in doubt whether she was a great goat, or a horned sow.

The two captains of his Majesty's ships accompanied these young men on shore. With some difficulty and a good wetting, and with the assistance of their conductors, they accomplished a landing through the surf, and were soon after met by John Adams, a man between fifty and sixty years of age, who conducted them to his house. His wife accompanied him, a very old lady blind with age. He was at first alarmed lest the visit was to apprehend him; but on being told that they were perfectly ignorant of his existence, he was relieved from his anxiety. Being once assured that this visit was of a peaceable nature, it is impossible to describe the joy these poor people manifested on seeing those whom they were pleased to consider as their countrymen. Yams, cocoanuts and other fruits, with fine fresh eggs, were laid before them; and the old man would have killed and dressed a hog for his visitors, but time would not allow them to partake of his intended feast.

This interesting new colony, it seemed, now consisted of about forty-six persons, mostly grown up young people, besides a number of infants. The young men all born on the island were very athletic and of the finest forms, their countenances open and pleasing, indicating much benevolence and goodness of heart: but the young women were objects of particular admiration, tall, robust, and beautifully formed, their faces beaming with smiles and unruffled good humour, but wearing a degree of modesty and bashfulness that would do honour to the most virtuous nation on earth; their teeth, like ivory, were regular and beautiful, without a single exception; and all of them, both male and female, had the most marked English features. The clothing of the young females consisted of a piece of linen reaching from the waist to the knees, and generally a sort of mantle thrown loosely over the shoulders and hanging as low as the ancles; but this covering appeared to be intended chiefly as a protection against the sun and the weather, as it was frequently laid aside—and then the upper part of the body was entirely exposed; and it is not possible to conceive more beautiful forms than they exhibited. They sometimes wreath caps or bonnets for the head in the most tasty manner, to protect the face from the rays of the sun; and though, as Captain Pipon observes, they have only had the instruction of their Otaheitan mothers, "our dress-makers in London would be delighted with the simplicity, and yet elegant taste, of these untaught females."

Their native modesty, assisted by a proper sense of religion and morality instilled into their youthful minds by John Adams, has hitherto preserved these interesting people perfectly chaste and free from all kinds of debauchery. Adams assured the visitors that since Christian's death there had not been a single instance of any young woman proving unchaste; nor any attempt at seduction on the part of the men. They all labour while young in the cultivation of the ground; and when possessed of a sufficient quantity of cleared land and of stock to maintain a family, they are allowed to marry, but always with the consent of Adams, who unites them by a sort of marriage ceremony of his own.

The greatest harmony prevailed in this little society; their only quarrels, and these rarely happened, being, according to their own expression, *quarrels of the mouth:* they are honest in their dealings, which consist of bartering different articles for mutual accommodation.

Their habitations are extremely neat. The little village of Pitcairn forms a pretty square, the houses at the upper end of which are occupied by the patriarch John Adams, and his family, consisting of his old blind wife and three daughters from fifteen to eighteen years of age, and a boy of eleven; a daughter of his wife by a former husband, and a son-in-law. On the opposite side is the dwelling of Thursday October Christian; and in the centre is a smooth verdant lawn on which the poultry are let loose, fenced in so as to prevent the intrusion of the domestic quadrupeds. All that was done was obviously undertaken on a settled plan, unlike to any thing to be met with on the other islands. In their houses too they had a good deal of decent furniture, consisting of beds laid upon bedsteads, with neat covering; they had also tables, and large chests to contain their valuables and clothing which is made from the bark of a certain tree, prepared chiefly by the elder Otaheitan females. Adams's house consisted of two rooms, and the windows had shutters to pull to at night. The younger part of the sex are, as before stated, employed with their brothers, under the direction of their common father Adams, in the culture of the ground, which produced cocoanuts, bananas, the bread-fruit tree, yams, sweet potatoes, and turnips. They have also plenty of hogs and goats; the woods abound with a species of wild hog, and the coasts of the island with several kinds of good fish.

Their agricultural implements are made by themselves from the iron supplied by the Bounty, which with great labour they beat out into spades, hatchets, crows, etc. This was not all. The good old man kept a regular journal in which was entered the nature and quantity of work performed by each family, what each had received, and what was due on account. There was, it seems, besides private property, a sort of general stock out of which articles were issued on account to the several members of the community; and for mutual accommodation exchanges of one kind of provision for another were very frequent, as salt, for fresh provisions, vegetables and fruit for poultry, fish, &c. Also when the stores of one family were low or wholly expended, a fresh supply was raised from another, or out of the general stock, to be repaid when circumstances were more favourable;—all of which was carefully noted down in John Adams's Journal.

But what was most gratifying of all to the visitors was the simple and unaffected manner in which they returned thanks to the Almighty for the many blessings they enjoyed. They never failed to say grace before and after meals, to pray every morning at sun-rise, and they frequently repeated the Lord's Prayer and the Creed. "It was truly pleasing," says Captain Pipon, "to see these poor people so well disposed, to listen so attentively to moral instruction, to believe in the attributes of God, and to place their reliance on divine goodness." The day on which the two captains landed was Saturday the 17th September; but by John Adams's account it was Sunday the 18th, and they were keeping the Sabbath by making it a day of rest and of prayer. This was occasioned by the Bounty having proceeded thither by the eastern route, and our frigates having gone to the westward; and the Topaz found them right according to his own reckoning, she having also approached the island from the eastward. Every ship from Europe proceeding to Pitcairn's island round the Cape of Good Hope will find them a day later—as those who approach them round Cape Horn, a day in advance, as was the case with Captain Folger and the Captains Sir T. Staines and Pipon.

The visit of the Topaz is of course, as a notable circumstance, marked down in John Adams's Journal. The first ship that appeared off the island was on the 27th December, 1795; but as she did not approach the land, they could not make out to what nation she belonged. A second appeared some time after, but did not attempt to communicate with them. A third came sufficiently near to see the natives and their habitations, but did not attempt to send a boat on shore; which is the less surprizing, considering the uniform ruggedness of the coast, the total want of shelter, and the almost constant and violent breaking of the sea against the cliffs. The good old man was anxious to know what was going on in the old world, and they had the means of gratifying his curiosity by supplying him with some magazines and modern publications. His library consisted of the books that belonged to Admiral Bligh, but the visitors had not time to inspect them.

They inquired particularly after Fletcher Christian. This ill-fated young man, it seems, was never happy after the rash and inconsiderate step which he had taken; he became sullen and morose, and practised the very same kind of conduct towards his companions in guilt which he and they so loudly complained against in their late commander. Disappointed in his expectations at Otaheite, and the Friendly islands, and most probably dreading a discovery, this deluded youth committed himself and his remaining confederates to the mere chance of being cast upon some desert island, and chance threw them on that of Pitcairn. Finding no anchorage near it, he ran the ship upon the rocks, cleared her of the live stock and other articles which they had been supplied with at Otaheite, when he set her on fire, that no trace of inhabitants might be visible, and all hope of escape cut off from himself and his wretched followers. He soon however disgusted both his own countrymen and the Otaheitans, by his oppressive and tyrannical conduct; they divided into parties, and disputes and affrays and murders were the consequence. His Otaheitan wife died within a twelvemonth from their landing, after which he carried off one that belonged to an Otaheitan man, who watched for an opportunity of taking his revenge, and shot him dead while digging in his own field. Thus terminated the miserable existence of this deluded young man, who was neither deficient in talent nor energy, nor in connexions, and who might have risen in the service, and become an ornament to his profession.

John Adams declared, as it was natural enough he should do, his abhorrence of the crime in which he was implicated, and said that he was sick at the time in his hammock; this, we understand, is not true, though he was not particularly active in the mutiny: he expressed the utmost willingness to surrender himself and be taken to England; indeed he rather seemed to have an inclination to revisit his native country, but the young men and women flocked round him, and with tears and entreaties begged that their father and protector might not be taken from them, for without him they must all perish. It would have been an act of the greatest inhumanity to remove him from the island; and it is hardly necessary to add that Sir Thomas Staines lent a willing ear to their entreaties, thinking, no doubt, as we feel strongly disposed to think, that if he were even among the most guilty, his care and success in instilling religious and moral principles into the minds of this young and interesting society, have, in a great degree, redeemed his former crimes.

This island is about six miles long by three broad, covered with wood, and the soil of course very rich: situated under the parallel of 25° S. latitude, and in the midst of such a wide expanse of ocean, the climate must be fine, and admirably adapted for the reception of all the vegetable productions of every part of the habitable globe. Small, therefore, as Pitcairn's Island may appear, there can be little doubt that it is capable of supporting many inhabitants; and the present stock being of so good a description, we trust they will not be neglected. In the course of time the patriarch must go hence; and we think it would be exceedingly desirable that the British nation should provide for such an event by sending out, not an ignorant and idle evangelical missionary, but some zealous and intelligent instructor, together with a few persons capable of teaching the useful trades or professions. On Pitcairn's island there are better materials to work upon than missionaries have yet been so fortunate as to meet with, and the best results may reasonably be expected. Something we are bound to do for these blameless and interesting people. The articles recommended by Captain Pipon appear to be highly proper;—cooking utensils, implements of agriculture, maize or the Indian corn, the orange tree from Valparaiso, a most grateful fruit in a warm climate, and not known in the Pacific islands; and that root of plenty, (not of poverty, as a wretched scribbler has called it,) the potatoe; bibles, prayer books, and a proper selection of other books, with paper, and other implements of writing. The visitors supplied them with some tools, kettles, and other articles, such as the high surf would permit them to land, but to no great extent; many things are still wanting for their ease and comfort. The descendants of these people, by keeping up the Otaheitan language, which the present race speak fluently, might be the means of civilizing the multitudes of fine people scattered over the innumerable islands of the Great Pacific. We have only to add, that Pitcairn's island seems to be so fortified by nature as to oppose an invincible barrier to an invading enemy; there is no spot apparently where a boat can land with safety, and, perhaps, not more than one where it can land at all; an everlasting swell of the ocean rolls in on every side, and breaks into foam against its rocky and iron bound shores.

O happy people! happy in your sequestered state! and doubly

happy to have escaped a visit from "Captain Porter of the United States frigate Essex!" May no civilized barbarian lay waste your peaceful abodes; no hoary proficient in swinish sensuality rob you of that innocence and simplicity which it is peculiarly your present lot to enjoy!

APPENDIX E: JENNY'S STORY (1829)

This account of the Bounty *mutineers, given by one of their Tahitian companions, was first published in the* United Service Journal and Naval and Military Magazine, *1829, Part II, 589–593.*

PITCAIRN'S ISLAND—THE BOUNTY'S CREW.

In our July number we presented our readers with an account of the Mutiny on board the Bounty. We have been favoured by Capt. Dillon with the subjoined narrative of events connected with this interesting subject, communicated to him by an Otaheitan woman, named Jenny, the wife of Isaac Martin, one of the mutineers, in the presence of Mr. Nott, a missionary, who resided on Otaheite for twenty-seven years. Capt. Dillon also speaks the Otaheitan language fluently, and has acquired perhaps a more intimate acquaintance with the manners and customs of the South-Sea Islanders, than any other person living, from his having been in constant correspondence with the natives in the course of his numerous voyages.

As all accounts hitherto received respecting his Majesty's ship Bounty, have only been obtained from John Adams, who, it is more than likely, would have his own private motives for deviating from the truth in many important particulars, for perverting many facts, and suppressing others, the following details will no doubt be read with much curiosity, and we see no reason why they should not be entitled to some degree of credit.

It appears that Jenny remained on Pitcairn's Island about thirty years, that she left it in the American ship, Sultan, Capt. Rogers, for the Coast of Chili, and thence for the Marquesas, and afterwards returned to Otaheite, after an absence of thirty-one years. But let her speak for herself:—

"The day on which the Bounty returned to Otaheite, in charge of the mutineers, I went on board of her at Matavai: we shortly afterwards sailed towards Tabouai, and in a few days made that island, and came to an anchor in the mouth of the harbour. Four days after, we weighed anchor and hauled the ship farther upwards, between the reef, and anchored again. We went on shore the next day, and commenced the building of a very long house and two smaller ones; also began to erect a fort. Part of the crew wished to destroy the ship. This was opposed by Capt. Christian and some others, who said, that if the vessel might be the means of their detection, she might also be the means of their escape. One of the Otaheitans, who belonged to the Bounty, proposed to the Tabouai people, that in case the Englishmen should settle on the island, they should unite and take the ship, murder the crew, and share the property. This coming to the ears of Christian's wife, she informed him of the plot, but did not tell him that an Otaheitan was the contriver of it. The secret having transpired, led to a battle between the mutineers and the Tabouai people, in which the latter were defeated with considerable loss. One of the mutineers was mortally wounded with a spear.

"After this affray the mutineers were afraid to remain on Tabouai, and embarked in the Bounty, and sailed for Otaheite, where several of them proposed to stop.* In a few days we reached Matavai, where some of the crew went on shore, and took a proportion of the property with them. Only nine remained on board, attracted by the native females who were in the ship, about nineteen in number, and told the women that the vessel was to proceed to Paré, the king's district, the next morning.

"The same evening, while the women were below at supper, the mutineers cut the cable and stood to the northward. Four natives of Otaheite and two Tabouai men were then on board. When the ship got about a mile outside the reefs, one of the women leaped overboard and swam ashore. Next morning the vessel was off Tethuroa, a low island to the northward of Otaheite, but not so near as to permit any of the women venturing to swim ashore there, which several of them were inclined to do, as they were much afflicted at being torn from their friends and relations.

"The ship now tacked and stood to the southward, and next morning was close in with the island of Eimeo, about five or six

*The men who remained at Otaheite were taken off by Capt. Edwards, of the Pandora; some of them were brought to England, and executed.

leagues distant from Otaheite. A canoe shortly afterwards came off, and six of the women, who were rather ancient, were allowed to depart in her: twelve then remained on board. Next morning they were out of sight of land, and sailed before the wind to the westward. After many days had elapsed, a small island was discovered, called by the natives Purutea. A canoe came off, bringing a pig and cocoa-nuts. One of the natives ventured on board, and was much delighted at beholding the pearl-shell buttons on the jacket of Capt. Christian, who, in a very friendly manner, gave the man the jacket. The latter stood on the ship's gunwale, showing the present to his countrymen, when one of the mutineers shot him dead: he fell into the sea. Christian was highly indignant at this; but could do nothing more, having lost all authority, than reprimand the murderer severely. The other natives in the canoe immediately picked up their dead companion, and paddled towards the shore, uttering loud lamentations.

"In a few days we saw one of the Tongataboo, or Friendly Islands. Several canoes came off with abundance of hogs, yams, and poultry. The natives said that Totee (Capt. Cook) had been there, and that the horned cattle left by him were living. Continued our course to leeward, and discovered a small low island, where Christian proposed to stop. The boat was sent on shore to ascertain whether it was inhabited. Before the crew had time to land, people were seen on the beach. After landing and remaining awhile on shore, the boat returned to the ship with the news. Had this been an uninhabited island, Christian would have destroyed the ship and remained there. Finding the inhabitants were numerous, they sailed away that night to windward. Two months elapsed before land was again seen, during which time all on board were much discouraged: they therefore thought of returning to Otaheite. Pitcairn's Island was at length discovered in the evening. It was then blowing hard, and no landing could be effected till the third day, when the boat was lowered down, and the following persons went on shore, Christian, Brown, Williams, McKoy, and three of the Otaheitan natives.

"The ship now stood out to sea, and returned towards the island the second day, by which time the boat returned. The crew reported that there were no natives on the island; that it abounded with cocoanuts and sea-fowl, and that they had found traces of its having been once inhabited. Charcoal, stone axes, stone foundations of houses, with a few carved boards, were discovered. Christian got the vessel under a rocky point and came to anchor. The mutineers began to discharge the ship, by means of the boat and a raft made out of the hatches. The property from the ship was landed principally on the raft, by means of a rope fastened to the rocks. When all they wanted was brought on shore, they began to consider what they should do with the vessel. Christian wished to save her for awhile. The others insisted on destroying her, and one of them went off and set fire to her in the fore part. Shortly after two others went on board and set fire to her in different places. During the night all were in tears at seeing her in flames. Some regretted exceedingly they had not confined Capt. Bligh and returned to their native country, instead of acting as they had done. The next morning they began to build some temporary houses. Between the huts and the sea-shore were a number of trees, which concealed them from the view of any vessel that might pass.

"After a few weeks they ventured upon the high land, and began to erect more substantial buildings; to plant sweet potatoes and yams, the seed of which they brought with them. They shortly after divided the ground, and allotted to each his proportion. The cloth plant of the South Sea Islands was discovered growing upon one of the lots, about which some squabbling took place, but they afterwards agreed to divide it equally among them. One of the women who lived with Williams died of a disease in her neck about a year after their arrival. The Taro-root plant was found on the island, and means were immediately taken to cultivate it. Christian had a son born about this time, whom he named Friday;* he was baptized by Brown.

"Williams, whose wife died, now proposed to take one of the Otaheitan men's wives, there being only two among them; and lots were drawn which it should be. The chance fell on the wife of an Otaheitan, called Tararo. Williams accordingly took her from her husband, who was in consequence much afflicted, and betook himself to the hills. After three days, he returned and got his wife away, and took her to the mountains with him. The native men now proposed to kill the English, who were, however, upon their guard: three of the principals in the plot thought proper to seek refuge in the mountains. One of the natives who remained with the English, was sent by

---

*This differs from all the other accounts. His name, according to Sir T. Staines and Capt. Folger, is Thursday October Christian.

Christian to the mountains, for the purpose of shooting the principal conspirator, whose name was Oopee, promising to reward him handsomely if he succeeded, but, if he did not, he was to lose his own life. This man took a pistol with him as directed: he found Oopee among the craggy precipices and killed him. Tararo, who had taken his wife from Williams, and was still in the mountains, was shot by order of the Europeans: his wife now returned to Williams. After this the mutineers lived in a peaceable manner for some years, (it must be recollected there were now only four native men remaining).

The next affair of consequence that occurred was that of Manarii, the Otaheitan, who stole a pig belonging to McKoy, for which offence the English beat him severely. Teimua afterwards stole some yams, and one of the women informed of him. He was also severely chastised.

The natives again concerted among themselves to murder the English, and went about from day to day with their muskets, on a pretence of shooting wild-fowl. The mutineers did not suspect their intentions: Williams was the first man shot, while putting up a fence round his garden. The natives next proceeded to shoot Christian: they found him clearing some ground for a garden, and while in the act of carrying away some roots, they went behind him and shot him between the shoulders—he fell. They then disfigured him with an axe about the head, and left him dead on the ground.

The natives next proceeded to another enclosure, where they found Miles and McKoy: the former was shot dead, but McKoy saved himself by flight. They now went to Martin's house and shot him: he did not fall immediately, but ran to Brown's house, which was not far off. He was there shot a second time, when he fell; they beat him on the head with a hammer till he was quite dead. Brown at the same time was knocked on the head with stones, and left for dead. As the murderers were going away, he rose up and ran. One of them pursued and overtook him. He begged hard for mercy, or that they would not kill him until he had seen his wife. They promised they would spare his life; however, one with a musket got behind him and shot him dead. Alexander Smith (*alias* John Adams) was next fired at in his own house; the ball grazed his neck and broke two of his fingers. He was saved by the women, who were at this time assembled. The murderers, after wounding him, permitted him to take farewell of his wife. The women threw themselves on his body, and at their entreaties his life was spared. Teimua, one of the four natives, was next shot by his countryman Manarii. McKoy and Matthew Quintil were still concealed, in the mountains. One of the mutineers was spared by the murderers, and lived with Smith and the woman.

"Manarii was now afraid of his two surviving countrymen; he therefore fled to the mountains, joined Matthew Quintil and McKoy, and told them that they must not attempt to go down, as the other two Otaheitans would be sure to kill them. He offered them his musket, and said he would remain in concealment with them. One or two of the women now went in quest of McKoy and Matthew Quintil. They met with them, and strongly advised them to kill Manarii, which was accordingly done that night. The two remaining Otaheitan men next went in search of McKoy and Quintil to kill them; they found them among the mountains, shot at them, and supposed that one was wounded; this however, was not the case.

"The Otaheitans proceeded to the house where the women, with Smith and Young, were, and boasted that they had wounded McKoy. One of the women proposed to her two countrymen to go into the mountains, and see if this was the case, and bring them correct information. To this proposal they gladly acceded; but the real object of the woman was to advise McKoy and Quintil to come privately at a certain time that night, and assist the women to kill the two remaining natives. The Englishmen promised to do this, but did not keep their word. Next day the women agreed with Smith and Young to kill the two Otaheitans. About noon, while one of the Otaheitan men was sitting outside of the house, and the other was lying on his back on the floor, one of the women took a hatchet and cleft the skull of the latter; at the same instant calling out to Young to fire, which he did, and shot the other native dead. Thus ended the whole of the six Tahitans and Tabouaians. There now remained on the island eleven Otaheitan women, and four Englishmen, viz. Alexander Smith, McKoy, Young, and Matthew Quintil. They soon began to distil a spirituous liquor from the tea-root. In a drunken affray, Matthew Quintil was killed by his three countrymen. McKoy came by his death through drinking spirits, which brought on derangement, and caused him to leap into the sea, after having tied his own hands and feet. Young died a natural death on a Christmas-day. Sunday was observed by Christian, and divine service read. He left his wife and three children: she had more children by another husband.

"A ship was seen before Matthew Quintil was killed, and after the death of Christian, when only four of the mutineers were left. A long time after, another vessel appeared, and sent a boat on shore to take off cocoa-nuts; the people on shore beckoned to the ship to send the boat a second time, she did not do so, but stood out to sea. The next ship that arrived was the Topaz, Capt. Folger. He promised to return in eight months. A vessel may anchor where the Bounty did; wind at south and south-east. The island abounds in yams, taro, tea-root, cloth-plant, bread-fruit, hogs, poultry, &c."

Such were the fatal consequences of a crime foreign to the character of British seamen, and originating in the abuse of the extensive authority necessarily vested in the commander of a man-of-war, for the preservation of good order and discipline; furnishing a memorable example of the effects of undue severity in the first instance, and the absence of salutary control in the end.

APPENDIX F: JOHN ADAMS'S STORY (1831)

The most extensive version of John Adams's account of the mutiny and settlement of Pitcairn was published by Frederick W. Beechey in Narrative of a Voyage to the Pacific and Beering's Strait *(London: Colburn and Bentley, 1831), 66–95.*

THE interest which was excited by the announcement of Pitcairn Island from the mast-head brought every person upon deck, and produced a train of reflections that momentarily increased our anxiety to communicate with its inhabitants; to see and partake of the pleasures of their little domestic circle; and to learn from them the particulars of every transaction connected with the fate of the Bounty: but in consequence of the approach of night this gratification was deferred until the next morning, when, as we were steering for the side of the island on which Captain Carteret has marked soundings, in the hope of being able to anchor the ship, we had the pleasure to see a boat under sail hastening toward us. At first the complete equipment of this boat raised a doubt as to its being the property of the islanders, for we expected to see only a well-provided canoe in their possession, and we therefore concluded that the boat must belong to some whaleship on the opposite side; but we were soon agreeably undeceived by the singular appearance of her crew, which consisted of old Adams and all the young men of the island.

Before they ventured to take hold of the ship, they inquired if they might come on board, and upon permission being granted, they sprang up the side and shook every officer by the hand with undisguised feelings of gratification.

The activity of the young men outstripped that of old Adams, who was consequently almost the last to greet us. He was in his sixty-fifth year, and was unusually strong and active for his age, notwithstanding the inconvenience of considerable corpulency. He was dressed in a sailor's shirt and trousers and a low-crowned hat, which he instinctively held in his hand until desired to put it on. He still retained his sailor's gait, doffing his hat and smoothing down his bald forehead whenever he was addressed by the officers.

It was the first time he had been on board a ship of war since the mutiny, and his mind naturally reverted to scenes that could not fail to produce a temporary embarrassment, heightened, perhaps, by the familiarity with which he found himself addressed by persons of a class with those whom he had been accustomed to obey. Apprehension for his safety formed no part of his thoughts: he had received too many demonstrations of the good feeling that existed towards him, both on the part of the British government and of individuals, to entertain any alarm on that head; and as every person endeavoured to set his mind at rest, he very soon made himself at home.*

The young men, ten in number, were tall, robust, and healthy, with good-natured countenances, which would any where have procured them a friendly reception; and with a simplicity of manner and a fear of doing wrong, which at once prevented the possibility of giving offence. Unacquainted with the world, they asked a number of questions which would have applied better to persons with whom they had been intimate, and who had left them but a short time before, than to perfect strangers; and inquired after ships and people we had never heard of. Their dress, made up of the presents which had been given them by the masters and seamen of merchant ships, was a perfect caricature. Some had on long black coats without any other article of dress except trousers, some shirts without coats, and others waistcoats without either; none had shoes or stockings, and only two possessed hats, neither of which seemed likely to hang long together.

They were as anxious to gratify their curiosity about the decks, as we were to learn from them the state of the colony, and the particulars of the fate of the mutineers who had settled upon the island, which had been variously related by occasional visiters; and we were more especially desirous of obtaining Adams' own narrative; for it was peculiarly interesting to learn from one who had been implicated in the mutiny, the facts of that transaction, now that he considered himself exempt from the penalties of his crime.

I trust that, in renewing the discussion of this affair, I shall not be

*Since the MS. of this narrative was sent to press, intelligence of Adams' death has been communicated to me by our Consul at the Sandwich Islands.

considered as unnecessarily wounding the feelings of the friends of any of the parties concerned; but it is satisfactory to show, that those who suffered by the sentence of the court-martial were convicted upon evidence which is now corroborated by the statement of an accomplice who has no motive for concealing the truth. The following account is compiled almost entirely from Adams' narrative, signed with his own hand, of which the following is a fac-simile.

John Adams.

But to render the narrative more complete, I have added such additional facts as were derived from the inhabitants, who are perfectly acquainted with every incident connected with the transaction. In presenting it to the public, I vouch, only, for its being a correct statement of the above-mentioned authorities.

His Majesty's ship Bounty was purchased into the service, and placed under the command of Lieutenant Bligh in 1787. She left England in December of that year, with orders to proceed to Otaheite,* and transport the bread fruit of that country to the British Settlements in the West Indies, and to bring also some specimens of it to England. Her crew consisted of forty-four persons, and a gardener. She was ordered to make the passage round Cape Horn, but after contending a long time with adverse gales, in extremely cold weather, she was obliged to bear away for the Cape of Good Hope, where she underwent a refit, and arrived at her destination in October 1788. Six months were spent at Otaheite, collecting and stowing away the fruit, during which time the officers and seamen had free access to the shore, and made many friends, though only one of the seamen formed any alliance there.

In April 1789, they took leave of their friends at Otaheite, and proceeded to Anamooka, where Lieutenant Bligh replenished his stock of water, and took on board hogs, fruit, vegetables, &c., and

---

*This word has since been spelled *Tahiti*, but as I have a veneration for the name as it is written in the celebrated Voyages of Captain Cook—a feeling in which I am sure I am not singular—I shall adhere to his orthography.

put to sea again on the 26th of the same month. Throughout the voyage Mr. Bligh had repeated misunderstandings with his officers, and had on several occasions given them and the ship's company just reasons for complaint. Still, whatever might have been the feelings of the officers, Adams declares there was no real discontent among the crew; much less was there any idea of offering violence to their commander. The officers, it must be admitted, had much more cause for dissatisfaction than the seamen, especially the master and Mr. Christian. The latter was a protegé of Lieutenant Bligh, and unfortunately was under some obligations to him of a pecuniary nature, of which Bligh frequently reminded him when any difference arose. Christian, excessively annoyed at the share of blame which repeatedly fell to his lot, in common with the rest of the officers, could ill endure the additional taunt of private obligations; and in a moment of excitation told his commander that sooner or later a day of reckoning would arrive.

The day previous to the mutiny a serious quarrel occurred between Bligh and his officers, about some cocoa-nuts which were missed from his private stock; and Christian again fell under his commander's displeasure. The same evening he was invited to supper in the cabin, but he had not so soon forgotten his injuries as to accept of this ill-timed civility, and returned an excuse.

Matters were in this state on the 28th of April 1789, when the Bounty, on her homeward voyage, was passing to the southward of Tofoa, one of the Friendly Islands. It was one of those beautiful nights which characterize the tropical regions, when the mildness of the air and the stillness of nature dispose the mind to reflection. Christian, pondering over his grievances, considered them so intolerable, that any thing appeared preferable to enduring them, and he determined, as he could not redress them, that he would at least escape from the possibility of their being increased. Absence from England, and a long residence at Otaheite, where new connexions were formed, weakened the recollection of his native country, and prepared his mind for the reception of ideas which the situation of the ship and the serenity of the moment particularly favoured. His plan, strange as it must appear for a young officer to adopt, who was fairly advanced in an honourable profession, was to set himself adrift upon a raft, and make his way to the island then in sight. As quick in the execution as in the design, the raft was soon constructed, various useful articles were got together, and he was on the point of launching it, when a young officer, who afterwards perished in the Pandora, to whom Christian communicated his intention, recommended him, rather than risk his life on so hazardous an expedition, to endeavour to take possession of the ship, which he thought would not be very difficult, as many of the ship's company were not well disposed towards the commander, and would all be very glad to return to Otaheite, and reside among their friends in that island. This daring proposition is even more extraordinary than the premeditated scheme of his companion, and, if true, certainly relieves Christian from part of the odium which has hitherto attached to him as the sole instigator of the mutiny.*

It however accorded too well with the disposition of Christian's mind, and, hazardous as it was, he determined to co-operate with his friend in effecting it, resolving, if he failed, to throw himself into the sea; and that there might be no chance of being saved, he tied a deep sea lead about his neck, and concealed it within his clothes.

Christian happened to have the morning watch, and as soon as he had relieved the officer of the deck, he entered into conversation with Quintal, the only one of the seamen who, Adams said, had formed any serious attachment at Otaheite; and after expatiating on the happy hours they had passed there, disclosed his intentions. Quintal, after some consideration, said he thought it a dangerous attempt, and declined taking a part. Vexed at a repulse in a quarter where he was most sanguine of success, and particularly at having revealed sentiments which if made known would bring him to an ignominious death, Christian became desperate, exhibited the lead about his neck in testimony of his own resolution, and taxed Quintal with cowardice, declaring it was fear alone that restrained him. Quintal denied this accusation; and in reply to Christian's further argument that success would restore them all to the happy island, and the connexions they had left behind, the strongest persuasion he could have used to a mind somewhat prepared to acquiesce, he recommended that some one else should be tried—Isaac Martin for instance, who was stand-

*This account, however, differs materially from a note in Marshall's Naval Biography, Vol. ii. Part ii. p. 778: unfortunately this volume was not published when the Blossom left England, or more satisfactory evidence on this, and other points, might have been obtained. However, this is the statement of Adams.

ing by. Martin, more ready than his shipmate, emphatically declared, "He was for it; it was the very thing." Successful in one instance, Christian went to every man of his watch, many of whom he found disposed to join him, and before daylight the greater portion of the ship's company were brought over.

Adams was sleeping in his hammock, when Sumner, one of the seamen, came to him, and whispered that Christian was going to take the ship from her commander, and set him and the master on shore. On hearing this, Adams went upon deck, and found every thing in great confusion; but not then liking to take any part in the transaction, he returned to his hammock, and remained there until he saw Christian at the arm-chest, distributing arms to all who came for them; and then seeing measures had proceeded so far, and apprehensive of being on the weaker side, he turned out again and went for a cutlass.

All those who proposed to assist Christian being armed, Adams, with others, were ordered to secure the officers, while Christian and the master-at-arms proceeded to the cabin to make a prisoner of Lieutenant Bligh. They seized him in his cot, bound his hands behind him, and brought him upon deck. He remonstrated with them on their conduct, but received only abuse in return, and a blow from the master-at-arms with the flat side of a cutlass. He was placed near the binnacle, and detained there, with his arms pinioned, by Christian, who held him with one hand, and a bayonet with the other. As soon as the lieutenant was secured, the sentinels that had been placed over the doors of the officers' cabins were taken off; the master then jumped upon the forecastle, and endeavoured to form a party to re-take the ship; but he was quickly secured, and sent below in confinement.

This conduct of the master, who was the only officer that tried to bring the mutineers to a sense of their duty, was the more highly creditable to him, as he had the greatest cause for discontent, Mr. Bligh having been more severe to him than to any of the other officers.

About this time a dispute arose, whether the lieutenant and his party, whom the mutineers resolved to set adrift, should have the launch or the cutter; and it being decided in favour of the launch, Christian ordered her to be hoisted out. Martin, who, it may be re-

membered, was the first convert to Christian's plan, foreseeing that
with the aid of so large a boat the party would find their way to England, and that their information would in all probability lead to the
detection of the offenders, relinquished his first intention, and exclaimed, "If you give him the launch, I will go with him; you may as
well give him the ship." He really appears to have been in earnest in
making this declaration, as he was afterwards ordered to the gangway
from his post of command over the lieutenant, in consequence of
having fed him with a shaddock, and exchanged looks with him in-
dicative of his friendly intentions. It also fell to the lot of Adams to
guard the lieutenant, who observing him stationed by his side, exclaimed, "And you, Smith,* are you against me?" To which Adams
replied that he only acted as the others did—he must be like the rest.
Lieutenant Bligh, while thus secured, reproached Christian with in-
gratitude, reminded him of his obligations to him, and begged he
would recollect he had a wife and family. To which Christian replied,
that he should have thought of that before.

The launch was by this time hoisted out; and the officers and seamen of Lieutenant Bligh's party having collected what was necessary
for their voyage,† were ordered into her. Among those who took
their seat in the boat was Martin, which being noticed by Quintal, he
pointed a musket at him, and declared he would shoot him unless he
instantly returned to the ship, which he did. The armourer and carpenter's mates were also forcibly detained, as they might be required
hereafter. Lieutenant Bligh was then conducted to the gangway, and
ordered to descend into the boat, where his hands were unbound,
and he and his party were veered astern, and kept there while the ship
stood towards the island. During this time Lieutenant Bligh requested some muskets, to protect his party against the natives; but
they were refused, and four cutlasses thrown to them instead. When
they were about ten leagues from Tofoa, at Lieutenant Bligh's request, the launch was cast off, and immediately "Huzza for Otaheite!" echoed throughout the Bounty.

There now remained in the ship, Christian, who was the mate,

---

*Adams went by the name of Alexander Smith in the Bounty.
†Consisting of a small cask of water, 150 lbs. of bread, a small quantity of rum and
wine, a quadrant, compass, some lines, rope, canvas, twine, &c.

Heywood, Young, and Stewart, midshipmen, the master-at-arms, and sixteen seamen, besides the three artificers, and the gardener; forming in all twenty-five.

In the launch were the lieutenant, master, surgeon, a master's mate, two midshipmen, botanist, three warrant-officers, clerk, and eight seamen, making in all nineteen; and had not the three persons above-mentioned been forcibly detained, the captain would have had exactly half the ship's company. It may perhaps appear strange to many, that with so large a party in his favour, Lieutenant Bligh made no attempt to retake the vessel; but the mutiny was so ably conducted that no opportunity was afforded him of doing so; and the strength of the crew was decidedly in favour of Christian. Lieutenant Bligh's adventures and sufferings, until he reached Timor, are well known to the public, and need no repetition.

The ship, having stood some time to the WNW, with a view to deceive the party in the launch, was afterwards put about, and her course directed as near to Otaheite as the wind would permit. In a few days they found some difficulty in reaching that island, and bore away for Tobouai, a small island about 300 miles to the southward of it, where they agreed to establish themselves, provided the natives, who were numerous, were not hostile to their purpose. Of this they had very early intimation, an attack being made upon a boat which they sent to sound the harbour. She, however, effected her purpose; and the next morning the Bounty was warped inside the reef that formed the port, and stationed close to the beach. An attempt to land was next made; but the natives disputed every foot of ground with spears, clubs, and stones, until they were dispersed by a discharge of cannon and musketry. On this they fled to the interior, and refused to hold any further intercourse with their visiters.

The determined hostility of the natives put an end to the mutineers' design of settling among them at that time; and, after two days' fruitless attempt at reconciliation, they left the island and proceeded to Otaheite. Tobouai was, however, a favourite spot with them, and they determined to make another effort to settle there, which they thought would yet be feasible, provided the islanders could be made acquainted with their friendly intentions. The only way to do this was through interpreters, who might be procured at Otaheite; and in order not to be dependent upon the natives of Tobouai for wives, they determined to engage several Otaheitan women to accompany them. They reached Otaheite in eight days, and were received with the greatest kindness by their former friends, who immediately inquired for the captain and his officers. Christian and his party having anticipated inquiries of this nature, invented a story to account for their absence, and told them that Lieutenant Bligh having found an island suitable for a settlement, had landed there with some of his officers, and sent them in the ship to procure live stock and whatever else would be useful to the colony, and to bring besides such of the natives as were willing to accompany them.* Satisfied with this plausible account, the chiefs supplied them with every thing they wanted, and even gave them a bull and cow which had been confided to their care, the only ones, I believe, that were on the island. They were equally fortunate in finding several persons, both male and female, willing to accompany them; and thus furnished, they again sailed for Tobouai, where, as they expected, they were better received than before, in consequence of being able to communicate with the natives through their interpreters.

Experience had taught them the necessity of making self-defence their first consideration, and a fort was consequently commenced, eighty yards square, surrounded by a wide ditch. It was nearly completed, when the natives, imagining they were going to destroy them, and that the ditch was intended for their place of interment, planned a general attack when the party should proceed to work in the morning. It fortunately happened that one of the natives who accompanied them from Otaheite overheard this conspiracy, and instantly swam off to the ship and apprised the crew of their danger. Instead, therefore, of proceeding to their work at the fort, as usual, the following morning, they made an attack upon the natives, killed and wounded several, and obliged the others to retire inland.

Great dissatisfaction and difference of opinion now arose among the crew: some were for abandoning the fort and returning to Otaheite; while others were for proceeding to the Marquesas; but the majority were at that time for completing what they had begun, and

*In the Memoir of Captain Peter Heywood, in Marshall's Naval Biography, it is related that the mutineers availing themselves of a fiction which had been created by Lieutenant Bligh respecting Captain Cook, stated that they had fallen in with him, and that he had sent the ship back for all the live stock that could be spared, in order to form a settlement at a place called Wytootacke, which Bligh had discovered in his course to the Friendly Islands.

remaining at Tobouai. At length the continued state of suspense in which they were kept by the natives made them decide to return to Otaheite, though much against the inclination of Christian, who in vain expostulated with them on the folly of such a resolution, and the certain detection that must ensue.

The implements being embarked, they proceeded therefore a second time to Otaheite, and were again well received by their friends, who replenished their stock of provision. During the passage Christian formed his intention of proceeding in the ship to some distant uninhabited island, for the purpose of permanently settling, as the most likely means of escaping the punishment which he well knew awaited him in the event of being discovered. On communicating this plan to his shipmates he found only a few inclined to assent to it; but no objections were offered by those who dissented, to his taking the ship; all they required was an equal distribution of such provisions and stores as might be useful. Young, Brown, Mills, Williams, Quintal, McCoy, Martin, Adams, and six natives (four of Otaheite and two of Tobouai) determined to follow the fate of Christian. Remaining, therefore, only twenty-four hours at Otaheite, they took leave of their comrades, and having invited on board several of the women with the feigned purpose of taking leave, the cables were cut and they were carried off to sea.*

The mutineers now bade adieu to all the world, save the few individuals associated with them in exile. But where that exile should be passed, was yet undecided: the Marquesas Islands were first mentioned; but Christian, on reading Captain Carteret's account of Pitcairn Island, thought it better adapted to the purpose, and accordingly shaped a course thither. They reached it not many days afterwards; and Christian, with one of the seamen, landed in a little nook, which we afterwards found very convenient for disembarkation. They soon traversed the island sufficiently to be satisfied that it was exactly suited to their wishes. It possessed water, wood, a good soil, and some fruits. The anchorage in the offing was very bad, and landing for boats extremely hazardous. The mountains were so difficult of access, and the passes so narrow, that they might be main-

---

*The greater part of the mutineers who remained at Otaheite were taken by his Majesty's ship Pandora, which was purposely sent out from England after Lieutenant Bligh's return.

tained by a few persons against an army; and there were several caves, to which, in case of necessity, they could retreat, and where, as long as their provision lasted, they might bid defiance to their pursuers. With this intelligence they returned on board, and brought the ship to an anchor in a small bay on the northern side of the island, which I have in consequence named "Bounty Bay," where every thing that could be of utility was landed, and where it was agreed to destroy the ship, either by running her on shore, or burning her. Christian, Adams, and the majority, were for the former expedient; but while they went to the fore-part of the ship, to execute this business, Mathew Quintal set fire to the carpenter's store-room. The vessel burnt to the water's edge, and then drifted upon the rocks, where the remainder of the wreck was burnt for fear of discovery. This occurred on the 23d January, 1790.

Upon their first landing they perceived, by the remains of several habitations, morais, and three or four rudely sculptured images, which stood upon the eminence overlooking the bay where the ship was destroyed, that the island had been previously inhabited. Some apprehensions were, in consequence, entertained lest the natives should have secreted themselves, and in some unguarded moment make an attack upon them; but by degrees these fears subsided, and their avocations proceeded without interruption.

A suitable spot of ground for a village was fixed upon with the exception of which the island was divided into equal portions, but to the exclusion of the poor blacks, who being only friends of the seamen, were not considered as entitled to the same privileges. Obliged to lend their assistance to the others in order to procure a subsistence, they thus, from being their friends, in the course of time became their slaves. No discontent, however, was manifested, and they willingly assisted in the cultivation of the soil. In clearing the space that was allotted to the village, a row of trees was left between it and the sea, for the purpose of concealing the houses from the observation of any vessels that might be passing, and nothing was allowed to be erected that might in any way attract attention. Until these houses were finished, the sails of the Bounty were converted into tents; and when no longer required for that purpose, became very acceptable as clothing. Thus supplied with all the necessaries of life, and some of its luxuries, they felt their condition comfortable even beyond their most sanguine expectation, and every thing went on peaceably and prosperously for about two years, at the expiration of which Williams, who had the misfortune to lose his wife about a month after his arrival, by a fall from a precipice while collecting birds' eggs, became dissatisfied, and threatened to leave the island in one of the boats of the Bounty, unless he had another wife; an unreasonable request, as it could not be complied with, except at the expense of the happiness of one of his companions: but Williams, actuated by selfish considerations alone, persisted in his threat, and the Europeans not willing to part with him, on account of his usefulness as an armourer, constrained one of the blacks to bestow his wife upon the applicant. The blacks, outrageous at this second act of flagrant injustice, made common cause with their companion, and matured a plan of revenge upon their aggressors, which, had it succeeded, would have proved fatal to all the Europeans. Fortunately, the secret was imparted to the women, who ingeniously communicated it to the white men in a song, of which the words were, "Why does black man sharpen axe? to kill white man." The instant Christian became aware of the plot, he seized his gun and went in search of the blacks, but with a view only of showing them that their scheme was discovered, and thus by timely interference endeavouring to prevent the execution of it. He met one of them (Ohoo) at a little distance from the village, taxed him with the conspiracy, and, in order to intimidate him, discharged his gun, which he had humanely loaded with powder only. Ohoo, however, imagining otherwise, and that the bullet had missed its object, derided his unskilfulness, and fled into the woods, followed by his accomplice Talaloo, who had been deprived of his wife. The remaining blacks, finding their plot discovered, purchased pardon by promising to murder their accomplices, who had fled, which they afterwards performed by an act of the most odious treachery. Ohoo was betrayed and murdered by his own nephew; and Talaloo, after an ineffectual attempt made upon him by poison, fell by the hands of his friend and his wife, the very woman on whose account all the disturbance began, and whose injuries Talaloo felt he was revenging in common with his own.

Tranquility was by these means restored, and preserved for about two years; at the expiration of which, dissatisfaction was again manifested by the blacks, in consequence of oppression and ill treatment, principally by Quintal and McCoy. Meeting with no compassion or redress from their masters, a second plan to destroy their oppressors was matured, and, unfortunately, too successfully executed.

It was agreed that two of the blacks, Timoa and Nehow, should desert from their masters, provide themselves with arms, and hide in the woods, but maintain a frequent communication with the other two, Tetaheite and Menalee; and that on a certain day they should attack and put to death all the Englishmen, when at work in their plantations. Tetaheite, to strengthen the party of the blacks on this day, borrowed a gun and ammunition of his master, under the pretence of shooting hogs, which had become wild and very numerous; but instead of using it in this way, he joined his accomplices, and with them fell upon Williams and shot him. Martin, who was at no great distance, heard the report of the musket, and exclaimed, "Well done! we shall have a glorious feast to-day!" supposing that a hog had been shot. The party proceeded from Williams' toward Christian's plantation, where Menalee, the other black, was at work with Mills and McCoy; and, in order that the suspicions of the whites might not be excited by the report they had heard, requested Mills to allow him (Menalee) to assist them in bringing home the hog they pretended to have killed. Mills agreed; and the four, being united, proceeded to Christian, who was working at his yam-plot, and shot him. Thus fell a man, who, from being the reputed ringleader of the mutiny, has obtained an unenviable celebrity, and whose crime, if any thing can excuse mutiny, may perhaps be considered as in some degree palliated, by the tyranny which led to its commission. McCoy, hearing his groans, observed to Mills, "there was surely some person dying"; but Mills replied, "It is only Mainmast (Christian's wife) calling her children to dinner." The white men being yet too strong for the blacks to risk a conflict with them, it was necessary to concert a plan, in order to separate Mills and McCoy. Two of them accordingly secreted themselves in McCoy's house, and Tetaheite ran and told him that the two blacks who had deserted were stealing things out of his house. McCoy instantly hastened to detect them, and on entering was fired at; but the ball passed him. McCoy immediately communicated the alarm to Mills, and advised him to seek shelter in the woods; but Mills, being quite satisfied that one of the blacks whom he had made his friend would not suffer him to be killed, determined to remain. McCoy, less confident, ran in search of Christian, but finding him dead, joined Quintal (who was already apprised of the work of destruction, and had sent his wife to give the alarm to the others), and fled with him to the woods.

Mills had scarcely been left alone, when the two blacks fell upon him, and he became a victim to his misplaced confidence in the fidelity of his friend. Martin and Brown were next separately murdered by Menalee and Tenina; Menalee effecting with a maul what the musket had left unfinished. Tenina, it is said, wished to save the life of Brown, and fired at him with powder only, desiring him, at the same time, to fall as if killed; but, unfortunately rising too soon, the other black, Menalee, shot him.

Adams was first apprised of his danger by Quintal's wife, who, in hurrying through his plantation, asked why he was working at such a time? Not understanding the question, but seeing her alarmed, he followed her, and was almost immediately met by the blacks, whose appearance exciting suspicion, he made his escape into the woods. After remaining there three or four hours, Adams, thinking all was quiet, stole to his yam-plot for a supply of provisions; his movements however did not escape the vigilance of the blacks, who attacked and shot him through the body, the ball entering at his right shoulder, and passing out through his throat. He fell upon his side, and was instantly assailed by one of them with the butt end of the gun; but he parried the blows at the expense of a broken finger. Tetaheite then placed his gun to his side, but it fortunately missed fire twice. Adams, recovering a little from the shock of the wound, sprang on his legs, and ran off with as much speed as he was able, and fortunately outstripped his pursuers, who seeing him likely to escape, offered him protection if he would stop. Adams, much exhausted by his wound, readily accepted their terms, and was conducted to Christian's house, where he was kindly treated. Here this day of bloodshed ended, leaving only four Englishmen alive out of nine. It was a day of emancipation to the blacks, who were now masters of the island, and of humiliation and retribution to the whites.

Young, who was a great favourite with the women, and had, during this attack, been secreted by them, was now also taken to Christian's house. The other two, McCoy and Quintal, who had always been the great oppressors of the blacks, escaped to the mountains, where they supported themselves upon the produce of the ground about them.

The party in the village lived in tolerable tranquillity for about a week; at the expiration of which, the men of colour began to quarrel about the right of choosing the women whose husbands had been killed; which ended in Menalee's shooting Timoa as he sat by the side of Young's wife, accompanying her song with his flute. Timoa not dying immediately, Menalee reloaded, and deliberately despatched him by a second discharge. He afterwards attacked Tetaheite, who was condoling with Young's wife for the loss of her favourite black, and would have murdered him also, but for the interference of the women. Afraid to remain longer in the village, he escaped to the mountains and joined Quintal and McCoy, who, though glad of his services, at first received him with suspicion. This great acquisition to their force enabled them to bid defiance to the opposite party; and to show their strength, and that they were provided with muskets, they appeared on a ridge of mountains, within sight of the village, and fired a volley which so alarmed the others that they sent Adams to say, if they would kill the black man, Menalee, and return to the village, they would all be friends again. The terms were so far complied with that Menalee was shot; but, apprehensive of the sincerity of the remaining blacks, they refused to return while they were alive.

Adams says it was not long before the widows of the white men so deeply deplored their loss, that they determined to revenge their death, and concerted a plan to murder the only two remaining men of colour. Another account, communicated by the islanders, is, that it was only part of a plot formed at the same time that Menalee was murdered, which could not be put in execution before. However this may be, it was equally fatal to the poor blacks. The arrangement was, that Susan should murder one of them, Tetaheite, while he was sleeping by the side of his favourite; and that Young should at the same instant, upon a signal being given, shoot the other, Nehow. The unsuspecting Tetaheite retired as usual, and fell by the blow of an axe; the other was looking at Young loading his gun, which he supposed was for the purpose of shooting hogs, and requested him to put in a good charge, when he received the deadly contents.

In this manner the existence of the last of the men of colour terminated, who, though treacherous and revengeful, had, it is feared, too much cause for complaint. The accomplishment of this fatal scheme was immediately communicated to the two absentees, and their return solicited. But so many instances of treachery had occurred, that they would not believe the report, though delivered by Adams himself, until the hands and heads of the deceased were produced, which being done, they returned to the village. This eventful day was the 3d October, 1793. There were now left upon the island, Adams, Young, McCoy, and Quintal, ten women, and some children. Two months after this period, Young commenced a manuscript journal, which affords a good insight into the state of the island, and the occupations of the settlers. From it we learn, that they lived peaceably together, building their houses, fencing in and cultivating their grounds, fishing, and catching birds, and constructing pits for the purpose of entrapping hogs, which had become very numerous and wild, as well as injurious to the yam-crops. The only discontent appears to have been among the women, who lived promiscuously with the men, frequently changing their abode.

Young says, March 12, 1794, "Going over to borrow a rake, to rake the dust off my ground, I saw Jenny having a skull in her hand: I asked her whose it was? and was told it was Jack William's. I desired it might be buried: the women who were with Jenny gave me for answer, it should not. I said it should; and demanded it accordingly. I was asked the reason why I, in particular, should insist on such a thing, when the rest of the white men did not? I said, if they gave them leave to keep the skulls above ground, I did not. Accordingly when I saw McCoy, Smith, and Mat. Quintal, I acquainted them with it, and said, I thought that if the girls did not agree to give up the heads of the five white men in a peaceable manner, they ought to be taken by force, and buried." About this time the women appear to have been much dissatisfied; and Young's journal declares that, "since the massacre, it has been the desire of the greater part of them to get some conveyance, to enable them to leave the island." This feeling continued, and on the 14th April, 1794, was so strongly urged, that the men began to build them a boat; but wanting planks and nails, Jenny, who now resides at Otaheite, in her zeal tore up the boards of her house, and endeavoured, though without success, to persuade some others to follow her example.

On the 13th August following, the vessel was finished, and on the 15th she was launched: but, as Young says, "according to expectation she upset," and it was most fortunate for them that she did so; for had they launched out upon the ocean, where could they have gone? or what could a few ignorant women have done by themselves, drifting upon the waves, but ultimately have fallen a sacrifice to their folly? However, the fate of the vessel was a great disappointment, and they continued much dissatisfied with their condition; probably not without some reason, as they were kept in great subordination, and were frequently beaten by McCoy and Quintal, who appear to have been of very quarrelsome dispositions; Quintal in particular, who proposed "not to laugh, joke, or give any thing to any of the girls."

On the 16th August they dug a grave, and buried the bones of the murdered people: and on October 3d, 1794, they celebrated the murder of the black men at Quintal's house. On the 11th November a conspiracy of the women to kill the white men in their sleep was discovered; upon which they were all seized, and a disclosure ensued; but no punishment appears to have been inflicted upon them, in consequence of their promising to conduct themselves properly, and never again to give any cause "even to suspect their behavior." However, though they were pardoned, Young observes, "We did not forget their conduct; and it was agreed among us, that the first female who misbehaved should be put to death; and this punishment was to be repeated on each offence until we could discover the real intentions of the women." Young appears to have suffered much from mental perturbation in consequence of these disturbances; and observes of himself on the two following days, that "he was bothered and idle."

The suspicions of the men induced them, on the 15th, to conceal two muskets in the bush, for the use of any person who might be so fortunate as to escape, in the event of an attack being made. On the 30th November, the women again collected and attacked them; but no lives were lost, and they returned on being once more pardoned, but were again threatened with death the next time they misbehaved. Threats thus repeatedly made, and as often unexecuted, as might be expected, soon lost their effect, and the women formed a party whenever their displeasure was excited, and hid themselves in the unfrequented parts of the island, carefully providing themselves with fire-arms. In this manner the men were kept in continual suspense, dreading the result of each disturbance, as the numerical strength of the women was much greater than their own.

On the 4th of May 1795, two canoes were begun, and in two days completed. These were used for fishing, in which employment the people were frequently successful, supplying themselves with rock-fish and large mackarel. On the 27th of December following, they were greatly alarmed by the appearance of a ship close in with the island. Fortunately for them, there was a tremendous surf upon the rocks, the weather wore a very threatening aspect, and the ship stood to the SE, and at noon was out of sight. Young appears to have thought this a providential escape, as the sea for a week after was "smoother than they had ever recollected it since their arrival on the island."

So little occurred in the year 1796, that one page records the whole of the events; and throughout the following year there are but three incidents worthy of notice. The first, their endeavour to procure a quantity of meat for salting; the next, their attempt to make syrup from the tee-plant (*dracaena terminalis*) and sugar-cane; and the third, a serious accident that happened to McCoy, who fell from a cocoa-nut tree and hurt his right thigh, sprained both his ancles and wounded his side. The occupations of the men continued similar to those already related, occasionally enlivened by visits to the opposite side of the island. They appear to have been more sociable; dining frequently at each other's houses, and contributing more to the comfort of the women, who, on their part, gave no ground for uneasiness. There was also a mutual accommodation amongst them in regard to provisions, of which a regular account was taken. If one person was successful in hunting, he lent the others as much meat as they required, to be repaid at leisure; and the same occurred with yams, taros, &c., so that they lived in a very domestic and tranquil state.

It unfortunately happened that McCoy had been employed in a distillery in Scotland; and being very much addicted to liquor, he tried an experiment with the tee-root, and on the 20th April 1798, succeeded in producing a bottle of ardent spirit. This success induced his companion, Mathew Quintal, to "alter his kettle into a still," a contrivance which unfortunately succeeded too well, as frequent intoxication was the consequence, with McCoy in particular, upon whom at length it produced fits of delirium, in one of which, he threw himself from a cliff and was killed. The melancholy fate of this man created so forcible an impression on the remaining few, that they resolved never again to touch spirits; and Adams, I have every reason to believe, to the day of his death kept his vow.

The journal finishes nearly at the period of McCoy's death, which is not related in it: but we learned from Adams, that about 1799 Quintal lost his wife by a fall from the cliff while in search of birds' eggs; that he grew discontented, and, though there were several disposable women on the island, and he had already experienced the fatal effects of a similar demand, nothing would satisfy him but the wife of one of his companions. Of course neither of them felt inclined to accede to this unreasonable indulgence; and he sought an opportunity of putting them both to death. He was fortunately foiled in his first attempt, but swore he would repeat it. Adams and Young, having no doubt he would follow up his resolution, and fearing he might be more successful in the next attempt, came to the conclusion, that their own lives were not safe while he was in existence, and that they were justified in putting him to death, which they did with an axe.

Such was the melancholy fate of seven of the leading mutineers, who escaped from justice only to add murder to their former crimes; for though some of them may not have actually embrued their hands in the blood of their fellow-creatures, yet all were accessary to the deed.

As Christian and Young were descended from respectable parents, and had received educations suitable to their birth, it might be supposed that they felt their altered and degraded situation much more than the seamen, who were comparatively well off: but if so, Adams says, they had the good sense to conceal it, as not a single murmur or regret escaped them; on the contrary, Christian was always cheerful, and his example was of the greatest service in exciting his companions to labour. He was naturally of a happy, ingenuous disposition, and won the good opinion and respect of all who served under him; which cannot be better exemplified than by his maintaining, under circumstances of great perplexity, the respect and regard of all who were associated with him up to the hour of his death; and even at the period of our visit, Adams, in speaking of him, never omitted to say *"Mr. Christian."*

Adams and Young were now the sole survivors out of the fifteen males that landed upon the island. They were both, and more particularly Young, of a serious turn of mind; and it would have been wonderful, after the many dreadful scenes at which they had assisted, if the solitude and tranquility that ensued had not disposed them to repentance. During Christian's lifetime they had only once read the church service, but since his decease this had been regularly done on every Sunday. They now, however, resolved to have morning and evening family prayers, to add afternoon service to the duty of the Sabbath, and to train up their own children, and those of their late unfortunate companions, in piety and virtue.

In the execution of this resolution, Young's education enabled him to be of the greatest assistance; but he was not long suffered to survive his repentance. An asthmatic complaint, under which he had for some time laboured, terminated his existence about a year after the death of Quintal, and Adams was left the sole survivor of the misguided and unfortunate mutineers of the Bounty. The loss of his last companion was a great affliction to him, and was for some time most severely felt. It was a catastrophe, however, that more than ever disposed him to repentance, and determined him to execute the pious resolution he had made, in the hope of expiating his offences.

His reformation could not, perhaps, have taken place at a more propitious moment. Out of nineteen children upon the island, there were several between the ages of seven and nine years; who, had they been longer suffered to follow their own inclinations, might have acquired habits which it would have been difficult, if not impossible, for Adams to eradicate. The moment was therefore most favourable for his design, and his laudable exertions were attended by advantages both to the objects of his care and to his own mind, which surpassed his most sanguine expectations. He, nevertheless, had an arduous task to perform. Besides the children to be educated, the Otaheitan women were to be converted; and as the example of the parents had a powerful influence over their children, he resolved to make them his first care. Here also his labours succeeded; the Otaheitans were naturally of a tractable disposition, and gave him less trouble than he anticipated; the children also acquired such a thirst after scriptural knowledge, that Adams in a short time had little else to do than to answer their inquiries and put them in the right way. As they grew up, they acquired fixed habits of morality and piety; their colony improved; intermarriages occurred: and they now form a happy and well-regulated society, the merit of which, in a great degree, belongs to Adams, and tends to redeem the former errors of his life.

FOR THE BEST IN PAPERBACKS, LOOK FOR THE

In every corner of the world, on every subject under the sun, Penguin represents quality and variety—the very best in publishing today.

For complete information about books available from Penguin—including Puffins, Penguin Classics, and Compass—and how to order them, write to us at the appropriate address below. Please note that for copyright reasons the selection of books varies from country to country.

In the United Kingdom: Please write to *Dept. EP, Penguin Books Ltd, Bath Road, Harmondsworth, West Drayton, Middlesex UB7 0DA.*

In the United States: Please write to *Penguin Putnam Inc., P.O. Box 12289 Dept. B, Newark, New Jersey 07101-5289* or call 1-800-788-6262.

In Canada: Please write to *Penguin Books Canada Ltd, 10 Alcorn Avenue, Suite 300, Toronto, Ontario M4V 3B2.*

In Australia: Please write to *Penguin Books Australia Ltd, P.O. Box 257, Ringwood, Victoria 3134.*

In New Zealand: Please write to *Penguin Books (NZ) Ltd, Private Bag 102902, North Shore Mail Centre, Auckland 10.*

In India: Please write to *Penguin Books India Pvt Ltd, 11 Panchsheel Shopping Centre, Panchsheel Park, New Delhi 110 017.*

In the Netherlands: Please write to *Penguin Books Netherlands bv, Postbus 3507, NL-1001 AH Amsterdam.*

In Germany: Please write to *Penguin Books Deutschland GmbH, Metzlerstrasse 26, 60594 Frankfurt am Main.*

In Spain: Please write to *Penguin Books S. A., Bravo Murillo 19, 1° B, 28015 Madrid.*

In Italy: Please write to *Penguin Italia s.r.l., Via Benedetto Croce 2, 20094 Corsico, Milano.*

In France: Please write to *Penguin France, Le Carré Wilson, 62 rue Benjamin Baillaud, 31500 Toulouse.*

In Japan: Please write to *Penguin Books Japan Ltd, Kaneko Building, 2-3-25 Koraku, Bunkyo-Ku, Tokyo 112.*

In South Africa: Please write to *Penguin Books South Africa (Pty) Ltd, Private Bag X14, Parkview, 2122 Johannesburg.*